Consultancy Skills for Mission and Ministry

DAVID DADSWELL

Consultancy Skills for Mission and Ministry

scm press

© David Dadswell

Published in 2011 by SCM Press
Editorial office
13–17 Long Lane,
London, EC1A 9PN, UK

SCM Press is an imprint of Hymns Ancient & Modern Ltd
(a registered charity)
13a Hellesdon Park Road
Norwich NR6 5DR, UK

www.scmpress.co.uk

British Library Cataloguing in Publication data

A catalogue record for this book is available
from the British Library

978-0-334-04373-7
Kindle edition 978-0-334-04457-4

Typeset by Regent Typesetting, London
Printed and bound by
CPI Group (UK) Ltd, Croydon, CR0 4YY

Contents

Acknowledgements

Many people have helped in the production of this book and I am grateful to them all. I would have got nowhere on my journey as a consultant without the insights, rigour and wisdom of Ian Macdonald of Macdonald Associates as my initial trainer and continuing friend and colleague. As will be seen, I owe a huge debt to George Lovell in understanding that it is possible to offer consultancy to the churches with integrity, warmth and vision. The collaborative learning community over ten years on the Consultancy for Mission and Ministry course at Cliff College and then the York Institute for Community Theology with the tutors, Helen Cameron, Richard Andrew, Ian Johnson, Martin Atkins and Stuart Jordan, and generations of students has helped me immensely in grasping the range of knowledge that leads to good consultancy practice. Helen and Richard have spent many an hour picking over drafts of this book and given challenging, yet sensitive feedback. Many of the ideas in this book have also been tested with or derived from conversations with colleagues in the Macdonald Associates network across the globe, especially Philip Bartlett, Hilton and Rod Barnett, Philip Biggs, Tony Dunlop, Michael Evers, Roy Feltham, Michelle Forbes-Harper, Joe Grimmond and Ken McDonald. Thanks are also due to my close colleagues, Griff Dines and Carolyn Nahajski, for looking over the complete drafts to see whether the book made sense as a whole. Many people have given time to offer input or reflect on themes, including Lynda Barley, Paul Bayes, Johanna Clare, Ian Fishwick, Keith Lamdin, Tim Ling, Kathryn Morgan and colleagues in the Oxford Diocesan Work Consultants Network. Thanks to all of them and to Natalie Watson at SCM Press. Obviously, the final decision of what was in and out was mine and so any deficiencies in the text land at my door. Finally, thank you to Stuart without whose patience, encouragement, support and cups of tea this book would never have been finished.

Introduction

I had just taken up a role as a management consultant in a small, international consultancy, which dealt mostly with Australian mining companies. I had been recruited not just to work down mines but also to develop the consultancy's work in the not-for-profit sector, especially the churches. I was an ordained minister who had worked in a parish and then as a university chaplain for some 13 years and with a solid conviction in the value of the consultancy theory and practice I was using, I wondered how difficult it could be. However, as soon as I started to look for opportunities to help as a consultant, I quickly realized how complicated and difficult the churches as organizations are. Commercial organizations normally have an element of clarity around structure and role relationships, strategy and plans, external aims and internal expectations, however poorly implemented. Such never seemed to be the case in tackling church situations. How are you supposed to work with the perplexing organizational concoction of religious structures and their porous boundaries, with paid and voluntary workers unclear about who is in control, with the battle between centralizing and centrifugal pressures, with rules that exist to be broken or significantly bent, with independent-minded, local staff shouting their belief in community and all operating under wildly diverging notions of what they are for and how to do it? And I had been, variously, a member, voluntary worker and paid employee of this organization all my life. Stuart Macdonald of the University of Sheffield puts it well:

> [Church] workers might well take exception to performance indicators or measures of efficiency. What measures should be used to determine, say, whether a funeral is conducted efficiently? What indicators disclose level of performance in coping with bereavement? The very order and efficiency that is central to so much consultancy advice sits awkwardly with an ecclesiastical tradition that values diverse opinion and encourages criticism of the sort that would lead to instant dismissal in other organizations.
>
> (2006, p. 418)

There was, however, an answer to be found in the work and writings of George Lovell. Lovell is a Methodist minister who has spent half a century, with his main colleague, Catherine Widdicombe, a Roman Catholic laywoman, patiently and imaginatively building a clear set of concepts and tools to support the work of consultants in church and community settings. Getting to know him and working in his team on the Consultancy, Mission and Ministry course, then at Cliff College in Derbyshire, opened the possibility for me of an ethical, rigorous and useful approach to consultancy in a church setting. Watching him support, coach and teach generations of consultancy students from very different backgrounds and with very different theologies underlined the truths of the influential psychologist, Kurt Lewin, that there is nothing as practical as a good theory and that human behaviour has to be seen as a function of the person within his or her environment. Lovell constantly pushes for a theory that informs developing, reflective practice alongside a practice that feeds growing, disciplined theory. Yet, all the time there is an absolute respect in theory and practice for the autonomy of the other person, the focus of the help being offered.

Take, for example, Lovell's invention and use of the term 'consultor' where often 'client' is the norm. The term 'consultor' (which will be the standard term in this book for the person who has requested consultancy) encourages a way of thinking in which the process of consultancy is seen as a non-hierarchical, collaborative process in which there is, in Carl Rogers' words (1959, p. 239), an 'unconditional, positive regard for the other', particularly the other's skill and knowledge in solving their own problems. Like many others I have benefited hugely from George's clarity and coherence. So, to be clear about what the subject matter of this book is, this is Lovell's definition of consultancy:

> Consultancy is a process of seeking, giving and receiving help aimed at aiding a person, group, church or organization to achieve their purposes in specific situations and circumstances. Analyses and designs are produced through the creative interplay between consultors and consultants as they focus on their work, the what and why and how of what they want to achieve in the circumstances in which they operate.
>
> (2000, p. 23)

Consulting on work

The key issue for the consultancy we are talking about here is that it is *work* consultancy. Ministers and other church workers call on help from a range of approaches and disciplines, spiritual direction, supervision and counselling among them. As a helping discipline, work consultancy is different in its content and its focus. While talking about their work and its context, ministers and other church workers will inevitably need to deal with issues of faith, self-esteem or personality. A consultant needs to be able to be happy talking about these areas, but the subject matter is the work the consultor is engaged in, its problems, their solutions and the learning that comes from thinking the problems through. The overlap may be greater with approaches such as coaching, accompaniment and mentoring. These different activities draw on the same skills, theories and approaches, so it is important to be clear about what we think we are doing. Such clarity is a key aim of this book.

Who are these work consultants?

The standard picture of a consultant is of an external expert who comes in to help us do something we can't do, either because we don't know how or because we don't have the resources. (The question of whether a consultant is an expert will be dealt with in a later chapter.) Certainly, there are consultants who are brought in from outside our church or denomination. Yet there are many roles and functions now in the churches where someone stands alongside people involved in front-line ministry to help them think through how their work is going and how best to meet its continuing challenge. The growth of appraisal and review schemes for those in ministry produces a need for appraisers who are skilled in processes that raise the right questions, identify relevant patterns and encourage productive reflection. A well-informed listening ear can be of enormous help at the initial stages of the establishment of new forms of church such as church plants or Fresh Expressions. Traditional churches can benefit from someone who will accompany them as they work out how they might continue to offer mission and ministry in situations where the supply of ordained ministers and congregation members is dwindling fast. Such skills are key in the work of development or evangelism advisors, mission officers, vocations directors, youth work advisors and social responsibility officers. Those historically seen as hierarchs such as an archdeacon, a regional minister or a district chair find themselves needing to find effective means of encouraging a local minister to develop their ability to reflect on their work. How can that minister do so in a way that is consistent with their declared theological beliefs in order that their ministry can be more authentic and effective? Rather than barking orders at their charges or quietly hoping they are doing the right thing, many church leaders and decision-making bodies are seeing the benefit of providing consultants to work with individuals, teams and congregations both in tackling specific problems they are faced with and in their development over time as self-aware, mission-focused workers for the gospel. It suits the spirit of a more democratic age and appears to deliver better results. There are increasing numbers of examples where a district, diocese, region or indeed a national church is investing in a network of consultants. Building such a resource may mean not just training up your own ministers and employees but also using well-qualified volunteers from congregations and supportive local businesses.

Recent years have seen a growth in the number of consultants and leaders from secular organizations who provide consultancy services to the churches. Some are doing this in a voluntary capacity and some see it as part of their portfolio of income-generating work. As has already been said, there are significant differences between running or consulting to a commercial organization and running or consulting to a church. Yet the insights that can be brought in from the private and public sectors and from other voluntary organizations have yielded significant lessons for the churches in recent years. A critical issue is to make sure that the secular consultant has sufficient grasp of the context in which any consultation takes place. The Church uses many secular experts, such as accountants and architects, who work much more effectively if they can understand what makes their client tick. This book is designed to support their work. It may be, given their background, that different sections have greater relevance than those that are new insights for the church worker as consultant. This book aims to be of help both to consultants who are working inside the churches already and those who are invited in from outside. It is intended to support the work of those who have 'consultant' explicitly in their job title as well as those who employ consultancy skills and approaches in the regular work of their role. My work portfolio means that I am sometimes an insider and sometimes an outsider as a church consultant. This has meant that I have had access to a range of consultancy interventions which I have used as feedstock for this book. The stories and examples that I have used in this book come mostly from my experience and that of my colleagues over the years. In some cases names and details have been changed to protect the confidentiality and identity of the people involved.

Conscious, theory-based consultants

Consultants will only be of use to the consultor if they can integrate a range of disciplines. It may be necessary to draw on theology, biblical studies, ecclesiology, missiology, sociology, organizational studies, congregational studies, psychology, group dynamics, management and anthropology, to name but a few. A gifted consultant will be able to handle a relevant, healthy interaction of these disciplines. They will need to be able to use them effectively in live situations with a range of skills learnt from a number of helping styles. An ethical consultant will be reflective enough to recognize when the skills or bodies of knowledge required are beyond their personal capability and will address that issue honestly with the consultor. For me this is a key issue: that a consultant can articulate and justify their model of consultancy, its strengths and its limits. The professional practice of consultancy involves knowing what we can do and owning up to what we can't. Some consultants I have come across claim that they can do anything the consultor wants – just to get work.

So, a central aim of this book is to encourage those working as consultants to be self-conscious and articulate about their model of consultancy. What do they do when consulting and why? How is it supposed to reach a useful outcome? How does what they do enact what they believe to be God's way of working and purpose? What is the balance between knowledge, theory, skills, practice and experience? And how do these elements inform and feed each other in a developmental, reflective progress?

One of the joys of getting to know George Lovell and then others who are involved in consultancy with the churches was seeing what riches there are in the variety of styles and models of consultancy being helpfully employed. Lovell identifies very clearly with a non-directive model but has done considerable work in categorizing other models of consultancy such as management consultancy, the psychodynamic approach, systems thinking and complexity theory. The idea of this book is not to push any one model as the one to use but to encourage analytical rigour about the theory and practice we are using as consultants. This book should raise the sorts of questions and issues that will need to be recognized, tackled and continuously resolved by an effective consultant. The order of the chapters may not be as expected. The first two chapters set out the context in which a church consultant works – the wider social context the church sits in and some discussion of what we mean by church as organization – before tackling the nature and then the practice of consultancy. The order of the chapters is meant to be a logical sequence but it is for the reader to choose the order they are read in. The order of the material is, however, meant to indicate that a lot needs to be in place before a consultant can start to be effective. A book like this will not produce a perfectly formed church consultant just as a result of reading its pages. It is offered, nevertheless, as a support to the constant search for developing and improving practice by professional, integrative, effective consultants who can support the people and mission of the Church.

I

The Consultant as Practical Theologian

Consultancy happens in context. Consultants need understanding, capability and skills to work in that context. This first chapter lays out some features of the contemporary, secular and church context, and different general aspects of a consultant's capability by looking at:

- the context for church consultancy
- the consultant as interdisciplinary thinker
- the consultant as reflective practitioner
- the consultant as practical theologian.

A good start when working as a consultant with a new organization is just to wander around. Looking at the state of a church building or a person's office or watching people's habitual behaviour can provide invaluable data to discuss and check in conversation with the individual or group you're working with. One of the key insights is how consistent what you see and experience is with the avowed principles and intent of the consultor. 'We are a welcoming, friendly, inclusive church' according to the noticeboard outside, but, as you arrive up the steep steps, you are given a hymn book, a service book, a sheaf of papers (the notices, a song that is not in the hymn book, an advert for a coffee morning), no indication of where you are supposed to sit or how to know what to do when. Everyone up front is the same gender and there is no one to take you to coffee afterwards. In another place, the church building smells and looks clean and cared for in a congregation that says it values the beauty of holiness. As an outsider, it is often remarkable that the people who are there day by day, week by week, have ceased to notice what strikes the visitor with force. In training, a good tool is to video participants as they do activities. It is often a huge shock for participants when they see how their normal, habitual behaviour looks projected up on the screen. Consistency and the lack of it between what is espoused and what is visible symbolically and behaviourally is a common challenge in churches. Churches and Christians are typically accused of hypocrisy because of the mismatch between what they are seen to stand for and how they behave.

What you are doing by just watching and looking for the match between words and deeds is to *reflect*, that is, to stand back a little to consider what is being done and how it matches the aspirations for the activity. A bishop recently asked me what I thought consultancy was aiming to do in the Church. My response was that people normally call on consultancy in three situations. The first is when they are in trouble with a problem they need help solving. The second is when they are contemplating a big project or challenge and they would like someone to help them through it. The third is when an individual, team or organization wants a companion to be with them as a matter of course to help them reflect on what they are doing in their work. This means they can look backwards to check they are doing things well and, by learning from the past, modify their behaviour and understanding, so that they get progressively better at what they do. While not dismissing the first two, the third is my ideal for consultancy. If church ministers and leaders are regularly and productively reflective on what they are doing, it is much more likely that they will be effective in the work of mission and ministry in their context.

The same holds true for the consultant. This chapter will discuss what that reflective quality means in the case of a consultant. By looking at the context of a consultant's work in the modern church and by considering the consultant as an interdisciplinary thinker, a reflective practitioner and a practical theologian, the groundwork will be set for a discussion of the nuts and bolts of work as a consultant in church settings. There is a growing literature behind each of these areas and so a short chapter such as this can only give an introductory view of the range of areas that impact on the consultant as reflective, practical theologian. Recommendations in the text offer avenues to go down to explore these topics further.

The context for church consultancy

I joined a choral society recently and found myself (in my fifties), as is often the case at church events, among the youngest attending. After practising our Handel for an hour or so, it was time for the half-time break. Naturally, as I was expecting email, I got my mobile phone out of my pocket. Looking around I realized I was the only one of the 150 people checking their phone. I was shocked. That's what most people do when I am running a session with a company or a group of leaders.

As soon as you say, 'Let's break for coffee', out come the BlackBerries and mobiles. That's what happens when people get on a train or are waiting for the film at the cinema. I was evidently in a different context and culture. It would be necessary to check and adjust my assumptions about what people believed and how to behave. A consultant working with a person or a team needs to be sensitive to the context in which the consultancy is taking place and how that context influences what has happened and could happen. Martyn Atkins, the General Secretary of the British Methodist Church, once suggested to a group of consultancy students that they imagine themselves saying, 'Well, they would say that, wouldn't they?' when trying to understand an individual or a church group. The trick he went on to say is to investigate why they would. What is it in their setting, background and self-understanding that leads to them talking and behaving like that?

The postmodern, globalized context

If consultants are to be useful in helping consultors make sense of their issues, their work must include making sense of the context that surrounds the consultor's activity. This context is set in a web of large, often controversial understandings of the way our world and its societies are moving. One is the description of present-day uncertainty offered by postmodernism. A postmodern analysis sees a growth in the mistrust of the big certainties, what are often called metanarratives, high-level, overarching theories that account for all that is going on. Science offers us the solution to anything we can think of, if we give it time. Yet, we seem to be sure of very little in a world where shared meaning is limited and ambiguous, if not contradictory, and where the interconnections are fluid and incomprehensibly complex. So, while seeing all the benefits that scientific and technological advances are bringing us, some of us express mistrust in the positive direction of scientific progress. Grand, coherent themes which bind us together as a society are replaced by anxiety in the face of increasingly rapid change leading us to worry about whether anything we know or value will endure. It feels as if all that matters now has little depth, being based on consumerism and celebrity. Objective, universal truth apparently no longer exists, and it doesn't matter how we behave or what we believe as long as we don't actually harm anyone else. Metanarratives such as capitalism, communism and religion are treated with suspicion. Yet, at the same time, millions of people are seen to continue to adhere to religious belief and it could be said that new metanarratives such as

Christian and Muslim fundamentalism/radicalism are on the increase. (For further reading, Glenn Ward provides a helpful, accessible introduction to postmodernism in *Understand Postmodernism* (2010) in the *Teach Yourself* series.)

Although the analysis offered by postmodernism is debatable, it can help understand how perplexed many involved in ministry can be as they struggle to promote universal values and behavioural norms, feeling besieged by apparent societal chaos, fragmentation and moral relativism. So how does the theological worker in contemporary mission proceed with Christian claims of a biblical metanarrative concerning a Christ who transforms and heals individuals and societies? The critical conversation between Christianity and culture continues, but where does the consultant help the consultor locate it in, say, Niebuhr's five categories through Christian history: Christ against Culture, Christ of Culture, Christ above Culture, Christ and Culture in Paradox, and Christ Transforming Culture? Is the authentic Christian response to stand over against the fluidity or to engage with it from the inside?

Yet, there are some grand themes that dominate modern living such as globalization, climate change, pluralism/multiculturalism and technology. Many of the outworkings of these add to our anxiety but can promote both positive and negative responses. Climate change anxiety is a response to the fear that the planet will not be habitable in the future but is also a spur to increasing community action to change our habits individually, nationally and globally to reverse the trend. Globalization supported by modern communications technology can lead to a world economic collapse with disastrous consequences for those in rich and poor nations alike. Many businesses of the types with whom I work as a commercial consultant are moving their production facilities from western countries to the Asian subcontinent, China and other parts of South East Asia. Manufacturing is decimated here, while dubious practices around safety, working terms and conditions and sustainability from the early industrial age here reappear in the developing world. At the same time, widely available technologies for contacting people in your town or on the other side of the world can foment a revolution and stop a corrupt government in its tracks. New laws and policies allow those excluded on the grounds of gender, ethnicity, class, disability and sexuality to get closer to contributing their full potential while the same laws and policies leave some feeling threatened, even excluded, by the loss of a traditional knowledge of where everyone stands and what the shared values are. The way younger members of society now communicate by text, social networking sites and by playing multiplayer games on the internet offers new opportunities to connect with high-quality information technology but also challenges traditional forms of meeting, sharing, supporting, learning and forming community.

Secularization

A particular challenge for the Christian consultor from the modern context is what has been called secularization, that process where society gradually becomes less and less dependent on a religious explanation of the world. Again, like postmodernism, this is a disputed topic, which, nevertheless, helps us examine carefully the nature of changes in our society. Sociologists of religion raise big questions about what is happening in terms of religious adherence in our society today. Christianity is becoming marginalized socially, in its influence on politics, its presence in our institutions and its priority in individuals' personal lives. Bruce (2003) paints a grim picture of decline. In 1851, between 40 and 60 per cent of the British attended church. By 1999, it was 8 per cent. Among these, the balance is more heavily weighted towards the elderly than in the population as a whole. From 1900 to 2000, the number of religious professionals dropped by 25 per cent, during which time the population nearly doubled. At the beginning of the twentieth century, over 80 per cent of weddings in England and Wales took place in church. By the end of the century, less than 40 per cent did. In politics, it is significant that none of the developed assemblies of the United Kingdom has recreated anything like the position of the Church of England bishops in the House of Lords. It looks as if the influence of a basic Christian culture will become increasingly attenuated. Bruce's final prediction is that Britain will be a secular society by 2030.

It is possible to counter this argument by looking at Europe as an exception to the global picture. In North America the churches appear to be flourishing. Examples can be brought in from Africa and Asia of stable and growing churches. Those churches, such as some black churches in Britain, that reflect an American or African influence are seen as examples of continuing vigour. Some well-known sociologists like Grace Davie (2006) predict a significant and central future for religion in European and British society, although in a changed way. Rather than the established, traditional approach that she says will persist for a few decades, it is likely to be a much more USA-style, market approach tempered to some extent by the historical role of churches. You go to church as a voluntary, consumer choice rather than as an obligation or a cultural norm in a culture where church operates as a utility. For the consultant and consultor looking at this context, an important aspect she brings out is the effect secularization has on reducing the general religious literacy of the population. People will simply not understand what they are talking about when they come to discuss the place of religion in society, even the religion they identify with. Thus, in a multicultural or pluralistic society, for many of those who identify themselves as Christians, dialogue with the increasing numbers, for example, of religiously literate, European Muslims will become ill-informed and dangerously lacking in nuance.

New forms of church

Some thinkers come at this shifting context in a different, less defeated way, seeing a creative new world of blurred boundaries, liquid, emerging church, the third space, the hybrid encounter. In *Entering the New Theological Space* (Reader and Baker, 2009) the editors offer

> essays which seek to break out of the constraints of an uncritical and teleological account of a triumphant secularism that predicts the eventual collapse of organized religion and the disappearance of Christianity in the public domain. Its main thesis is that this secular meta-narrative of inexorable decline has always associated rapid social change as a crisis for the church, and defined Christians only as those people it can count in attendance and membership statistics. What this meta-narrative underestimates is the ability of Christianity, as both a cultural system and an institution, to mutate itself in surprisingly robust and relevant ways.
>
> (2009, p. 6)

In order to bridge the gap between contemporary culture and the Church, alternative ways of worship and being church are being tested. Influential initiatives such as the Church of England Report, *A Mission-Shaped Church* (Cray *et al.*, 2004), which describes and promotes fresh expressions of church, are springing up. These *emerging* churches draw on a range of tradition, practice and theologies in unconventional ways to respond to the surrounding culture and its postmodern features of consumerism, uncertainty, individualism, and immediacy and information technology. A contextual approach to theology means that it is difficult to pin these new forms down to any one coherent category. In a survey of some of these Fresh Expressions in the Anglican Church, Mobsby concludes:

Fresh Expressions are able to respond to the opportunities and challenges of this form of contextual mission, namely, a renewed hunger for relating; new forms of spirituality resultant from information technology that engage with mysticism, new forms of communication, listening and dialogue through experiential events; experience through the arts; engaging and reframing consumption; enthusiasm for experimentation; renewed interest in the relevance of ancient spirituality; positive engagement with social change; renewal of public space and engagement with the stranger.

(2007, p. 91)

These understandings have influenced large-scale mission strategy. For example, the Church of England in 2010 adopted Archbishop Rowan Williams' vision of a mixed-economy church where traditional church would sit alongside Fresh Expressions and emerging congregations where church is being re-imagined in response to changes in the context. A significant initiative, which has both contributed to and benefited from this new approach, has been the Church of England's Weddings Project. Acting on anxiety that the number of church weddings was falling dramatically faster than civic weddings, couples and clergy were interviewed systematically, revealing that more than half the population believe that church is the proper place for a wedding to happen. Yet, their lack of regular attendance made them reluctant to request a church wedding. It seems that deep spirituality, however inarticulate, and the desire to recognize that God is present in key points of life, are still common. Thus the aims of the Weddings Project, in supporting, resourcing and training ministers and churches, became

[f]irstly to let people know that the church is there for them and that they are welcome, not only in the lead-up to the wedding, but also afterwards. Secondly to work with clergy and their colleagues in parishes to ensure that people are made welcome and that their spiritual seriousness (which is very real) is itself taken seriously.

(Bayes, 2010, pp. 1–2)

These topics are very large and beset by controversy and disagreement. A brief survey such as this across these vast fields of study and debate may induce a headache even though designed just to point to fruitful areas to explore. The analysis they provide, however, and the frameworks they employ can offer illumination for the consultant working with a local church, for example on a congregation's mission strategy or with a minister on their pastoral approach.

Later chapters will suggest how the consultant might examine the closer, local, social and ecclesiological context with the consultor, but the purpose of this section is to underline the importance of understanding the broad context of the consultor's work. Both the nature of this context and consultors' assumptions and beliefs about their place in their context are key factors to take into account when looking at how to respond to work challenges. It is important for the consultant to be aware of their own assumptions and beliefs about this wider context and how that might affect their collaboration with the consultor.

The consultant as interdisciplinary thinker

Although the work of people like George Lovell and Catherine Widdicombe has been available to the churches for decades, there is often still an assumption that proper consultants come from outside the Church. In the Church of England, newly appointed bishops are offered a series of coaching sessions with expert coaches from the world of business. If a denomination or other church organization is looking to provide work consultancy for their ministers and other workers, they will often look for resources from anywhere but their own clergy. To be able to call on experienced consultants or former leaders from the commercial or public sector brings in helpful expertise. Often such people, frequently church members, are willing to give their time in a genuine attempt to help the church concerned operate more effectively. However, in my experience working in a diocesan network of consultants and with cohorts of students on a masters course in consultancy for mission and ministry, it is clear that there are significant, highly capable resources among those who already work for the Church as ministers, officers and advisors. Among these groups, the interplay between the church workers with a history of full-time ministry and those who come from a background in consultancy or leadership in secular organizations creates a rich mixture of insights, interpretative frameworks and skills. This enhances the consultancy practice of both groups. In such a network of consultants, the individual consultant will be all the more effective since they can call on a wide range of fields of knowledge and skill to inform their practice.

Consultants need to be explicit and coherent about their praxis. Praxis can be seen as the way theory and practice feed each other in building effective consultancy in a healthy, reflective, iterative, cyclical process. This combination of theory and practice will be a different mixture for each consultant. It depends on their capability, preferences, and the skills and knowledge they have built up through a work life of learning, training and experience, as well as the opportunities they have for work as a consultant. Some will be experts in particular technical areas such as youth work, fundraising, working in teams or leadership. They will bring a technical knowledge of the analytical frameworks that help diagnose the problems in their expert area and assist in constructing solutions and plans. This being said, they still need to be sensitive to the context. Otherwise, a secular consultant can be left puzzled and frustrated about why what works perfectly well in the bank or factory they work in most days will not work in a church. A competent consultant in any field working in any but the narrowest way with the most limited, technical subjects will be drawing on understandings of how to listen, the way groups work, how organizations are structured, how change comes about, how to plan, how systems help, and so on. This would indicate that they have engaged seriously with disciplines such as individual and social psychology, change management, theories of learning and training, management studies, organizational behaviour, all often mixed in with some financial, commercial and project-management theory. The added ingredient for a consultant setting to work in churches is the whole area of theology, mission and ecclesiology. Often credibility for a consultant from outside church circles is based on their work in secular organizations. However, it is very easy for the ordained consultor to dismiss someone they perceive as an outsider as not understanding that the Church is an organization unlike any other, with a different history, with different aspirations and perspectives and with different types of role relationships. Even for consultants with a background in the voluntary sector, consultors can see churches as very different animals. Often there is a basic truth in this. Yet, there are some practices and assumptions in the way churches traditionally operate which deserve challenge from good quality, secular theory. Similarly, if churches draw on their own workers as consultants, they will come with a ready-made understanding of theology, mission and ecclesiology. They will often also come with skills and knowledge used in common with other caring professions, such as counselling or social work. What they will need over and above this, however, may well come from the secular disciplines and the theories and models of consultancy.

Being able to handle a range of disciplines productively is not easy. There is always the danger of claiming an unrealistic facility and depth of understanding based on a surface acquaintance with a particular field. Balance needs to be sought in knowing enough to be able to use the skills and insights ethically without having to be a world expert. The major benefit of calling on a range of disciplines is how they help to analyse a situation by looking at qualitatively different dynamics in explaining what is going on. The skill is not just in being able to do the analysis but also to work with the complex, interacting impacts that the different analyses bring, assessing their relevance and significance. It can be very helpful to make notes and go away to reflect, but often the most telling interventions by a consultant can be when they suddenly realize they have been approaching the issue from one angle when another theoretical framework might shed more light on the situation. They then test that out with the consultor in the session. For example, the sticky issue of the youth group leaders not running the Friday meetings very well may not be an organizational structure or leadership training problem. It may be a psychological issue all about the pastor's need to feel wanted by the people by whom he's always been affirmed. It's not that the youth leaders will not take up the responsibility; it is that there is something in the dynamic that is about the pastor not letting go. It can be quite a pressure, but being able to undertake this interdisciplinary analysis live is very helpful to a consultancy session.

Tragical – Comical – Historical – Pastoral

The leadership team of an Anglican team ministry in which I was one of the self-supporting clergy were having difficulty understanding how to deal with the antagonistic relationship between two of the churches in the team. The team's regular consultant, Judi, had worked with us through a difficult time of change and reshaping of the parishes in the team ministry. For this meeting she suggested we constructed a timeline. Along this timeline we were to position stories that went as far back as we could remember or as far back as we had heard stories. Some of the staff were clergy appointed to posts in the team. Others were ordained and lay leaders who had lived in the area for quite some time. Memories were shared and positioned on the long timeline on the roll of paper on the floor. One of the self-supporting ministers, June, who had lived in the town for a long time, recounted stories about how, 50 or 60 years ago, choristers from the two currently unco-operative churches used to stand on either side of the street and throw stones at each other. Others then added that the received wisdom was that this was because the newer church had been built for the use of the servants of the wealthy people who attended the older church and so symbolized a class division between the two congregations. This was a signifi-cant, penny-dropping moment. The technique of viewing the his-torical structure of the churches' relationship with telling and shar-ing stories led the staff to draw on insights from the dynamics and psychology of organizations. We could now see the same patterns being perpetuated, repeated and reinforced in the new context of the present changes. Looking for help with contemporary obstacles, a multidisciplinary reflection on the past illuminated the present and opened up a deeper analysis on which to plan future strate-gies. Just assuming that Christians will get along with each other in what looks like a reasonable way was, evidently, not a good place to start.

Drawing on a range of disciplines does not mean that their insights are accepted uncritically. The act of drawing on different approaches means that it is possible to set up a dialogue between them. There may be assumptions in some approaches in the social sciences that are antithetical to some theological assumptions. A well-used schema in understanding people individually and in organizations is Maslow's hierarchy of needs. It sees our priority as human beings in a pyramid moving from the basic, physiological needs (breathing, food, sleep …) through safety needs (protection from danger, shelter ...), needs of love, affection and belonging, needs for esteem (self-esteem and esteem from others) to needs for self-actualization (achieving individual potential). It is commonly accepted that humans need to have the earlier ones satisfied before they perceive the need to satisfy the higher ones. So, if a person is ill, all they care about is getting better. In *Christ in the Marketplace* (2008), a study of how the Church might engage with the world of business, Bridget Adams shows, by using insights from theology, Scripture and religious experience, that Maslow's analysis is sometimes not correct. Again and again, for example, Christians and those of other faiths have relegated the basic need for food or security below finding self-fulfilment, purpose and communion with God, often at the cost of their lives. She quotes John 6.68, when the disciples are confronted with the cost of discipleship: 'Lord, to whom shall we go? You have the words of eternal life.'

A useful example of interdisciplinary thinking is contained in the format of Cameron *et al.*'s *Studying Local Churches* (2005). This is designed as a handbook in the field of Congregational Studies. It looks at a series of issues such as studying the local church, resources and people, power and the local and global context of a church. Each topic is handed over to a sociologist, an anthropologist, an expert in organizational studies and a theologian so that the reader gets four distinct academic approaches to the same issue side by side, as well as a sense of the dialogue between them. What they offer is high-level analysis by experts. It may be too much to expect every consultant to develop and maintain a similar expertise. However, as part of their regular, professional reflection, consultants need to check that they are sufficiently knowledgeable and up to date to be able to apply relevant interdisciplinary fields of knowledge in an integrated fashion. A later chapter in this book looks at models of consultancy in the hope that church consultants will be conscious and thoughtful about the models they are using in their practice. Although it is common for consultants to identify themselves with a particular family or mode of consultancy (complexity theory or a psychodynamic approach, for example), many make use of a mixture of approaches as well as drawing on insights from numerous disciplines. It is to be hoped that consultants consider the consistency and effectiveness of the mixture they are using and their ability to deploy it helpfully.

The consultant as reflective practitioner

A common experience among working people, whether in churches or in secular organizations, is that they are very busy. In the rush to get everything done they finish one task and then jump straight into the next. What is typically missed out is any form of review. It is an understandable reaction to the pressure of being minister in charge of ten rural chapels, or not just the vicar but the area dean as well. Yet, the consequence can be a loss of effectiveness and efficiency. If we don't reflect on what we have just done, we will not benefit from any lesson our success or failure can teach us, and we are likely to repeat the same mistakes. It is a matter of slowing down for a while in order to speed up overall. This notion of reflective practice is increasingly seen as an essential part of a professional's regular work. The worker's ability to do their job is directly connected with their ability to learn from what they have done and to use that learning to improve their work. David Kolb (1984) suggested this reflection and development happens ideally in an Adult Learning Cycle. The process of learning, he says, builds up through four steps (see Figure 1.1).

At a slight distance from work we have just done we can observe what we have experienced and arrive at analysis and judgements about

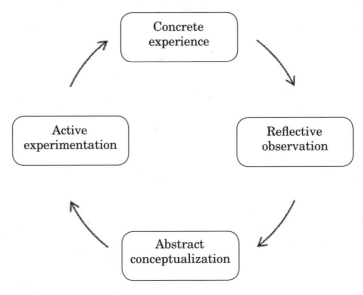

Figure 1.1 Kolb's Adult Learning Cycle

D. Kolb, 1984, *Experiential Learning: Experience As A Source of Learning and Development*, 1st edn, p. 21. Reprinted by permission of Pearson Education Inc., Upper Saddle River, NJ.

what is working and what not. We can bring in analytical tools, theories and frameworks from books and experts to help us reflect. From that, the process derives abstract concepts, principles and models that will, in turn, allow us to form a plan, an experiment as to how we operate the next time. The process is more a spiral than a cycle as it assumes that the next action, which has benefited from the reflective learning, will become, in its turn, the object of observation, reflection, conceptualization, and lead to further modifications in the approach to the task in a continuing flow of improvement. It is important to note that the assumption behind Kolb's approach is that, to be of maximum benefit, the driver of this learning is the individual concerned. It is much more about learning than teaching or training and is a lifelong activity. This is not to say that, as a result of this experiential learning process, the individual may not identify a need for being taught or trained.

In Christian circles, many people are familiar with the pastoral cycle as a means of reflection and planning. For a helpful discussion of how this can be used, and further similar models, see Judith Thompson's *SCM Studyguide: Theological Reflection* (2008). Put simply, the steps are *See – Judge/Reflect – Act*, or, in a more developed way, *Experience – Analysis – Reflection – Action – Celebration*. This approach, evidently similar to Kolb's, guards against both constant activism, where we are always beavering away but never checking whether we are effective or improving, and spending all our time reflecting but never actually getting anything done. Its emphasis on the individual or individuals concerned taking the initiative in looking at what they have been doing or intend to do has been used to great effect in supporting empowerment and liberation work in poor communities. It is a basic tool in liberation theology. Reflection on practice can very successfully be a group activity. This can form the process by which assessment of the present reality and planning future strategy happen, for example, in a church committee or working group or as a form of consultancy or supervision for a group who meet on a regular basis. Action research, which is a method used by many consultants to help an organization, can be seen as the same reflective process engaged in by members of a social group or situation in order to improve, as Carr and Kemmis say, 'the rationality and justice of their own practice, their understanding of these practices, and the situations in which these practices are carried out' (1986, p. 162).

Supports to reflective practice

The origins of these models are in the world of secular adult learning and learning organizations. There is a characteristic difference when it comes to learning and reflection in a Christian setting, particularly when we think about the theories and frameworks against which a consultor or a consultant will reflect on their experience of doing work. As has already been said, the consultant needs to be an interdisciplinary thinker, for example drawing on insights from a range of social sciences while using group work and active listening skills. The big difference is that the consultant and consultor reflect on what they are doing against biblical frameworks and models from theology. There will be a discussion in the next section on theological reflection itself when we look at the consultant as practical theologian, but the principles of being a reflective practitioner in this section are essential factors in how theological reflection can be of use. Considering, say, a biblical framework in an adult learning or pastoral cycle shows how such reflection can help a consultancy address issues of coherence, consistency and effectiveness. If a church declares that its purpose is to make disciples along the lines of the last verses of Matthew 28 or to work for justice in terms of Luke 4's account of Jesus in the synagogue at Nazareth, it is relatively clear how the core passage can be a lens through which to examine the congregation's strategies and behaviour. How exactly does the beetle drive or the minister's merry-go-round of visiting make disciples or build a just society?

The same process takes place with the more secular elements on which consultant and consultor can draw. A good example is your theory of change. It is possible to see all a consultant does as concerning change: how to help a consultor cope with changes around them, implement a desired change or keep themselves effective and improving over time. If the consultor is looking for change, there might be an assumption that the consultor is operating on the basis of some idea about how change happens or is brought about. It may be, however, that they are not and this becomes the basis of work between the consultant and the consultor. Is it a secular theory? Is it a theory from business or psychology? Is it a theory based on an understanding of the agency of God in the world as miraculous intervention, response to prayer, via the processes of creation or through the powerlessness of the cross? The consultant should consider whether the consultor might have a different change model from theirs. The way a consultant reviews their work as a consultant, therefore, needs to take into account, in this case, both their own theory of change and that of the consultor, assessing the effect of the interaction between them and how that has been handled. (For a detailed discussion of theories of change, see Chapter 6.)

In order to be as effective as possible, the consultant needs to reflect on what is happening on four levels:

1 the issues in the consultor's problem/case in context and the action taken
2 the nature and quality of the consultor's reflection on 1
3 the nature and quality of their own reflection on 1 and 2
4 the nature and quality of their reflection on their responses to and actions with the consultor.

This means that a consultant needs to be able to undertake what Argyris and Schön (1978) call 'double-loop' learning. 'Single-loop' learning means looking at what you have done, seeing whether it was successful or not and modifying your actions as a result of your analysis. Double-loop learning is an examination of the single-loop learning. It questions the assumptions, values and principles that informed the action in the first place with a view to reinforcing or modifying them according to whether they are helpful or not. A consequence of this may be the discovery of a contradiction between two theories of action, the 'espoused theory' – what you say are the principles and values behind how you operate – and the 'theory in use' – the way you actually operate, especially when under stress. This can be of invaluable help both in looking at the way the consultor is acting and in the consultant reflecting on their own interaction with the consultor.

One technique that many people find a useful support to their reflective learning is keeping a journal, a daily or regular account of what has happened, what the journaller feels and thinks about it on reflection and any developing themes and intentions for the future. It encourages the single-loop learning by giving a space and time for making a record of events and processing them. It also allows double-loop learning to happen as the continuing record (in a book, on sheets in a folder, on a blog or computer, on an audio or video recording) offers an overview of developing trends, repeating patterns and insights that stick out as major shifts in understanding – learning about the learning. Mark Smith, on www.infed.org, provides a helpful summary of journalling, with some good references to follow up.

Journalling in some form or other is heavily recommended by writers such as Frances Ward in her *Lifelong Learning* (2005). She sees it as a central tool in the worker's professional development in ministry and draws on key writers to provide a detailed toolkit for getting to grips with writing in this reflective way. Some consultants may, however, find that writing a journal does not help or is too difficult. So, they don't stick with it. Sometimes this is a matter of learning style. When considering how best to reflect, it may be helpful for the consultant to consider how they best learn. There are theories around learning styles on many a website where the way we take in information visually or verbally or in a tactile/physical way might point up difficulties with journalling. Perhaps it would be better to make diagrams or pictures. Some people do their reflecting by talking to someone else or in a group. Awareness of one's personality, as in, for example, Myers Briggs typologies, can explain what works for one person as against another. As always, such categorizations need to be taken as indicators of preferences rather than predictions of inability to work in any but the identified category. However, it may help to understand why a technique such as journalling might be more of a struggle for some than for others and how to gain the benefits of such a useful technique given an individual's basic preferences. For example, it may be easier to see journalling as a group activity or done with a guide or tutor, at least at first, rather than as a solitary activity.

Chapter 8 will look, among other topics, at the necessity of supervision for the consultant. It is of benefit for a number of reasons but, for the purposes of the present discussion, a central benefit is how it helps the consultant become, remain and improve as a reflective practitioner. Whether the supervision happens with an individual supervisor, with a work-based group or with an outside group, a central part of its function is to support the consultant in the double-loop learning that results from rigorous, imaginative reflection on practice. This should be an explicit part of the contract at the start of the supervision and part of any review of how the supervision is going.

The consultant as practical theologian

So, consultants are people aware of context, able to think in an interdisciplinary manner, drawing on a spectrum of sources including theology. They reflect carefully on what they are and have been doing in order to discover patterns and improve their praxis. This places their work in the field of practical theology. Historically, practical theology has been closely identified with that bit of ministers' college training where they were taught how to do the pastoral aspects of the job. More recently, with the move away from a clerical paradigm to an emphasis on the ministry of the whole Christian community in the world, practical theology has become much more generally about how Christian life and practice operates within the Church and within society as a whole. It depends on both an understanding of theology and of the social context, surfing on the ebb and flow of the dialogue between them. It can be seen as a very wide-ranging undertaking as it involves such things as theory, practice, the pastoral activity of ministers, issues of Christian truth in a pluralistic environment, and the meaning a church member looks for in being a faithful Christian in the workplace. The emphasis is on the interaction between ideas and practice and can start from either. It is possible to start with the theological concepts in order to look for principles behind proposed action or to start with a problem that needs addressing and look at the issue through the lens of the tradition of the Church and its understanding of God's purposes in the world. (For a good discussion of the history, theory and development of practical theology and many useful essays on how it works in practice, see Woodward and Pattison's *The Blackwell Reader in Pastoral and Practical Theology* (2000).)

A key aspect of practical theology is that it is contextual. It makes little sense if it is not helping understand and mould practical activity in the mission and ministry of the Church. Consultants support that activity by helping consultors address the problems, situations and challenges they face in that work in context. This means that they need, first, to be able to think about the work of the consultor in theological terms, helping them reflect productively, and, second, to be able to reflect theologically on their own activity as a consultant. Judith Thompson's book on theological reflection (2008), which has already been mentioned, offers an accessible introduction to a range of useful, reflective methods. Again, as with the discussion on reflective practice and learning styles, there is no one particular method of theological reflection that is the best or must be followed. There are varieties of ways of doing it, which go some way to catering for the different personalities and theological backgrounds found among consultants and consultors. Another useful resource is Graham, Walton and Ward's *Theological Reflection: Methods* (2005). This provides an overview of a series of well-used methods with examples of how each method has been used, with commentary on the strengths and weaknesses of each method.

The range of methods that can be used for theological reflection needs to respond to different personalities and learning styles. Some people will benefit from a contemplative or written method, whereas some will get more out of discussion or movement. Or it may be that certain reflective processes work better with groups than with individuals. Lovell, in *Diagrammatic Modelling: An Aid to Theological Reflection in Church and Community Development Work* (1991), describes a process based on diagrams developed by the William Temple Foundation in the late 1970s to do theological modelling and reflection. He says:

> The diagrams were a novel way of conducting a theological discussion: normally we relied entirely on words and theological exchanges that rely entirely on words so quickly become involved and abstract. Diagrams tend to make things concrete and objective. They make one think again. Of themselves, they display old truths in a different light. They help people to articulate what they cannot adequately describe.
>
> (Lovell, 1991, p. 42)

Diagrams can be a powerful tool in building the analyses and designs that are part of the consultancy helping process and have a particular value when consultor and consultant are trying to understand the relationships, causal and influential, between different factors in a situation. As Lovell says, often familiar situations can suddenly be enlightened by the construction of a diagram in understanding the reasons behind, consequences of, and the theological implications of a structure, system or pattern of behaviour.

For some consultants, particularly those who come from a secular background, it may feel that this is straying too far onto ground where they are not confident. Just asking the question may be enough to release the theological skills of the consultor with whom the consultant is working. In a non-directive sense, there is no problem in the consultor leading the theologically less expert consultant through a process of theological reflection on the issue on which they are working. As we shall see later, effective consultancy is a collaborative activity where as much use as possible is made of the skills of both consultant and consultor. However the process works, it is important that questions are addressed about what the consultor's activity implies in terms of grace, salvation, community, justice, hope, the Eucharist, bias to the poor, discipleship, atonement, forgiveness and so on. It can be vital to get to grips with the fact that the consultor's (or indeed the consultant's) espoused theology, that is, the theological principles and values they say they are following, is inconsistent with the operant theology, that is, the theological principles and values demonstrated in the way they are behaving.

In terms, then, of being a practical theologian, the work of the consultant in context can be seen as:

- *doxological* – supporting the work of those who are enabling the Church to be a channel of the worship and praise of God
- *missiological* – assisting those who are being Christ's hands, mouths and feet in the world to do that as effectively as possible
- *vocational* – helping those involved in the Christian project to be all they can on the way to reaching the potential God has given them
- *justice focused* – working constructively alongside those who are building a world where the poor hear good news, the blind see and the oppressed go free
- *transformational* – accompanying consultors through the internal and external blocks and challenges before them in their work of mission and ministry.

2

The Consultant and Church Organizations

> The Diocese of Oxford's unique combination of buildings, volunteers, voluntary giving and involvement in the lives of the community make it the largest self-funded voluntary organisation in the Thames Valley.
>
> (www.oxford.anglican.org)

This is a dramatic claim from a Church of England diocese's website. It opens up a multitude of questions that the church consultant needs to ponder before grappling with a presenting issue. What does it mean by organization? What does voluntary mean? Are the volunteers mentioned members? When you look around a church, there seem to be paid workers, unpaid workers, regular attenders and some more like occasional consumers. Why is there no mention of the word 'church'? There seems to be a connection between being a voluntary organization and involvement in the community, presumably of some benefit to that community. Why is being the biggest voluntary organization something to be proud of for a Christian body? Are we meant to assume this church body runs just like any voluntary organization? Does it run differently from a public body like a council or a school, and from a commercial entity such as a manufacturing company or a bank? Are all churches the same, given that they might be called Presbyterian, Methodist, Roman Catholic or Baptist? This way of talking about the diocese seems very secular. Aren't there more theological models from the Bible or elsewhere?

The answers to these questions are not simple but, if consultants are to be of any help, they will have, in their toolkit, ways of understanding or categories by which to get to understand how churches operate and how they perceive themselves. The aim of this chapter is to point the consultant to areas of the disciplines of organizational behaviour and organizational studies, of the relatively recent field of congregational studies, and of missiology and ecclesiology that will assist in acquiring the necessary tools.

The first section of this chapter looks at how churches might be classified in terms of organizational studies models. Using sociological terms, it asks whether they are bureaucracies or associations or something else. This leads to a discussion of the clergy whose role, both set apart, ordained and paid, yet still members alongside the laity, can be puzzling. The next section looks at some of the theological models and images of the Church and particularly at the development of the understanding of the Church as participant in, rather than initiator of, God's mission in the world. The third section examines different ways of understanding congregations of different sizes and styles and their work as collaborators in God's mission, spending some time on roles, relationships, systems, teams and personnel.

A few basic resources
for the consultant who wants to understand the
church as an organization

J. Shafritz and J. S. Ott (eds), 2010, *Classics of Organization Theory*, 9th edn, Belmont, CA: Wadworth – *a helpfully structured series of readings from key authors in the field of organizational studies which give a clear and authentic flavour of the major developments in this field.*

H. Cameron, P. Richter, D. Davies & F. Ward (eds), 2005, *Studying Local Churches*, London: SCM Press – *congregational studies seen as the interaction of anthropology, organizational studies, theology and sociology applied rigorously and practically to local churches, with a good review of the literature.*

D. Bosch, 1991, *Transforming Mission: Paradigm Shifts in Theology of Mission*, Maryknoll, NY: Orbis Books – *the classic text which includes a significant analysis of the Church's models of mission over the centuries and proposes the key features of mission in a post-modern world.*

M. Torry, 2005, *Managing God's Business: Religious and Faith-Based Organizations and their Management*, London: Ashgate – *a significant, useful review of the literature about the way religious organizations are managed.*

> www.alban.org – *the Alban Institute is an ecumenical, interfaith organization based in the United States which provides interdisciplinary resources and modelling on congregations through its community, publishing, research and consulting.*

What type of organizations are churches?

This question can be asked in two ways. What kind of organizations are churches, and what kind of organization is the Church? The consultant needs a range of models and frameworks through which to ask organizational questions. Otherwise, any consulting interventions may miss the mark. As has been said a number of times already, the wealth of material from the public sector and business world on the nature of organizations and what happens inside and around them tempts the organizational thinker to apply secular insights directly onto churches and faith-based organizations. As we have also seen, this does not always work. It would, therefore, be a good idea to explore organizational and ecclesiological approaches to the nature of churches before starting to consult on church issues. So what do we mean by organizations?

> We are born in hospitals, educated in schools, employed by business firms and government agencies, we join trades unions and professional associations, and are laid to rest in churches. In sickness and in health, at work and at play, life in modern industrialized society is increasingly conducted in organizational settings.
>
> (Haralambos and Holborn, 1990, p. 405)

Organizations are key features of our society. Whether they are modelled as systems, machines, institutions or organisms, organizations are basically social; that is, they are about people getting together to achieve tasks that are too big for one person alone. The larger and more complicated the task becomes and the more people who need to be involved, the more organizations need to be able to co-ordinate and manage the work through structure, authority and systems. In the early Church's case, the need to preach the gospel further and more widely, and to support the networks that grew up of people who believed in the gospel, meant that the work that needed to be done increased in quantity and complexity. Thus, the Church, as we meet it today, constitutes a sociological and organizational entity or multiple entities. Disciplines such as sociology and organizational studies may, therefore, hold useful insights for the consultant working with church issues, as the next few pages intend to demonstrate.

Are churches bureaucracies?

Max Weber, one of the founders of modern sociology, worked on the idea of organizations as entities designed to co-ordinate the work of a number of people who are tackling the same task in order to suggest the different forms organizations take. He is most associated with the form *bureaucracy*. He saw this as becoming the dominant form of organization in modern society, in that it is an efficient and effective way of implementing the tasks that need to happen in order to achieve its purpose. It involves a hierarchy of paid officials who control, manage and co-ordinate the network of different tasks needed and the distribution of the tasks in well-ordered, standardized specializations. Nowadays, bureaucracy is regularly talked about as negative, but when Weber was developing his theories, it was seen as the rational way of setting up entities that would achieve objectives through complex, interacting activities without the need for authoritarianism or arbitrary use of power. Weber's prediction has proved correct in that bureaucratic organizations are now found not just in business but also in government, education, the military and even churches. In contrast to other forms of action (*affective* where action is based on emotion, or *traditional* where action is based on what has been the custom), *rational* action, which has its best organizational expression in a bureaucracy, is seen by Weber as 'the methodical attainment of a definitely given and practical end by means of an increasingly precise calculation of adequate means' (in Gerth and Mills, 1991, p. 293).

Weber proposed the ideal form of bureaucracy but made no claims to its desirability or ease of operation. A more recent proponent of bureaucracy, Elliott Jaques, the organizational psychologist who started much of the organizational work at the Tavistock Institute, is well known for his assertions that, if an organization is built on a bureaucracy with a well thought-out and implemented managerial hierarchy, not only will the organization be effective, and if commercial, profitable, but it will be a place where employees are fulfilled in their work as they are in the right place where their capability is used to the full and they can trust those who manage them. The fact that this seems to have rarely, if ever, been the case, does not deter Jaques.

Hierarchy has not had its day. Hierarchy never did have its day. As an organizational system, managerial hierarchy has never been adequately described and has just as certainly never been adequately used. The problem is not to find an alternative to a system that once worked well but no longer does; the problem is to make it work efficiently for the first time in its 3,000 year history.

(Jaques, 1990, p. 231)

A central feature of a bureaucracy is that it is a system of control. This control depends on legitimate authority accepted by the managed in the organization both regarding their managers and in its rules, policies and systems. In affective action, that authority might come from the response to the charismatic leader – likely to be personal and short lived. In traditional action, authority might depend on kinship, class roles or social obligation. Under rational action, authority comes from the fact that accountability, task and position within the hierarchy are distributed in a logical fashion to people in roles or offices under a consistent system of rules. Thus, activities such as the supervision of the people over whom you have authority operate dispassionately according to the rules, which are based on rationally calculated, explicit factors. Offices are given to those who are capable of carrying them out. Weber saw bureaucracy as the most efficient way of allowing large organizations to carry out complex tasks. However, he was concerned with what this might mean in terms of human freedom, initiative, creativity and happiness. The elements of control inherent in the structure open the way for the abuse of authority and for the creation of a culture and of people who will only ever follow orders, particularly when bureaucracy is implemented by governments. As bureaucracy and hierarchy have been used to study and explain organizations since Weber's time, questions have been raised about some of its assumptions about organizations. Is, for example, a bureaucracy merely a reflection and reinforcement of existing patterns such as masculine, class-bound or western capitalist ways of running the world? Furthermore, in recent years the ease with which information flows and the ability to organize over very different geographical and social ranges permitted by developments in information technology may lead some to think that bureaucracies are no longer necessary.

Are churches associations?

An alternative organizational form for getting work done Weber identified is the *association*. There is no generally agreed definition of an association but Helen Cameron (2010, p. 27) has produced the following list of characteristics of associations from a survey of the literature on voluntary associations:

Voluntary associations
- are formally organized
- have offices filled by established procedures (often elections)
- hold scheduled meetings
- bestow membership on applicants who fulfil criteria
- have some formalized division of labour
- make decisions by democratic processes whether representative or participative
- expect members to pay towards the association normally by a subscription
- expect members to contribute their time to the work of the association
- can only ask members to leave the association if they break its rules
- may employ paid staff to support the work of the association, enabling the members to carry out the distinctive tasks for which they associate.

The distinction between associations and bureaucracies hinges, according to Knoke and Prensky (1984), around approaches to

- incentives to participate
- formal structure
- authority relations
- relationship to the environment
- criteria for organizational effectiveness.

It is important to keep these distinctions in mind as some organizations display characteristics of both associational and bureaucratic form. Significant numbers of organizations are governed ultimately by an association. British schools have boards of governors who are unpaid representatives of various sections of the community, who determine the overall policy and strategy of the school. They employ head teachers and staff in a bureaucratic hierarchy to effect the work of educating young people. Charities will have boards of trustees who are volunteers but are held accountable under charity law for the charity's work getting done even if that is actually done by paid managers and workers.

Whether churches are associations is a matter for discussion. Churches feel like voluntary organizations, but it seems, in many churches, to be the paid, employed workers (bishops, ministers, parish priests and pastors) rather than the members who make the decisions, even though there are church councils, committees and bodies of elders. The existence of the two organizational notions at the same time in the same organization can lead to confusion about how member/volunteer workers and employed workers are treated and how accountability works. I heard recently of a minister in an episcopally led church, who certain members of the congregation thought was not working hard or long enough, being threatened by those members at a church council with a time and motion study. Time sheets would have to be filled in to account for how the minister's day was spent. The minister politely declined.

Church – denomination – sect

Congregations can be distinguished by a number of recurrent forms of social organization that relate to theological dispositions. In this respect, sociologists have customarily drawn from models derived from Weber and developed by Troeltsch and (H. Richard) Niebuhr as ideal types. These encompass three organizational types – church, denomination and sect – which broadly correspond to the way power is distributed within Christian groups. Churches have a high ecclesiology, reflected in vertical top–down power structures. In terms of authority, they are both hierarchical and bureaucratic. Denominations tend to have more horizontal power structures, reflecting their associational nature and a more relativized approach to authority. Sects tend to rely more on authority deriving from 'charismatic' leadership, where there is strong emotional or affective commitment to leaders and, usually, a high degree of normative consensus which can be rigidly enforced. Bureaucracy tends to be weak and these groups are often fairly fissile.

(Paul Chambers in Cameron *et al.*, 2005, p. 200)

It is possible to distinguish between associations along the lines of who benefits from their activities. Does its activity benefit members like a society of bee-keepers or a trade union, or benefit the public, those who are not its members, like Meals on Wheels or a local Churches Together homelessness shelter? The distinction is not always clear. It may be thought that a church choir's aim is to assist in leading the worship of the people of God in that place. However, it is often the case that such choirs will only agree to sing what they like and want to sing. They don't turn up when their sort of music is not on the menu. The apparent public benefit has changed into member benefit. Clarity around this, achieved often by talking to the members and beneficiaries themselves, can be crucial if consultors with the help of their consultants are going to understand a situation.

The nature of church work often entails significant involvement in the community. This may be done directly or through charities, trusts or voluntary organizations set up to employ workers or to manage the interaction with other public, ecclesiastical or voluntary agencies. Examples could be a multi-agency youth project, an initiative around unemployment, a church cafe, the trust that runs the church/village hall as a community association, or a church social club with an alcohol and entertainment licence. What the consultant needs to look out for is how the different bodies within what may look like one organization are run. What is the nature of governance? How are decisions made? How are members, volunteers and employees held accountable for what they are expected to do? What happens if they don't do what they are supposed to? What is the relationship with external bodies in terms of funding, spending, service delivery, accountability and transparency? How is the difference from the way a church is governed and managed handled? How is governance different from what church members experience in their work lives? Those who are used to decisive managerial decision-making in their workplace often feel frustration when it comes to the long-winded, inclusive, consensual, meandering way decisions are reached in voluntary and church settings. As part of its constitutional set-up, the board of trustees of a charity may have service users as trustees. This provides crucial service-member input, but their approach to their role as trustees may be too close to the operational decisions that are the proper concern of the paid workers. It may be very difficult to maintain the overview distance that is desirable.

So, are we to conclude that the Church and churches are associations? In an article in an important book on congregational studies, Guest *et al.*'s *Congregational Studies in the UK: Christianity in a Post-Christian Context* (2004), Helen Cameron argues that, although congregations display some of the characteristics of associations, none seem to be exactly associations. Even within denominations there seem to be such differences between churches that applying the given literature about associations to them doesn't quite work. The way they make decisions and galvanize the resources of time and money from among their membership can be wildly different. This diversity is to be celebrated. As she says, 'in a culture where much of organizational life has been homogenized by managerialism, congregations stand out as a testimony to the variety of ways in which work can be organized and the range of beliefs and values it is therefore possible to enact' (Cameron, 2004, p. 148).

What about the clergy?

An issue that is probably getting more confused at the moment is the status of the clergy. Recent changes in many churches, sometimes in reaction to anxiety about new laws and the risk of litigation, have given the impression that clergy are employed by the churches. Traditionally, clergy have been regarded as office holders rather than employees. Elliott Jaques agrees strongly with this as a result of his work with the Church of England:

> Clergy are decidedly *not* employees of the Church. They are members of the Church, in the sense not only of being members of the Association, as are all parishioners, but special members in the sense of being ordained members. The only employees are the administrative and maintenance staff, choir members (sometimes), and some other members of staff who may or may not be members of the Church. Being members of an Association does not provide for being a manager of other members. There is no managerial hierarchy of clergy. The Bishop is not in a manager–subordinate relationship with the Parish Priest ... Nor does the fact that clergy receive financial recompense make them into employees, any more than partners, or professional athletes, or elected political representatives, are employees, even though they also receive money ... In short, clergy are members of the Church.
>
> (1994, pp. 3–4)

Developments in ministerial review, national and regional restructuring, the arrival of terms and conditions, and managerialist expectations on senior roles in churches may be giving the impression that the churches are becoming, or are already, bureaucratic hierarchies with clergy now straightforward employees as in any business. The most that can be said may be that the situation is confused, and clarifying what that confusion is in organizational terms is important work for any consultation affected by these issues. Malcolm Torry (2005, p. 111) suggests, from his survey of the literature, that there may be a distinction between the organizational experience at the local level, which has more of a community feel about it, and the regional or national level where it may be more bureaucratic. It is often a mistake to see churches as national or international organizations in the same way as you would a multinational corporation. Many denominations have a more or less congregationalist basis where authority is firmly rooted in the local assembly and local congregations pay their clergy. In contrast, the Anglican Church is often proclaimed as an episcopally led church, where congregationalism, however common, is not seen as the prime organizational model. The Church of England, with recent developments such as the Archbishops' Council, may look like a single institution. It becomes obvious, for example in the case of implementing national schemes such as the Ministerial Development Review, that the 43 dioceses (44 including the Diocese in Europe) are very much organizations of their own with bishops who happily and idiosyncratically determine what goes on in them according to their own vision.

Recognizing these differences will mean that it will be most productive to 'aim at best practice in all of them', emphasizing that 'methods believed to be appropriate at one level of an organization should not be assumed to be appropriate at another' (Torry, 2005, p. 111). Torry sees it as

> essential that we recognize that the governance of complex religious organizations is never going to be easy, for what constitutions exist are generally implied rather than explicit, there are different authority and compliance structures at work at the same time, change is threatening (because managing change in a complex organization is complex), and denial and avoidance set in; and in such a situation absence of communication is inevitable and sub-groups emerge and compete for resources. At the same time, the needs of neither the members nor the organization are met and the clergy's multiple roles become a source of conflict.
>
> (2005, p. 112)

There is, as can be seen, a significant danger of a consultant with a commercial or public background thinking that the recent changes mean that it is possible to see the clergy as either standard employees or as like professionals such as lawyers. The situation is more complex or perhaps more muddled than that.

There is, in addition to this, the question of whether the clergy are professionals. In a theological reflection in the Church of England report *Guidelines for the Professional Conduct of the Clergy* (2003), Francis Bridger is keen to hold together two ways of understanding *profession*. The first involves professing (standing for) a set of values or principles, and is closely connected with a sense of vocation. The second involves a set of principles, conventions, ethics and practices, which allow the individual to carry out their function professionally. Thus, professional, in the case of the clergy, indicates tangible, ethical service of God in and through the community in a way that responds vocationally to, and channels, God's love. Torry comments on a process of de-professionalization following a previous, partial and diverse professionalization. Interestingly, though, he sees clergy, who will be, for the foreseeable future, servants of small religious voluntary organizations, as moving into the 'role of listening as well as telling, of narrative knowledge, as well as rational knowledge; in fact the kind of "professionalism" which medical practitioners are now learning' (2005, p. 143). If this is a question in a consultancy, consultor and consultant may find it worthwhile to reflect on issues at stake in thinking about the clergy as professionals. Might it lead to a downgrading of the laity? Or, build a dependency culture? Might talk about clergy as the church professionals create assumptions among lay people, both professional and non-professional lay people, about the ways in which clergy will act and work?

Theological models and images of the Church

Access to a range of models or images of the Church can be helpful in getting people to think about what they are doing and being as a church or a member or leader of a local church. The first place many will look is in Scripture. In a study called *Images of the Church in the New Testament* (1960), Paul Minear identified 96 New Testament images of the Church, ranging from salt, through those on the road and the branches of the vine, to the Holy City. Examining the images, he builds a network that connects many of the pictures of the Church to four main images: the *people of God*, the *new creation*, the *fellowship in faith* and the *body of Christ*. Respectively these have different emphases: the first on the historical dimension coming out of Israelite origins; the second the cosmic element expressed in the new creation; the fellowship in faith concentrating on the personal, individual aspect; and the body picture underlining the corporate nature of the Church. These images are not complete or exclusive. Indeed, holding these different images together in tension will help to understand in biblical terms what might be happening and what might be missing. Using a range of biblical images with a consultor can reveal assumptions, causations and possibilities.

In an early work trying to link management theory with theological insights, *Ministry and Management: The Study of Ecclesiastical Management* (1964), the Australian Peter Rudge attempted to map Minear's four categories to standard theories of management, which he terms:

- *traditional theory* – the organization has a history and a life of its own which drives it on and keeps it whole and decisions and leadership continue what has always happened without much question
- *charismatic theory* – the focus is on the institution often of a prophetic leader who sets and controls what goes on among compliant followers
- *classical theory* – sees the organization as a machine that runs efficiently with a pyramidal structure and rationalized, routinized decision-making
- *human relations theory* – sees the organization as a series of face-to-face, group relationships populated by cultured, sophisticated people who provide momentum around shared goals
- *systemic theory* – sees the organization as a system, almost organic, composed of, but greater than, its constituent parts working through interdependence with leaders looking out for changes in the environment in order to help the system adjust appropriately.

Rudge finds that none of the New Testament images correspond with the classical model but suspects that some church structures and therefore ecclesiastical doctrines, particularly in the Roman Catholic Church, have developed since biblical times along classical lines. Writing at the same time as Vatican II, he suspects there might be some reshaping of structure and doctrine away from a classical model. It is interesting that influential texts about organizations such as Gareth Morgan's *Images of Organization* (2006) are relatively quick to dismiss the classical model as mechanistic, with its dominance in much organizational and leadership thinking being a big problem. It is a model he has to leave behind before exploring models that are more acceptable. Traditional theory, with its emphasis on what has always been, connects, for Rudge, with the people of God image. Charismatic theory connects with the new creation image with its emphasis on a new order: the old is uprooted and overthrown; the Kingdom breaks through. Human relations theory seems initially to connect with the fellowship of faith, focusing on the community of the faithful disciples living and praying together. However, for Rudge, the images gathered under the fellowship of faith point in a different direction, since human relations theory is based on relationships between people. The images are about a relationship with God in a church created by God on divine not human initiative. However, the way groups relate and interrelate may be influenced by the values that come out of the New Testament examples. Rudge's conclusion is that the fellowship of faith image may have more to do with a systemic theory or, if led in a charismatic fashion, to the charismatic theory. It seems for Rudge, following Minear's lead, that the connection between the systemic theory and the image of the body of Christ is the most satisfying, for example, in the strength of New Testament themes such as organic growth and transformation as the faithful are added to the body. Rudge, working at the relations between the different theories, suggests some of the theories are incompatible. A company cannot be run at the same time in a somewhat classical way and a somewhat charismatic way.

Although Rudge's work may not be wholly convincing in how he uses and applies the scriptural material to the management frameworks, what he does provide is an early, widely scoped, systematic attempt to map twentieth-century approaches to understanding and running organizations against the way we understand the Church. The typical ability of theology to hold contradictions in tension, for example as mysteries, is often the opposite of the tendency in management thinking to provide clear analytical frameworks without contradictions. The challenge in using biblical images is that somehow we have to handle the totality of the scriptural revelation at the same time and the variety of the ways it can be understood, using the tension between apparently contradictory material to illuminate our work. Working in this way with a consultor can offer rich, imaginative possibilities.

Rudge's optimism about Catholic thinking was not misplaced. In the wake of Vatican II and as a resource for systematic theology, Cardinal Avery Dulles produced an important study designed to help answer questions about the nature, purpose and form of the Church. Examining modern ecclesiologists from Protestant and Catholic traditions in *Models of the Church* (1974), he proposed five models through which to understand the Church, adding a sixth in later editions:

- *the Church as Institution* – emphasizing the order, structure and hierarchy of the Church, especially the clergy with clear roles and rules

- *the Church as Mystical Communion* – emphasizing the body/community nature of the Church
- *the Church as Sacrament* – emphasizing the Church as the visible sign that God is at work in the world through Christ
- *the Church as Herald* – emphasizing the Church's role and work as the messenger of the good news, proclaiming the gospel and the Kingdom
- *the Church as Servant* – the Church through its members and its actions lives out its faith in working for social justice
- *the Church as a Community of Disciples* – the Church as the community of the faithful who have a personal belief and faith commitment to follow Jesus in word and deed.

As with the New Testament images above, these models are not exclusive. The mystery of the Church is that somehow it has to blend the values from the different models in a critical conversation with each other. Most models will have a primary model and a number of influential secondary models. Individual, composite models of the Church may have any of the models as the primary model apart from the Church as Institution. Dulles says, 'of their very nature ... institutions are subordinate to persons, structures are subordinate to life' (1974, p. 187). People such as the missiologist David Bosch (1991, p. 372), in his search for an understanding of the missionary purpose of the Church, to which we turn now, took up the invitation to play around with such models. Like them, consultants and consultors will gain much by being able to draw on these sorts of models and frameworks during consultations.

The Church's mission and purpose

When a secular organization is looking at what it is really about and whether it is focused on the right things, it may look at its vision and mission. It may even use consultants to help it do so. Terms like vision and mission have a distinctly religious feel about them. They impart a sense of clear direction and some idea of what the future state should be when the organization gets there after all the present strategizing, effort and change. It then feels strange for us religious folk when secular models of consultancy encourage churches to pay some attention to defining their vision and mission. We were there first.

The danger with some visions and missions is that they can be vague, fantastical and, in the end, unhelpful. It is clearer to talk about purpose. What is the organization's purpose? A clear, short, focused purpose statement should tell you what will be achieved by an organization's existence and work. It sets the environment in which planning and day-to-day decisions can be made that will contribute to getting where the organization wants to be. There can be confusion between what an organization's purpose is and the conditions that it needs to fulfil that purpose. For example, many in the not-for-profit sectors will say, often dismissively, that a commercial business's purpose is to make money. I suggest that making a profit is one of the necessary conditions for a company to continue to achieve its purpose, as is complying with the law on employment, the environment, tax or safety. It will need continued investment from shareholders. It needs to be able to pay its employees. Its purpose, however, is to deliver a service or a product that fills a perceived need that makes the world better. If all it is concerned with is making a profit, it is likely to concentrate on the wrong things and go out of business. As Sir Rod Carnegie, an Australian mining executive, once said, 'I breathe in order to live; I don't exist to breathe.'

At present in the churches a similar conversation is happening. There are common debates around statements that the churches are about mission not maintenance. This is a crucial discussion on the purpose of church. It has influenced matters as diverse as the training of ministers, the distribution of money, staff and other resources, and even the shape and style of worship in new initiatives such as Fresh Expressions. Ministers who were trained in and esteemed for pastoral skill now feel pressurized to engage uncomfortably in unfamiliar, evangelistic adventures. This radical refashioning of the Church is documented clearly in Bosch's account of the development of the understanding of mission in *Transforming Mission: Paradigm Shifts in Theology of Mission* (1991). The centrality of mission to the nature of the Church has become the main principle of mission theology across Catholic, Orthodox and Protestant thinking. The Church participates in the outflowing of the love of the trinitarian God. It is its nature, not just an activity it undertakes. As the World Council of Churches expressed it in 1999:

It is God's design to gather all creation under the Lordship of Christ (Eph. 1:10), and to bring humanity and all creation into communion. As a reflection of the communion in the Triune God, the Church is called by God to be the instrument in fulfilling this goal. The Church is called to manifest God's mercifulness to humanity, and to restore humanity's natural purpose – to praise and glorify God together with all the heavenly hosts. As such, it is not an end in itself, but a gift given to the world in order that all may believe (John 17:21). Mission belongs to the very being of the Church.

(World Council of Churches, 1999, 1.B, paras 26 and 27)

Mission as expressed by the Church is characterized by being part of God's mission (*missio Dei*). Indeed the Church is only really the Church when it is being sent out into the world rather than fortifying itself against it or seeing itself as over against it. 'Mission was no longer merely an activity *of* the church, but an expression of the *very being* of the church' (Bosch, 1992, p. 494). Missiology, therefore, becomes, in Illich's definition,

> the science about the Word of God as the Church in her becoming; the Word as the Church in her borderline situations; the Church as a surprise and a puzzle; the Church in her growth; the Church when her historical appearance is so new that she has to strain herself to recognize her past in the mirror of the present; the Church where she is pregnant of new revelations for a people in which she dawns ... Missiology studies the growth of the Church into new peoples, the birth of the Church beyond its social boundaries; beyond the linguistic barriers within which she feels at home; beyond the poetic images in which she taught her children ... Missiology therefore is the study of the Church as surprise.
>
> (in Bosch, 1991, p. 493)

Ironically, then, given the discussion above, the Church's purpose seems to be mission, or rather participation in the mission that is already God's. Thus, the debate between maintenance and mission transforms into a discussion of how do we maintain churches in the condition that can support involvement in what Bosch calls 'the movement of God's love toward people' (1991, p. 390). If, however, the raising of money, the care of buildings, attention to ecclesiastical rules or even the evangelism and conversion of others in order to keep a church's numbers up become the central focus, that is, the purpose, then a consultant may well encourage discussion as to whether that church is still authentically church. Such questions also apply to systems of accountability that measure success in terms of, for example, regular Sunday attendance rather than how that attests to the harder, qualitative assessment of whether the work under inspection is authentically and effectively God's mission.

Mission and Messy Church

In the 1980s, the Anglican Communion developed what they called the Five Marks of Mission (Anglican Consultative Council, 1984, p. 49):

- to proclaim the Good News of the Kingdom
- to teach, baptize and nurture new believers
- to respond to human need by loving service
- to seek to transform unjust structures of society
- to strive to safeguard the integrity of creation and sustain and renew the life of the earth.

The Five Marks are often used as a template to reflect on how closely a church or church project is sticking to its missionary purpose. On the Messy Church website (www.messychurch.org.uk), Lucy Moore suggests a range of questions that messy people should be asking about what is happening in this Fresh Expression of church. In terms of proclaiming, she asks how members listen, learn and change as a result of what those who attend bring and say. As for teaching, she asks how far new believers are being baptized and encouraged on their journey of faith. In terms of service, are they doing Messy Church just to get bums on seats and is what they are doing really dealing with serious needs? How far is the principle of justice part of Messy Church in bringing in global and local issues? Are the congregation's understandings of justice embraced? On the matter of the earth, how does what happens at the meals that are so key to Messy Church, the use of food and its disposal, demonstrate good stewardship? Do the children get listened to with all their knowledge and wonder about the world?

Some of the Messy Church questions reveal an understanding of mission that would not have been the norm a century ago. Many of the questions in the blog involve listening to and being influenced, indeed changed, by those who can be seen as the focus of mission. Maintaining sensitivity to context and culture are now seen as important features of missionary activity as is openness to the value in what is seen as outside the Church. Inculturation, the ongoing dialogue between faith and culture, is a serious theological debate, for example in the Roman

Catholic Church where inflexibility led to disasters in mission fields such as seventeenth- and eighteenth-century China. In his encyclical *Redemptoris Missio* in 1990, Pope John Paul II confirmed inculturation as a respectable theological topic and an important factor in mission, describing the practice as 'a profound and all-embracing one, which involves the Christian message and also the Church's reflection and practice' and 'a difficult process, for it must in no way compromise the distinctiveness and integrity of the Christian faith' (section 52). Present debates about sexual ethics and euthanasia are often characterized as examples of where the tension of such openness, cross-boundary dialogue and questioning of rigid or flexible stances is felt painfully in the churches. The question of culture and especially the superiority of traditional western values, is also brought into question. The arrogance of much European and North American missionary thinking is challenged by the vigour and vibrancy of, for example, the African church. As Bosch says:

> There is no eternal theology, no *theologia perennis*, which may play the referee over 'local theologies'. In the past, Western theology arrogated to itself the right to be such an arbitrator in respect to third-world theologies. It implicitly viewed itself as fully indigenized, inculturated, a finished product. We are beginning to realize that this was inappropriate, that Western theologies (plural!) – just as much as all the others – were theologies in the making, theologies in the process of being contextualized and indigenized.
>
> (1991, p. 456)

A particular gift that the consultant brings to any consultation is an ability, as a relative or complete outsider, to help consultors check how conscious they are of any cultural assumptions in their individual and organizational behaviour. Churches spread or obstruct the gospel not just by what they say but also by their culture, the way they habitually behave, the values they display through the symbolic messages they transmit. Culture is like our spoken accent. We notice how different everyone else's is but not what ours is like or how strong it is – until somebody tells us or we hear it on an audio or video recording. Thus, the model of mission accompaniment promoted by the Churches Together in Britain and Ireland as consultancy (see Walker, 2005) recommends that the accompanier come from a different church, a different tradition, in order to be the helpful outsider.

The boiling frog

A common story to illustrate, among other things, the gradual nature of culture change is the *boiling frog*. It is claimed that experiments in the nineteenth century involved putting a frog in water. If the water was boiling, the frog would leap out straight away. If the water started at room temperature and slowly rose to boiling point, the frog stayed in the water and died. It is probably not true, but is a good story to illustrate a great danger for organizations of how their members don't notice gradual change happening while at the same time becoming used to it. If the culture of a church has transformed over some years away from what it is supposed to be and do, it will be no surprise (to the outsider) that it has lost its way. Furthermore, because the change has been slow and incremental, unnoticed poor or damaging behaviour may have been allowed to persist and so become an authorized, condoned norm.

The anatomy of a congregation

The range of types and forms of church can bewilder the consultant. If you were to go to a meeting of a local Churches Together, you might find Anglican and Catholic churches based on a traditional parish model. It may be that some of the Anglican team churches look as though they should be closed or merged. They struggle on, dependent on a few elderly couples mostly. Round the Catholic Church it's difficult to get a parking spot during Saturday evening Mass. There may be Methodist churches with one or two ministers, reasonably attended in the town, but clustered with rural chapels where the congregation numbers six. There may be a house church that meets in a warehouse on a commercial estate on the edge of town. It is growing mightily and sucks in all the young people and families from the town with its rock bands and youth ministries. There is an intriguing Baptist group that meets, apparently very informally, in the primary school on the new estate full of starter homes just beyond the ring road. The town centre Baptists planted it with some members of other churches in the town. There's the street pastor scheme, which operates on Friday and Saturday nights in the town centre among the pubs and clubs, led by a URC lay worker from their building near the night life. Some of these churches seem traditional and some quite unconventional. Some are growing, some dying. They seem to be very diverse but all claim to be church. If the consultant is going to be any use, he or she will need to have ways of understanding the forms and trajectories churches go through, particularly in this postmodern age of fresh and emerging expressions of church.

In looking for help, consultants and consultors may turn to the field of congregational studies. Over recent decades congregational studies has struggled out of being a footnote for sociologists and anthropologists and subsumed under ecclesiology to something of a discipline in itself. As may be seen in examples already mentioned in Cameron *et al.*'s *Studying Local Churches* (2005) and Guest *et al.*'s *Congregational Studies in the UK* (2004), people involved in congregational studies may come from a range of academic backgrounds (sociology, history, theology, psychology, etc.) and undertake research using methods from those disciplines, but the central focus is to work out what is going on in faith communities. The focus is not just on Christian context, although much of the research revolves around churches. For example, Margaret Harris's useful book *Organizing God's Work* (1998) has as its subtitle *Challenges for Churches and Synagogues*. Much of the utility for consultants of studies and theories in this area is the way they provide patterns against which to analyse the present state of congregations and to design their future. For example, one of the early key texts, Carroll *et al.*'s *The Handbook for Congregational Studies* (1986), among a treasury of advice around research methods and approaches, offers a four-factor approach to studying congregations by suggesting examining a congregation's

- *program* – those organizational structures, plans and activities through which a congregation expresses its mission and ministry both to its own members and those outside its membership
- *processes* – the underlying flow and dynamics of a congregation that knit it together in its common life and affect its morale and climate
- *social context* – the setting, local and global, in which a congregation finds itself and to which it responds
- *identity* – that persistent set of beliefs, values, patterns, symbols, stories and style that make a congregation distinctly itself.

(1986, pp. 11–12)

Underlying much of the approach here and in subsequent congregational theories was a systems approach, particularly an open systems approach where there is significant attention to the interaction with the congregation's context. One of the contributors to the *Handbook*, James Hopewell, developed a way of researching congregations through the use of narrative. He suggested that, by listening to the stories people tell of their congregation's culture, their beliefs and behaviour patterns would emerge that show God's intention for that community. In *Congregation* (1987), published from his notes some three years after his death, Hopewell, an anthropologist and historian of religions by training, offered a pattern that maps a church's stories and symbols, and the theological convictions behind them, through literary theory and classic story types (comic, romantic, tragic and ironic). From these he suggested that it was possible to locate where a congregation might be facing in terms of their belief:

- *Canonic* Reliance upon an authoritative interpretation of a world pattern, often considered God's revealed word or will, by which one identifies one's essential life. The integrity of the pattern requires that followers reject any gnosis of union with the pattern but instead subordinate their selfhood to it. (Tragic)
- *Gnostic* Reliance upon an intuited process of a world that develops from dissipation toward unity. The ultimate integrity of the world requires the deepening consciousness of those involved in its systemic outworking and their rejection of alienating canonic structures. (Comic)
- *Charismatic* Reliance upon evidence of a transcendent spirit personally encountered. The integrity of providence in the world requires that empirical presumptions of an ordered world be disregarded and supernatural irregularities instead be witnessed. (Romantic)
- *Empiric* Reliance upon data objectively verifiable through one's own five senses. The integrity of one's own person requires realism about the way things demonstrably work and the rejection of the supernatural. (Ironic)

(1987, p. 69)

Once more, it is not a matter of being exclusively in one category but operating dynamically in their own space somewhere in the field between the four extremes.

Consultants may be asked to work with congregations of different types of which a significant feature is size. Size matters in that it seems congregations tend to demonstrate particular characteristics and dynamics according to their numbers. One of the features of the growth in congregational studies has been the appearance of independent, not-for-profit organizations such as the Alban Institute who not only undertake research but also offer consultancy, publications and training. An influential area of the Alban Institute's work has been in the area of congregational size. What they have documented is the notion that, if you want to grow from one size of church to the next size up, some characteristics and patterns of behaviour that now predominate will have to change. In organizations of any kind there seem to need to be qualitative shifts from groups of about 12 (a family) to those of around 50 (a clan). When an organization gets to around 150, there need to be official roles, structures and systems. Nevertheless, bigger organizations work better if based on the smaller natural units. Following on the work of Arlin Rothauge, the Alban Institute has carried out extensive research and thinking around size which has had an influence beyond American shores. Steven Croft, formerly the Church of England's Archbishops' Missioner and Team Leader of Fresh Expressions and now Bishop of Sheffield, has developed the categories in *Ministry in Three Dimensions* (2008). His first category is the *Family Church* with 1–50 members, dominated by a small number of human dynasties and matriarchs/patriarchs who act as gatekeepers even to the minister who becomes a family chaplain. The second dynamic is the *Pastoral Church*, with 50–100 members (100 adults). Ministers are expected to provide pastoral care for everyone, and so there has to be a ceiling on what they can provide. The numbers limit may be expanded somewhat by the addition of an assistant minister, for example, a curate or a youth worker. A typical symptom of this type of church is overworked clergy as they try to fulfil the pastoral expectations of the congregation. The third is the *Programme Church*, with 150–400 members, with significant lay-led programmes, systems and networks for pastoral care and decision-making. The Alban Institute talks next about the *Corporate Church*, with 400–1,000 members, often with excellent music and worship, specialized, targeted programmes and often several distinct congregations. There is often a senior pastor who concentrates on preaching and managing a diverse team of paid staff. However, Croft, speaking from a UK perspective, sees the next types of church in a different way. The reality for many churches now is that they are family or programme-size churches bundled together in multiple church ministries. In this model, the options are for the ministers to rush around from church to church, often over considerable distances, trying to maintain the family or programme pastoral model. Croft suggests that models he calls the *Nurturing Communities Church* and the *Transforming Communities Church* are a better choice. In these, the ministers step back from providing direct pastoral care and set up lay leadership, systems and networks for pastoral support and local delivery, building community between members of a local church rather than between members and the minister. A concern in looking at church size (apart from watching a church decline and die) is how to grow. The pattern seems to be that, at a certain point whatever their size, churches reach equilibrium from which it takes significant dissonance and change in behaviour to move to the next stage.

Another angle the consultant and consultor can investigate, again with useful resources from, among others, the Alban Institute, is the life cycle of churches. Martin Saarinen (1998) takes the analogy (organic again) of a human life cycle to show stages a church goes through. This can help identify not only where a church sits but also what it needs to do to get to the next stage, or to avoid doing so, depending on where it is on the cycle. (In *What They Don't Teach You at Theological College* (2003), Malcolm Grundy summarizes and adapts the model for a British readership.) Through the stages of birth, infancy and adolescence the excitement and energy are matched by a need to set up programmes and systems. It may be that enthusiasm is overtaken by stress and burnout. As the stages reach the top of the bell curve there is the danger that structure, programmes and doing what we've always done leads to a loss of sense of mission and some defensiveness. Eventually factions and rigidity make it difficult for new people to join. In the death stage, it becomes an issue of desperately protecting objects and buildings. Acknowledging where a church might be on this arc can help in understanding why people are behaving as they are. It is often a puzzle to see how much energy, time and money a tiny number of people will devote to keeping a chapel open that is obviously without hope for the future. Combined with insights from the Family Church size model, Saarinen's death stage describes it perfectly.

So how does the consultant approach non-traditional types of church? Fresh Expressions and other initiatives influenced by the Church of England report *Mission-Shaped Church* raise questions about the form church should take to cope with a postmodern world of networks, mobility, consumerism, transience and diversity. Starting as a rationale for church planting, which had disturbed many assumptions about the parish system, the flexibility recommended in *Mission-Shaped Church* has moved into other areas of church life and encouraged the growth of forms of church outside traditional expectations. The talk is of Messy Church, Cafe Church, Biker Church, New Monasticism and alternative worship, often supported by ecumenical and para-church networks. Fresh Expressions as a body is a collaboration between the Church of England, the Methodist Church, the United Reformed Church and the Congregational Federation, among others. The freedom now granted has led to a blossoming of imaginative creativity in appealing in different ways to the unchurched and de-churched in local areas. However, some criticisms have been raised based on a range of features such as its perceived middle-class bias, its specialism and consumerism (Percy, 2010), and on it being about church-shaped mission ignorant of the contextual realities in which it stands (Hull, 2006). For the consultant working with Fresh Expressions, Martyn Percy, in *Shaping the Church*, raises some fundamental organizational issues around the generally welcomed emphasis on culturally appropriate forms of mission:

> The plethora of Fresh Expressions – dispersed forms of intensity – masks the retreat from the drudgery of engaging with older organizations, and in so doing critically undermines the very host body that sustains it. The core body appears to be too weak to resist the onslaught of 'alternatives'; yet the alternatives can only survive if the core body is sustained.
>
> (2010, pp. 75–6)

A study that aims to provide resources for local churches to understand themselves and to reflect on the range of issues they have to deal with is Helen Cameron's *Resourcing Mission* (2010). Taking a practical and reflective theology approach, she offers ways of thinking through practical issues such as time, money, buildings, risk and regulation, decision-making, leadership and partnership. One of the most interesting features of the book is the classification of organizational forms of church by mapping them against cultural, social phenomena suggested from academic studies of the postmodern world (Cameron 2010, pp. 24–37). These classifications are:

- *The parish as a utility* like the gas or water supplier; examples in Britain would be the Roman Catholic parish system and those of the Church of England and the Church of Scotland with an infrastructure that covers the whole country.
- *Gathered congregation as a voluntary association*; examples might be the Society of Friends, the Baptist Union and the Methodist Church.
- *Small-group church as book groups and party-plan groups* meeting in somebody's home; examples would be cell churches, home groups and base ecclesial communities.

- *Third-place church as secular third places*; examples would be groups meeting in neutral social spaces such as a coffee shop, a bar or a gym, where the lifestyle experience, symbolized by the venue, can offer, for example, the assurance of being 'cool' and psychological comfort and support.
- *Magnet church as parental choice of school*; examples might be where professional, middle-class people are attracted from a wide area to a church which has paid youth workers and which concentrates on family ministry.

The survival of the first two forms depends on assumptions that may be fading in society. Associations depend on members attending and contributing money and involvement. In a postmodern world, this is becoming a problem with a growing consumerist, transient approach to many things. The utility approach depends on assumptions of a church's right to be there and to offer services to everyone. This is undermined by, for example, the privatization of many utilities in the last few decades. Cameron underlines how useful a cultural way of thinking about churches can be to consultants and consultors:

> To compare churches with secular institutions may seem irreverent or to misunderstand the nature of church as holy and different. However, I want to emphasize that the church does have essential qualities, but, because these are wrapped in culture, it may be worth making comparisons that disrupt our thinking. The church is not a passive victim of culture but can scrutinize itself and, if it wishes, change things.
>
> (2010, p. 37)

The nature of church work

Attention to the nature of church work is a prerequisite for anyone attempting consultancy in a church context. The refashioned, contemporary emphasis on church as participating in God's mission has consequences for what we understand as the work of the Church at a macro and a local level. Consultants need to be aware of their assumptions about what the Church's work is for and how they describe, justify and evaluate the nature of church work. If they don't, there is a risk of confusion and an unreflective, if unconscious, imposition of their own beliefs. It is really helpful to go into a consultancy with a clear idea about what the nature of church work is and, therefore, in possession of frameworks to examine whether an issue is a matter of, for example, a mismatch between a minister and their church's understanding of mission and ministry or a situation where the church or the minister has simply lost their grasp of their characteristic purpose, identity and work. Developing an initial clarity around what constitutes the nature of church work is much less likely to lead to conflict in consultancy sessions as both parties should be able to build on their explicit, even if different, understanding of the nature of church work. The widening diversity of the Church's membership, of its ministry and of the ecclesiological forms it has taken in recent years has prompted an urgency to understand the nature of church work and its properties and forms.

George Lovell, in a seminar on church work at Cliff College, a Methodist Bible college in Derbyshire, offered the following description of the nature and properties of church work:

- Church work is personal and collective vocational involvement in redemptive and creative missiological activity. It is engagement in a divine–human enterprise directed by God and the Church.
- Its aim is to initiate, promote, foster and sustain to completion processes by which people and every aspect of their habitat become more like the Christian ideal.
- It involves engagement with human goodness and badness through working with and ministering to all kinds and conditions of people – personally and in all kinds of communities, socio-religious organizations and churches.
- This missiological work, essentially local, is a relational, personal, communal, organizational, ecclesiastical, contextual, language based, all life activity designed to meet all human personal, social and spiritual needs through a range of religious and secular programmes which aim to be inclusive and comprehensive.
- By nature and circumstance the work is voluntary in principle and practice, collaborative, participatory and multi-disciplinary and inter-professional.
- It is operational and reflective love-based action. It is an application of all our faculties and an outworking of Christian values through sub-political Christian institutions.
- Thus, church work is theological and mundane and holistically creative with its own culture and spirituality. It operates creatively on the inner and outer worlds of practitioners and those with whom they work and the complex relationships between them, their environment and God. It begins with a feeling of something

lacking, something desired ... something to be created, something to be brought into being ... in the environment and in the self and ends with the kingdom of God.

Working together to get the work done

Churches as social organizations depend on the interaction of members to achieve their mission, their purpose. This means that consultations need to examine questions of how that happens. Secular consultants, Tom Peters and Roger Waterman suggest that this happens through the interaction of seven variables. There is what they call the organizational hardware – Strategy and Structure – and the software – Style, Systems, Staff (people), Skills and Shared values (1982, pp. 10–11). Whether or not this applies exactly to churches, it does help understand why change can be difficult. The McKinsey 7 S Framework, as it is called, is based on the insight that if you try to change one of these variables, there is going to be movement in the others. If the initial change is going to take effect, the change in the others has to be supportive. The new emphasis on mission could be seen as a change in strategy and shared values for some churches. One of the problems the new emphasis on mission has come up against is the fact that many of the clergy were trained in a pastoral model and so some find the mission approach difficult. Thus, if the new strategy is going to succeed, changing the criteria in systems for recruiting candidates for ministry, training, developing, moving and reviewing ministers becomes necessary. By doing this, you are changing the staff and expecting a different style, the way people do their work and what they focus on.

The impact of systems is often underestimated. Karl Stewart is quoted in Ian Macdonald *et al.* (2006, p. 105) as coining the phrase 'systems drive behaviour'. If well designed, they encourage the organization's people to go about what they do in an authorized, consistent, productive way. If a system is poorly designed, it is very difficult for even the most skilled leader or organization member to counter its effect. Precision around the purpose of the system, how it is supposed to achieve its purpose (its theory), that is, how it will get the work it has to do done, clarity about the roles, authority and accountability in it and how you tell whether it is achieving what it is supposed to are all necessary if an organization is going to work well. In organizations like churches there will be a great variety of systems. Some of them will be big, overarching systems such as the selection of candidates for ministry or safeguarding. Some will be small, local systems about, say, how a church's marriage preparation course is run, or how the collection gets counted after a service. Systems can be divided into those that are authorized, in that they have been transparently, well and thoughtfully designed and carefully put into practice with all the right permissions with a good process of control and monitoring, and those that may have just developed over the years but are not written down in any handbook or set of policies. These just happen and people will say, 'That's the way we've always done it.' These systems often depend on an individual or a small group of people in the know. When they move on, nobody else knows how that work is done. Often such systems integrate poorly into or obstruct the operation of other systems. They may help locally but they may set unhelpful precedents when considering the bigger organization of which a local church might be part.

Often the reason behind systems operating counter-productively is that the social process analysis has not been done properly. Any attempt at systems design and implementation needs to investigate what the impact of any changed new system will be on the people concerned and therefore how they will react. When child protection systems were brought in during the 1980s, the logic behind making sure children in Sunday schools and youth clubs were not harmed was easy to understand. However, many people resisted the checking systems and some teachers and youth workers left those roles because they felt accused of being child molesters. Some had been in those roles for many years and had proved their trustworthiness. Now they were being treated like criminal suspects. If there is going to be an adverse reaction like this, the options are to change the system so the reaction does not happen, or to put in place consultations, meetings and one-to-one sessions to talk people through the new expectations. In the safeguarding children case there is no option. Thus, the second option has to be chosen and it becomes a matter of limiting damage and working out how to deal with the loss of workers. It is not just a matter of whether what is being proposed is right; it is a matter of working out how to implement it as effectively as possible. For further detail on systems design and implementation, Macdonald *et al.*'s *Systems Leadership* (2006) provides much practical help.

Teams, leaders and members

As has already been seen, churches involve people of all types and with all sorts of relationships coming together to get the work done. How this happens will depend on the way relationships are structured in terms of leaders, teams and the network of departments and subgroups in a church. There is no shortage of material on leadership in the churches and training schemes for those in leadership roles. Happily, there is also an increase in literature about collaborative working in churches. For the consultor and consultant, problems can often be unpicked by attending to assumptions about what the clergy do, what lay officers are for, and how governance, structures and leadership roles, paid and unpaid, interact. Many different principles and beliefs exist around the nature of priestly and ministerial authority set against or sometimes within the idea of the authority of all the people of God, every-member ministry, hierarchy, subsidiarity, delegation and inclusive democracy. Seeking clarity about these assumptions may free up both analytical and design possibilities. In addition to such structural and theological issues, there may be psychological and personality issues. Leslie Francis has done considerable work, using a Myers Briggs framework, on the impact personality type has on styles of ministry (see, for example, Francis and Robbins, *Personality and the Practice of Ministry*, 2004). It may, also, be that personality has an impact on the way ministry teams, church councils, leadership groups, and committees function. Many churches use Belbin's (1993) team roles framework. This suggests that a team needs a balance of roles, from those who are creative thinkers to those who are good at co-ordinating, to the co-operative ones, and the ones who actually make sure things get done. Reflecting on such a framework will help consultors understand why they and the people they are working with may, for example, be coming up with good ideas but never actually do anything substantial. Churches are often small, relying on a few key people. The message of these personality systems is not that they will not succeed if they don't have the right mix, but that the objective might be better achieved either by recruitment of what's missing or by members consciously working in a style that may not naturally be theirs. It is important to say that these types and roles are not inescapable. They are termed and seen as preferences.

Malcolm Torry, having trawled through the literature, comes to the conclusion that the major role of a leader is to 'ensure that governance structures are working and that their own work serves the organization through those structures rather than conflicts with them' (2005, p. 164). This involves a series of tasks. For Torry, these emanate from understanding the organization's values and governance systems in order to build goals and organizational structures, which align with those values and which can be delivered. It also involves managing change and conflict in a way that is consistent with those values and demonstrating those values in their own behaviour and lives. Church leaders should possess certain skills and qualities around communication and management, as well as individual, interpersonal skills. This assumes that the leader has the capability (cognitive, technical and social process) to understand, build and ensure delivery of the work. He suggests that the major difference between the leader of a religious organization and that of, say, a commercial company is the extent to which the former should be committed to the organization's values and puts them into practice. An interesting footnote to Torry's study is that the leader needs to be a 'good story-teller' (2005, p. 172). The leader should know, inhabit and develop the organization's narrative, retelling it to include new members and recasting it for the future when it has been forgotten or got stuck.

In much recent writing about leadership, a distinction has been made between leadership and management. In this, leadership is seen as transformational, charismatic and visionary, setting overall goals and direction and expects followers; management is about transactions, controlling and directing people and resources, and is a bit dull, if stable. There is a danger that the churches are adopting this division wholesale, which, I think, is unhelpful. Leaders at all levels need to be and do both. The person running a church's toddler group needs to make sure that someone has the keys to the hall and that the toys are put out, but also needs to understand how the group fits in with the church and the local context and to plan for its sustainable alignment with both. The senior pastor of an out-of-town mega-church needs to set the ten-year strategy and growth plan, but also needs to make sure that the people in charge of the various ministries are doing their job without stealing the money or working themselves into the grave.

A good start to looking at current thinking about church leadership in the churches would be two books published by MODEM, a body that looks at the transfer of learning between secular and religious leadership – *Creative Church Leadership* (Adair and Nelson, 2004) and *How to Become a Creative Church Leader* (Nelson, 2008). These sets of essays offer good reflections on a range of leadership issues by an interesting group of people and there are good bibliographies to take the reader further.

So, how does the consultant proceed?

This whirlwind tour of organizational issues and thinking may lead to excitement or to panic. The factors seem so multifarious and interconnected that it is difficult to know where to start when faced with an organizational issue in a consultancy. Blake and Mouton, in their classic work *Consultation* (1983), offer what they call the *Consulcube* (1983, p. 11). This is a three-dimensional matrix, like a Rubik's cube, which allows an interlinked analysis. The first dimension concerns the consultor. Is the consultor an individual, a group (established or ad hoc), intergroup (the interaction between two or more groups), a whole organization, or a larger entity such as a community? The second dimension looks at the focal issue. Is the issue being focused on concerned with power and authority, for example around decision-making? Is it to do with morale and cohesion, that is, organizational culture? Is it about norms and standards, how things are done? Or is it about goals and objectives, that is, why certain things are being done? The third dimension concerns the type of consultancy needed and maps the other two dimensions against Blake and Mouton's five kinds of consultancy intervention (theory/principles, prescriptive, confrontational, catalytic, and acceptant). Blake and Mouton's multidimensional analysis is worth looking at, not necessarily to adopt their particular approach, but to support the consultant and the consultor's desire to slow the analysis down until as clear and complex a picture as possible has been painted of the situation being addressed, so that the consultancy intervention is appropriate. Having laid out in this chapter, however briefly, the kaleidoscope of organizational considerations possible, it can only help to attend to ensuring that the consultancy is targeted at the right issue and works at the right level of complexity so that the outcome will be as useful as possible.

3

What is Consultancy?

One of the frustrations of those of us who are involved in consultancy in churches is the caricature that consultancy is just about applying a crass form of management consultancy that worked ten years ago in commercial companies in a way that is totally inappropriate in a body like the Church. To help show that this is not the case, this chapter attempts to define

- what work consultancy in the churches is
- what is meant by work
- what sort of metaphors might be helpful in understanding the nature and different approaches of work consultancy
- what biblical insights can inform its operation
- where work consultancy sits in a family of helping disciplines that are available to church workers.

Peter Block defines a consultant as a 'person in a position to have some influence over an individual, a group or an organization but who has no power to make changes or implement programs' (1999, p. 2). If they have that power, Block says, they are no longer consultants: they are managers. The authority to accept the advice of the consultant and to implement any plans that come out of a consultation must always stay with the consultor. The burden on the consultant is to provide as complete, nuanced and professional a service as they can. The collaborative process between consultor and consultant needs to be based on clear understanding of what consultancy can and cannot do and of the work that the two parties should do. For the safety of consultants, consultors and the mission of the Church, it is crucial to have some definitions and basic understanding about what consultancy is and what it offers. That is the aim of this chapter. Equally necessarily, the following chapter discusses the different roles of consultant and consultor.

Defining consultancy

Fly away Peter

A consultant colleague of mine shared with me the story of a consultancy which never got off the ground. This account changes the detail a little to protect confidentiality but illustrates the issue of different understandings of consultancy. Richard had just been appointed as the minister of a struggling church in a thriving city suburb. He was new to this sort of role, having been an engineer and then a junior minister in a group of rural churches and was keen to do well in the new job. He had a clear vision of the evangelistic and pastoral work he wanted to do and felt called to. One of the resources that was mentioned to him when he was interviewed and again in his introduction into the role was a work consultant, which his denomination would provide and pay for, if necessary. After a month or two he thought it would be a good idea to get some wise and experienced help. He set up monthly sessions with Peter, a highly respected work consultant trained in a non-directive, process style of consultancy. After four sessions of being asked open questions, being listened to carefully, having issues teased out and being encouraged to develop his own solutions and strategies, Richard had to admit that this wasn't working for him. What he wanted was for someone to advise him what to do, someone with tried and tested techniques and strategies, someone who knew from significant experience how to go about evangelism among these busy, middle-class people, not just questions about what he thought might be best. When he raised this with Peter, he said he was beginning to come to the same conclusion. What Richard was wanting and what Peter was offering did not match. They agreed that should be their last session.

Richard and Peter's ideas of what consultancy is about differ significantly. Richard is looking for expert advice. Tell me what I am supposed to do. Give me answers that will work. We might call this a 'content' type of consultancy. On the other hand, Peter's approach is based on the idea that the consultant supports the consultor in addressing and solving their problems by helping them think, by asking questions, by collaborating in framing hypotheses, in taking the situation apart, and assisting the consultor in coming up with his own solutions and plans. We might call this a 'process' type of consultancy. When it comes to defining consultancy and examining how a consultant offers consultancy support, this distinction between content and process models is important.

Why might it be that an individual, a group or an organization asks for help from consultants? If you were to look at, say, the Management Consultancies Association's website (www.mca.org.uk), you would find that what consultants bring is expertise, 'the creation of value for organizations, through improved performance, achieved by providing objective advice and implementing business solutions'. They fill a gap in knowledge, skill or experience that the consultor does not have or does not have in sufficient depth in order to achieve a productive end. This type of content approach is immediately applicable to, for example, the audiovisual consultant who is invited in to sort out the microphones, loudspeakers, amplification, projectors and screens in a church building. They have an expertise that the local congregation does not have. This does not mean that they do not have to listen carefully and help the congregation understand what is desirable and possible with their budget, building and worship pattern. The question being asked by the consultor is, 'I don't know how to do this. Show me how, or even do it for me.' The emphasis is heavily on expertise and content.

In a famous article, 'A General Philosophy of Helping: Process Consultation' (1990), Edgar Schein offers three models of helping as a consultant:

1 *Providing expert information*, where the consultor is buying in expert services or information. It depends for success on the accuracy of the consultor's diagnosis of their problem, on their selection of the correct consultant with the right expertise, and on their ability to own the consequences of the consultant's solution.

2 *Playing doctor*, where the consultor knows there is a problem but is not quite sure what it is or how to deal with it. Success depends on how accurately the sickness has been identified, how willing the consultor is to give the consultant all the relevant information, how willing they are to accept the diagnosis and the medicine prescribed, and then to take it. (This doctor/patient model is beginning to suffer as more and more doctors in medical practice see their work with patients as a collaborative partnership to diagnose and heal.)

3 *Process consultation* is more concerned with the process by which the consultor identifies problems and comes up with solutions. Success is based on the assumption that consultors look for help when they are not sure what the problem is or when they are not sure what is available to help them, that they understand what works best for

them and, therefore, benefit from being part of the diagnostic and problem-solving processes and that their intent is to engage productively in the process toward a productive outcome.

Schein places consultancy in a range of 'helping' interventions and encourages 'process consultation' as the initial mode of relationship when starting a consultancy and probably the most appropriate mode in most situations. He suggests that, at different times, a consultant may be operating under any of these models depending on conscious reflection on what the consultor needs and what their expertise can provide. His strong preference is for the process consultation model but recognizes that the consultant may have to persuade the consultor, who is looking for an immediate fix, that the benefits of his approach are worth waiting for and working towards.

However, this notion that a consultant can and should shift from a process method to an expert/content approach and back again is fraught with danger. Although a great admirer of Schein, Lovell disagrees fiercely on this point with him and others who think like him. For Lovell, the consultant is above all an encourager of reflective practice in the consultor through a collaborative, egalitarian process. Lippitt and Lippitt (1986, p. 59) produced a diagram in which the consultant is shown as on a continuum between process facilitator and technical expert. Lovell relegates this diagram to a footnote. He does not want to include in the main text of his book (Lovell, 2000, pp. 370–1) the notion that a consultant can slip easily back and forth, as if the qualitative distinction between the two modes of interaction is not important. A simple way that many consultants use to check where they are between the two approaches is to ask whether they feel they are giving advice or facilitating a process by which problems are being analysed and solved. If it feels like the former, further reflection will determine whether they are acting as an expert/content consultant or even as an advisor. The danger is that, as an expert or particularly as an advisor, you might be reducing the executive autonomy of the consultor and simply end up making decisions for them for which they take less and less ownership. Ironically, it is my experience that, in this case, it is much easier for the consultor to ignore the solutions and plans the consultancy has produced and lay the blame on the consultant if they go wrong.

Given this emphasis on the consultant as facilitator of process and the need for the consultor to come up with their own solutions with the consultant's help, Lovell provides a series of useful assumptions and basic understandings that underpin the practice of church work consultancy:

- Consultors or clients are those seeking consultancy help; consultants or facilitators are those offering it.
- Broadly speaking work consultancy is to reflective practitioners and their work what counselling is to people and their lives.
- Consultancy is a working relationship between two parties: consultants and consultors or clients. There are likely to be other parties implicated as well.
- Consultancy is effected through an alliance of minds which enables consultors and consultants to work together and separately more creatively and which enhances the ability of consultors to think for themselves, on their own and with others, and to think with and for others.
- Consultants are not responsible for doing the work about which they offer consultations. They help those who are responsible for doing the work, consultors or clients, without doing it for them or becoming colleagues or controlling them. Consultants and consultors are jointly responsible for consultations; consultors are responsible for their work.
- Consultors' work can be done in or through secular or religious organizations, communities and groups.
- The help sought and/or proffered can be on any practical, personal, theoretical, philosophical or theological aspect of a consultor's work.

(2006, pp. 19–20)

A common feature of the literature on consultancy is the difficulty of agreeing on a definition of consultancy. Greiner and Metzger offer three definitions which evidently struggle with the issue of whether consultancy should be or is expert or non-directive:

1 Management consulting is an advisory service contracted for and provided to organizations by specially trained and qualified persons who assist, in an objective and independent manner, the client organization to identify problems, analyse such problems, recommend solutions to these problems and help, when requested, in the implementation of solutions.

(1983, p. 7)

2 Management consulting is the temporary infusion of outside and credible talent to provide new ideas and additional personnel to the client organization, as well as to serve the special interests of those hiring the consultant.

(1983, p. 9)

3 Management consultancy is an uncertain and evolving process, conducted by a foreign intruder, who muddles through by performing various problem-solving activities, while trying to meet high professional standards and still attempting to meet the needs of the clients.

(1983, p. 9)

Often it seems that consultancy covers so wide a field of activity that only general definitions can function. Lippitt and Lippitt offer a definition which sounds good but is in danger of being so general it is of little use in distinguishing consultancy from other interventions:

Consultation is a two-way interaction – a process of seeking, giving, and receiving help. Consulting is aimed at aiding a person, group, organization, or larger system in mobilizing internal and external resources to deal with problem confrontations and change efforts.

(1986, p. 1)

A useful focus is given by the language of work consultancy, which is employed in a number of church consultancy schemes. This allows the production of helpful definitions from Malcolm Grundy:

Work Consultancy: a process of thinking through issues with a trained person as they relate specifically to you and your work/ministry.

Work Consultant: a trained and experienced person who helps you to analyse, understand and develop the work which you have been asked to do.

(2007, p. 160)

Consultancy on work

Recent years of recession have seen large numbers of people losing their jobs. As many of us will have experienced first or second hand, the stress this imposes on the redundant (a chilling word to use) is not just that their ability to bring in money for food and shelter is curtailed but also that they are cut off from a key source of self-esteem and self-expression. Work, whether paid or voluntary, offers the opportunity to deploy our ability to solve problems and make the world a different place. This feeds back into our sense of being of value and use. As Elliott Jaques, an organizational psychologist, put it:

> Work is an activity of the whole person. It is that behaviour which constitutes the primary plane of reality in which the individual relates his subjective world to the external world, transforming each in the process of creating some socially manifest output. It is a realization in the external work of a subjective project. It is the behaviour through which the individual experiences the reality of his core identity.
>
> (1976, p. 112)

When we work, as Jaques indicates, we are taking ideas and intentions we have, be it leading a funeral, developing a youth project, writing a report, restructuring a region or going to visit someone who is sick, and turning them into reality as successfully as we can. This involves drawing on a range of skills and knowledge, on predicting what might happen and what we need to have prepared, as well as dealing with the unexpected that crops up along the way. Handling this successfully is what Jaques sees as work in all its complexity, interactions and need for judgement. If we can meet the challenge and achieve a more or less satisfactory outcome, then we tend to feel good. If we fail to achieve what we see as success, we tend to feel bad, especially if that failure continues over time. Underachievement might be because we lack the intellectual capability or the necessary skills and understanding. It may be that the context, for example the systems, the other workers, our leaders or the structure we work in, makes success difficult or impossible. Then we feel emotions like frustration, anger, demotivation, hurt and insecurity.

Church consultors have a huge psychological investment in their work, often described by them as vocation. If their work is not going well, they will have a sense not only of not being able to express what they have to contribute as a human being but also of not being faithful to their calling. In work consultations it is very common for significant levels of emotion to be attached by consultors to the matters under discussion. Work consultancy sessions need to be places where feelings such as grief, frustration, disappointment, even hate, can be spoken of and dealt with safely. A handy box of tissues is a must for any consultant.

However, the activity is not counselling. The attendant emotion is a significant part of the context for the work done in any session. It often offers data that can illuminate why an unproductive situation has gone wrong. The hope is that the analysis of the situation and the design of solutions and plans will, by improving the consultor's experience of achievement, reduce the potency of such negative feelings.

In work consultancy certain assumptions underline this concentration on the consultor's work, such as:

- Work is an essential, therefore God-given, characteristic of human nature.
- Work is a response to and expression of what God does in creating, building, healing and redeeming.
- Mission is work, as is ministry.
- Churches are organizations which perform work.
- The work of mission and ministry is achieved by a variety of people (who are in a variety of relationships with churches) applying their skills and gifts faithfully and effectively.

Thus, the proper focus of consultancy on an individual's or group's work supports the mission of God in the world through the diversity of the Church. By helping the work get done as effectively as possible, work consultancy contributes both to continuing mission and to individual church workers' health and well-being.

When might a consultancy be helpful for your church?

a. When a church wants to review its health and direction
  - Vision/Mission/Value/Goal Statements
  - Are we achieving our aims?
  - Do we need to review our leadership structure/model?
  - Review of effectiveness of leadership/pastoral team
  - Evaluation of effectiveness/appropriateness of current direction of church and its ministries
b. When a church is going through a period of change
  - When the church has reached a plateau
  - When new pastoral staff is being considered
  - When restructuring is being planned
  - When the church is declining

- When the church is growing and needs to change structures to cope
- In other times of significant change
c. When assistance is needed in times of difficulty
  - In times of conflict and/or crisis
  - When there is a need for outside perspective: consultants can help a church see the real issues
  - When a church is struggling with a specific issue that could hinder unity and growth.

(From the *Church Consultancy Manual* (2007) of the Baptist Churches of New South Wales and the Australian Capital Territory)

Metaphors of consultancy

Many different images and metaphors for consultants are used consciously and unconsciously by those who use consultants and by consultants themselves. It is often useful to reflect on what metaphor or metaphors fit our own work and style as consultants and any consultants we have encountered. Metaphors often help to express in shorthand what is seen as admirable or unacceptable about consultancy praxis. Here are some commonly used examples:

- Doctor
  I can diagnose what's wrong with you and recommend the treatment that will cure it.
- Guru
  I have acknowledged wisdom from years of experience and study and you will benefit from listening to and following my wise words.
- Fool
  I can tell the King (anyone at any level) unacceptable truths that no one else would get away with.
- Witchdoctor/fairy godmother
  I have mystical powers and access to magical remedies so I can make all your problems go away.
- Someone who steals your watch to tell you the time
  I will listen to you and study your organization and tell you what you knew already.

- Critical friend
  I am here to listen to you talk about your work and to offer supportive, yet brave feedback.
- Detective
  My skill is to discover and fit together all the clues that constitute your unsolvable problem.
- Salesperson
  I have well-tested ways of dealing with your type of issues, which I will convince you to buy.
- Travel agent
  You're going on an unfamiliar journey and I know about routes, means of transport, good places to go and life-threatening diseases; I can help you plan your journey so you get there safely and in good shape.
- Scapegoat
  You can bring me in to force unwelcome change and dump all the blame on me.
- Catalyst
  I will come in as the outsider who will promote change, then move out leaving the consultor/organization to get on with it.
- Midwife
  I will help you through the pain of delivering your answer to your problem.
- Missionary
  I have the truth of how things should be done which will solve all your problems and I want you to see the light.
- Expert
  I have the technical knowledge you need and am here to fix your issues even though you may not quite understand how I did it.
- Mercenary
  I can do anything you need just as long as you keep employing me.

Metaphors have obvious limitations. Indeed, it may be necessary to use a mixture of images. The list of possible metaphors is potentially endless but this range of metaphors reveals different balances between:

- the nature of the work to be done
- the nature of the relationship between consultant and consultor
- the consultant's and the consultor's approaches to the work
- the expected outcomes of the consultancy from the consultant's and the consultor's point of view

- the view of the consultor's expertise and the view of the consultant's expertise
- organizational culture and personal beliefs of the consultor and of the consultant.

Chapter 6 will discuss different models of consultancy. A consultant working without a rigorous, theory-based underpinning for what they do with individuals and groups can be very dangerous. Looking at the metaphors that might apply to a consultant's work can help in constructing their praxis model and in reflecting how well they are following that model. The use of metaphors may help identify when the way we think we are operating (the espoused model) and the way we are actually functioning (the operant model) are not the same (see Watkins *et al.*, 2009, p. 3). Metaphors may also help in the conversation with consultors about exactly what their consultant is aiming to provide. A consultant can be subject to huge pressure both explicit and unspoken to perform to the metaphor(s) the consultor is wedded to. Pictures, images and metaphors may provide a way out of unhelpful misunderstandings.

When I was at theological college, I remember the biblical scholar, C. F. D. Moule, telling us that the key to understanding the New Testament was studying the prepositions – being 'on the way' or 'in Christ'. The same approach can be taken with consulting. When you listen to people talking about consultancy, it can be very important to be aware of whether a consultant sees their work as, for example, 'with', 'to', 'for', 'alongside', 'on behalf of', or even 'in spite of'. In the contrast between an expert/content and a process style of consultancy the basic dilemma is typically between doing consulting 'for' and doing it 'with' the consultor. Noticing what language a consultant and a consultor instinctively use, especially the prepositions, may reveal their fundamental understanding of the work and how it is being carried out.

Are there biblical models and metaphors for consultancy?

As theologically aware operators supporting the ministry and mission of the Church, it is natural for consultants to look to Scripture for examples, models and principles on which to build their consultancy practice. While trying to avoid anachronistic analysis, there are certain biblical characters and events that can be mined for guidelines and frameworks against which to reflect. The Bible is full of people who provide advice and who help others tussle with the issues in their daily life that are holding them back. Leaders in Israel's history and in the New

Testament church depended on wise people who provided construct-ive insights into how their behaviour and decisions might support or obstruct their struggle to be faithful and successful in mission. The Old Testament prophets, sometimes from inside the establishment, some-times from outside, offered support and critique to kings specifically and to the nation in general based on their personal charism and their understanding of the context within God's purposes. For example, the letters of Paul provided guidance, among much else, about the nitty-gritty, organizational issues of building, maintaining and nurturing the fledgling Christian communities around the Mediterranean. Whether they can be treated precisely as examples of consultancy is debatable, but studying their insight, authority, techniques, persistence, faith and courage can be instructive. For the most part consultants will be look-ing for general principles about the way God as Trinity is seen to oper-ate in the biblical witness. This may be through theological themes and patterns. It may be in Jesus' and others' general approaches to engaging with people, for example in teaching, questioning and leadership. It may be in helpful and challenging scriptural metaphors and models.

The person often quoted as the biblical consultant and the first con-sultant in history is Jethro, Moses' father-in-law. He meets the jour-neying Israelite nation in the desert just before Moses receives the Ten Commandments on Mount Sinai. He is an example of an outsider, in this case a non-Jew, who arrives on the scene, intervenes constructively and leaves. The way he works with Moses as the leader of such a tur-bulent organization in Exodus 18.7–28 offers some important insights about consultancy process.

Consider Jethro's process:

1 He listened to Moses' story.
2 He rejoiced at Moses' achievements in a way that Moses could hear.
3 He watched Moses at work all day without comment.
4 He got Moses' thoughts about the way he works, using an open ques-tion (Why...?). This elicited important information about Moses' understanding of his work.
5 He showed courage in challenging Moses' work style. 'What you do is not good.' This was out of concern for Moses. His workload was going to wear him out.
6 He offered sound organizational analysis, both in terms of the struc-ture of Moses' organization and of Moses' understanding of the work to be done:

(a) Moses was micromanaging. The work needed to be categorized, separated out and delegated so that Moses did the work that only he needed to do.

(b) Moses needed to appoint the right people to do lower-level work. Jethro offered selection criteria – they should be God-fearing, trustworthy and honest. Thus Moses could be sure that the work was being done to his satisfaction.

(c) Moses needed to give these judges sufficient authority to make their judgements, and clear guidance so that they knew when issues were too big for them.

7 He gave Moses the reason behind all this: that Moses would be able to keep going and his people would be content with the judgements they received.

8 He judged correctly that Moses was reflective, confident and humble enough to take his advice.

9 He understood finally that he had done his job and left. He was not there to take over. Moses was the leader who had the role-based, executive authority to make the decision, implement the change and manage the consequences.

Looking at Jesus' interactions with people, there seem to be some clear habits. He used stories and parables, which invited engagement and reflection. Even the signs in John were used to engender discussion out of wonder. Characteristically he asked questions, expecting the interlocutor to engage and do some work in addressing their own issue. The psychologist Gordon Lawrence (1994), in fathoming what a group might expect from a consultant, talks about consultancy as working through the politics of salvation or the politics of revelation. If you are operating within the politics of salvation, what you expect from a consultant is that they will save you, coming in with all the answers and, in a sense, doing all the thinking and decision-making for you on the basis of their greater wisdom, knowledge and experience. The consultant does not need to draw on your expertise or even consult you that much. As Arbuckle (1993, p. 107), using Lawrence, puts it when talking about Jesus' leadership, if you are operating within the politics of revelation, the aim is to 'develop those processes that encourage the responsible exercise of authority, both individually and collectively, so that people become generative of ideas and agents of their own growth and that of the group'. It can be seen that this is typical of the way Jesus deals with people. He does not impose his solutions. He asks the man beside the Pool of Bethesda whether he wants to be well again

(John 5.6) and responds when the man begs for healing. He asks the rich young ruler (Luke 18.18–23) searching questions and challenges him, but leaves the decision entirely up to him. When the young man walks away saddened, he lets him go. Jesus seems to encourage people to make up their own mind with utter respect for their independence. There are passages of significant and sometimes lengthy, direct teaching, but it is interesting how the testimony that comes down to us contains so many conversational interactions such as meals or journeys on foot. Gempf (2003) has discovered that, of the 67 discussions related in Mark's Gospel, 50 involve Jesus using questions. He suggests that Jesus' intent was to provoke rather than convince, to offer or even force a choice. Doors of possibility are opened, the imagery is taken up in Revelation 3.20 where Jesus stands at the door knocking, offering to come in if the choice is made to invite him in.

A common theme, from the Old Testament prophets through Jesus' work to the letters of the New Testament, is the frustration of working with people who, having the option to follow straightforward advice or carefully reached, collaborative conclusions, chose to continue to go in the direction in which they were already going, sometimes to their doom. That is certainly a biblical pattern that consultants regularly identify with.

Consultancy in the family of helping disciplines

Front-line ministers will rely on a range of support mechanisms to keep themselves effective, sane and developing. Among these, work consultancy is one that is increasingly available. Yet, as the aim of the present discussion is to define what consultancy is, it is important to distinguish it from disciplines that may look like they are doing the same thing or where the boundaries may be somewhat blurred. Indeed, a significant ethical and professional consideration for both consultant and consultor revolves around being clear when what is needed or requested is beyond the scope of work consultancy. Consultancy specifically focuses on issues concerning the consultor's work (whether the consultor is an individual or a group). It may be that the capacity of an individual to carry out their work to the best of their ability is compromised by psychological problems. As many consultants working in church settings have a background in pastoral work and counselling, it can be tempting to tackle those issues as well. The same may be true of issues around a minister's prayer life, given that those same consultants may be clergy or spiritual teachers themselves. However, the consultant needs to

Helping disciplines – related but not the same		
Work consultancy	Therapy and counselling	Spiritual direction
Mentoring	Coaching	Supervision
Training	Facilitating	Mediation
Co-consultancy, action learning sets and cell groups	Mission accompaniment	Evaluation, appraisal, assessment or review

Figure 3.1 The family of helping disciplines

work with the consultor to make sure that they are not wandering into areas that are not properly consultancy territory, such as counselling, therapy or spiritual direction. Thus, work consultancy constitutes one of a range of disciplines in the family of helping activities. While doing different things, they are working with individuals to help them achieve what they want to be (see Figure 3.1).

What makes this family more likely to encourage confusion is that they share many techniques and principles. Whether you are consulting, counselling or offering supervision, you are involved in a collaborative search for solutions that calls for active listening, the formation of hypotheses and reflective analysis. Lovell talks about this family in these terms:

> Each member's activity seeks to stimulate and facilitate within people themselves creative engagement with their inner selves about things to do with their being and personal and vocational doing which at the time is of critical importance to their well-being, effectiveness and destiny. They all concentrate on this. Those who practise the various disciplines stimulate people to move inwards and outwards. They promote contextual introspection. The interface between the inside and outside worlds of human and spiritual dynamics is charged with creative potential: it is a fulcrum for development. Overall effectiveness is closely related to getting human and spiritual dynamics working well in relation to the inner and outer worlds of people and the interaction between them. This kind of existential engagement is of the essence of Christian living.
>
> (2000, p. 369)

It is not a case of the various disciplines working against each other or replacing each other. The ideal situation is where the insights gained from each feed into each other, freeing up access to potential solutions to the relevant, presenting issues. It is a professional issue for the consultant particularly, but also for the consultor, to monitor whether the type of help being offered is appropriate. Some essential checks on continuing clarity about whether what is being undertaken is right are:

- clear contracting from the start about what the issues are that are being addressed and with what approach
- both the consultant and the consultor reflecting throughout the process
- regular, explicit, open process review involving both the consultant and the consultor
- the consultant using their supervisor to check any indicative anxieties or hunches.

Two areas, that are normally clearly understood in terms of the needs they address and their techniques and methods, are spiritual direction and counselling. *Spiritual direction*, according to the website of the Spiritual Direction Network,

> is about taking the time to meet with another person and talk about one's spiritual journey, prayer and search for God. It can be a way to make better sense of your faith journey, to find clarity and support at times of significant life choices, and to respond more deeply to God's presence and move forward towards wholeness and freedom.
>
> (www.soulfriend.org.uk)

Sometimes when working with a consultor, the consultant becomes aware that there are serious psychological issues that are constraining the consultor's ability to perform in their work. In these cases the consultant has to get involved in what Lovell calls 'first aid-cum-pastoral counselling' (2000, p. 69). The aim is to encourage the consultor towards the appropriate, specialist help from *psychotherapy, counselling* or *psychiatry*.

Many caring professions such as counselling or social work impose an obligation on their practitioners to have regular *supervision* where a professional with acknowledged supervision skills will talk through the worker's practice with them to ensure that they are operating effectively, professionally and developing. Some ministers and church workers may respond to this approach for their work as ministers. It does depend on the supervisor being an expert in the same field, who can stretch the supervisee in their technical discipline.

A regular feature of working as a consultant with ministry teams, work departments or church councils is conflict between the individuals and groups involved. Often this is perfectly adequately and helpfully dealt with in the course of the sessions held with the consultant. Sometimes, sadly in churches, it may have reached such an immovable, bitter level that it has to progress from straightforward consultancy to *mediation*. This is a highly skilled activity well left to the experts.

The discipline that has the greatest potential overlap with consultancy is *coaching*. In recent years there has been a huge increase in the provision of coaching, coaching consultancies and coaching courses. So, what is different about coaching? Martyn Snow and Huw Thomas, in their booklet *Coaching in the Church*, talk about coaching as:

> Deploying a distinct set of skills where the coach enables someone to unlock the gifts and potential they have ... The coach's job is to enable someone to overcome and get past interference (such as their lack of confidence or their inability to work with others) in order to maximise performance.
>
> (2008, p. 5)

Classically in organizations, coaching is a function of the leader. It is about developing performance. If a worker is struggling with a task, is being asked to do something they have never done before, or could be even more effective than they are in some way, it is their leader's work to provide coaching, either by working with them themselves or by drawing in some other appropriate person. Snow and Thomas are clear that coaching should be part of the day-to-day work of local church leaders in order to develop the people of God in that place as effective workers for Christ. Quoting Bryn Hughes, they prescribe that 'a mentality of personal development ... needs to be continuous, high profile and rooted in the workplace' (2008, p. 3).

In many secular organizations nowadays coaching support is brought in from outside. It is increasingly seen as a benefit that a good employer provides for its staff. In talking to coaches from the companies that provide this, both in secular and religious organizations, and on looking at their websites, the impression is that coaching is now seen as much more to do with the worker as person rather than the task or work that person is undertaking. It is about what is blocking you from being all you could be in your specific work and in your career in general. For example, coaches can be very useful when people are considering a career or lifestyle change. As such, a feature of the use of coaching, as suggested by Clare Huffington (Campbell and Huffington, 2008, p. 16), is that individuals often seek it for themselves, even if the employer does not provide it. Their lack of trust in the long-term future and level of care of their organization means they have to attend to their career themselves. Huffington also suggests that coaching may be the new alternative to organizational consultancy, 'a discrete, relatively cheap, controllable form of organizational consultancy compared with the large-scale major change consultancy in the 1980s and 1990s' (2008, p. 16).

One danger in sourcing coaching from outside is that leaders will shy away from coaching as a key part of their work with those whom they manage. The leaders in churches are so thinly spread and apparently so busy with a wide range of duties that evidence of them doing any coaching is hard to find. I suspect it would be difficult to find, say, a bishop, district chair, regional commander or any similar role who spends time regularly coaching their front-line ministers. Hence, church hierarchies increasingly provide internal and external work consultants and coaches. In secular settings a leader who feels isolated because they are, for example, the chief executive of a business or the sole paid worker in a small community charity will use a work consultant over many years, because such support is not available, safe or appropriate within the organization. It is a feature of work consultancy in church settings that, very often, sessions between a work consultant and a local minister will persist for many years – even for ministers in teams, groups and circuits. This may be due, in part, to the organizational structure of churches as well as to their being collections of workers where independence of thought, belief and action have been part of the culture for centuries.

So, it appears that coaching is used to refer to a number of normally one-to-one activities:

- providing someone who works with or for you help that makes them more effective at the task or role they are doing
- working with a person as an outsider to tackle specific work problems, challenges or ambitions in their present work in place of their manager
- working with a person as an outsider to help that person overcome blocks to being all they can be in their life, especially their work life and career.

Mentoring has traditionally involved pairing a younger or less experienced worker with someone older or more experienced who has done the same or a similar job but who is not the worker's manager. This off-line relationship allows the worker to talk through, analyse and plan their work capitalizing on the wisdom and knowledge of the mentor. External agencies such as the coaching firms mentioned above often also provide, or double up as, mentors, but they are unlikely to have experience in exactly the job the mentee occupies. Thus, mentoring in church terms can be either working with someone who has done the job you are in or with someone who has a helpful, general wisdom. This is an interesting issue for the provision of coaches, mentors and work consultants. For example, when asked what sort of person they would like to work with, a new country vicar seeking help will often specify a coach, mentor or consultant who has been a rural minister.

Allied activities

Group methods such as *Action Learning Sets* and *cell groups* will often provide help similar to consultancy using a group of people who, for example, trained together or are in similar roles in different settings. Action Learning Sets are now increasingly used and promoted by leadership programmes in some churches as a way of encouraging continuing reflection and learning among leaders in the Church. A group of peers, normally with a trained facilitator, meet regularly and listen to each other presenting situations or problems against a rigorous set of process rules. This encourages reflective practice and allows for the generation of options with empathetic, knowledgeable but challenging peers.

Consultants are often used for certain apparently different activities. The first is carrying out *appraisals*. Most denominations are embarking on systems of *review* in a genuine effort to ensure both that church workers are held accountable for delivering quality work in their ministry and that they are supported, especially when they are struggling or when they want to progress. Most churches, having decided that it is impossible for the hierarchical leaders to do this work as regularly as would be normal in secular organizations, have needed to recruit suitable people to carry out these sessions. One useful source of personnel is those who are already known as consultants. They seem ideally suited, as they are skilled at talking to people in a helpful way about their work. Many of the same skills are involved, but there are significant differences in terms of who the consultant is doing the work for and how information flows concerning the contents of the sessions.

Another activity, which it is common to see consultants undertaking, is *training*. Consultants will often possess generic, technical knowledge about organizational behaviour, systems, strategy development, team working or personality analysis. They may have specific expertise in evangelism, youth work, stewardship or liturgy. They will often, therefore, be involved in training groups in these areas. The training may indeed be an essential component of the consultancy they are involved in. If, as part of a parish audit, the project involves an assessment of what is needed and already provided in the local community, a group of parishioners may be recruited to investigate, interview and survey. The consultant may have to train those people in questionnaire design, interview techniques and data recording. It may be an explicit object- ive of the consultancy that the training results in the acquisition of knowledge and skills that make the local congregation more capable of carrying out their mission.

A common request from ministry teams, working groups and com- mittees is *facilitation*. Often a consultant who is skilled in group work will be an ideal person to attend to the process of a meeting or an away day. They have no expert involvement in the subject matter of the day but their handling and safe holding of an effective process for the ex- ploration and decision-making allows those involved to concentrate on the content. This can be useful if the local minister or manager, who would normally chair such an event, wants to be free to provide input, express opinions and join in the process in a truly collaborative way. A critical issue is getting clarity on whether the facilitator is also seen as a consultant, especially if they are seen as an expert consultant. The roles are not the same.

A final definition

In *The Priestlike Task* (1985), Wesley Carr offers his reflection on min- istry in the Church of England. Part of this is suggesting a model for ministry. Surprisingly, the model he opts for is that of a consultant. Although he is trying to elucidate the work of a priest, he offers some helpful insights for our present discussion. He sees the consultant as more of an interpreter than an expert. Although 'such a person has skills ... he chiefly uses what he feels and experiences in his role as consultant to offer interpretations to those with whom he is working' (1985, p. 15). (His masculine pronouns reveal that this comes from a time when there were only male priests in the Church of England.) The central piece of work for the consultant is to hold what is being presented, worked on and talked about together in the context of the overall task. Sometimes the consultor may get so involved in what is happening then and there that they forget the purpose of the entire enterprise. The consultant keeps holding the whole picture in front of people whose grasp of it becomes more and more fragmented as their emotional experience in the present gets more intense. The consultant is certainly involved in that emotion but needs to keep interpreting what is happening against what Carr calls 'a transcendent point of reference, namely the task' (1985, p. 15). However, this means that consultants are vulnerable because success in their work depends on their own judgements and interpretations, which are constantly being scrutinized by those with whom they are working. Their only authority lies in the fact that what they say or do is right. It may be a grand ambition and something more than Carr was claiming for consultancy, but in seeing consultancy as a distinct Christian ministry, a definition of consultancy starts from the assumption that

[consultancy's] chief components are the total involvement of the church in each situation afresh; its ability to hold a transcendent reference to which people may then relate their fragmented and incoherent experience; and this awareness that its authority is demonstrated by the accuracy of its interpretations of people's experiences in life.

(Carr, 1985, p. 17)

4

Roles in Consultancy

It is quite common to hear a minister say, 'My work consultant says I should ...' Talking through work habits, issues and approaches with a work consultant can have an immense influence on church workers' judgements and choices in their day-to-day activity. For a co-worker or a church member, hearing their minister quote their work consultancy like this can provoke a range of reactions from, 'Great, she's really dealing with those things that are holding her back', to 'What right does some overpaid outsider have to dictate how my minister deals with me?'

If it is working well, what goes on in a consultancy process is precious, productive, personal, powerful and liberating, and carries an authority by which its insights can be applied back in the work situation. It can have a continuing positive effect on the shape of the consultor's approach to their work. It is important, therefore, that consultancy is based on rigorous theory, ethical, professional practice and self-aware process. Central to this is clarity about who does what in the consultation process. Subsequent chapters will examine the process, consultancy models and ethics, but this chapter will concentrate on the roles and relationships in a consultancy. The aim is to shed light on:

- the nature of the relationship(s) during a consultancy
- consultancy as a collaborative activity
- the roles of consultant, consultor and observer
    the work of each role
    the authority of each role
    the capability needed to fulfil each role
    issues around more than one person being in each or any of the roles.

The nature of the consultancy relationship

When a consultancy involves a single consultant and a single consultor working together in a room on their own, it is possible to see the two actors as isolated individuals. However, it is often helpful to see them both as systems that overlap as a result of and for the purpose of the consultancy. A unique mixture of personality, experience, history, relationships, communities and adherences accompanies a church worker who comes as a consultor to a consultancy process. They stand as a person who has been raised, educated, trained and employed in a range of roles and organizations. They will be working in a particular setting at the nexus of their own objectives and ambitions. The desires and hopes of their superiors, their church members, the communities surrounding their setting and their family will all influence. Sometimes a key task in a consultancy is to discover the range of interests and ambitions that the worker represents in their daily work. Church ministers often feel significant pressure from their position at the centre of multiple hopes and anxieties, many of which are not their own. Similarly, the consultant is a system, but a different system, much of which is useful and available in tackling the issue that the consultor wants to address. However, some of the consultant system may have the potential for obstructing the success of the consultancy, such as their being in a hierarchical role in the consultor's organization. Thus it is important to recognize and work with, if possible, the hinterland that consultor and consultant bring. ('System', as we shall find in the discussion of consultancy models, is a word that is used to mean a range of different things in organizations and consultancy and so needs to be used with care as to exactly what is meant.)

More often than not, the issues that a consultor brings involve the people, structures and behaviour that they are connected with in their organization. It may be that the consultant is working within the same organization with several people individually or with individuals and groups at the same time. The issues may relate to the individual's personal work challenges or may concern the relationships and interactions between people or within a team. However, it may be that the resolution of the issues depends on giving attention to organizational structures, systems, processes and the relationships between entities such as departments within the organization or even with other organizations. As can be seen below by Schein's classification, the nature and focus of the work changes according to the type of consultor system that is involved. Part of the consultant's work is to identify with the consultor the level of the issue and therefore the nature of the consultancy. Are the conditions in place to tackle it? Do they have the right capability? It has to be said, though, that part of a consultancy may be acknowledging that, however justified an individual's frustrations with major processes or policies of a church, they may possess little effective ability to alter them. The work may need to be on an individual level to work out how to focus on change they can influence, effect and control.

Schein's types of consultors by levels of issues

1 Individual level

The individual level can be thought of as the 'intra-psychic' issues that a given person has for which the relevant intervention is some form of individual counselling and may include the fundamental problem of bonding with others, of membership in an organization or community.

2 Inter-personal level

This level contains problems or issues that pertain to the relationship between the individual and other members of the organization or consultor system.

3 Face-to-face group level

This level shifts to problems or issues that are lodged in how a group or team functions as a group.

4 Inter-group level

This level focuses on problems or issues that derive from the way in which groups, teams, departments, etc., relate to each other and co-ordinate their work on behalf of the organization or larger consultor system.

5 Organizational level

This level pertains to problems or issues that concern the mission, strategy and total welfare of the whole consultor system, whether that be a family unit, a department, an organization or a whole community.

6 Inter-organizational level

This level deals with important interventions that influence organizational sets, consortia, industry groups, and other systems where the members of the system are themselves complete organizational units but are working in some kind of alliance or joint venture with each other.

7 Larger system level

This level would pertain to problems or issues that involve the wider community or society where the consultant may be working with social networks, with organizational sets, or with community groups that involve a wide variety of issues pertaining to the health of larger systems, even the planet.

(Adapted from Schein, 1997, pp. 3–6)

Craig Lundberg, in the article 'Towards a General Model of Consultancy' (1997), sees the consultant and consultor as overlapping systems in the terms described above. He describes a consultor as a human system feeling anxious because they are experiencing some kind of uncertainty. So, the consultor asks for help. The definition of help is when a human system perceives that its anxiety has been reduced. A consultant, then, is a human system that responds and offers to provide such help. Because uncertainty is subjective, the consultor needs to define what the help is that will relieve their anxiety. The two systems interact and overlap in seeking to define and reduce the consultor's anxiety. The consultancy can be seen as a system itself and has an interdependent existence with the consultor and consultant's systems. As a consequence, since anxiety is a result of uncertainty, the consultant is likely to experience anxiety both from the uncertain effort to help the consultor and to some extent from the consultor's initial anxiety. The consultancy then becomes a system that experiences anxiety. Because it has a life of its own, the consultancy system has to deal with, for example, the fact that all the interconnecting human systems are unstable. They are always changing, transforming and adapting. The consultancy as a system will, consequently, transform with time in its own right, necessitating that consultor and consultant help reduce each other's anxiety. In working together, the traffic is not one way.

A consultancy relationship can become something very special to both consultor and consultant. Sometimes, when I have been engaged in organizational reviews, which depended on interviewing a cross section of a workforce, the senior managers have expressed doubts whether many of the workers would talk to a consultant. My experience is that workers (sometimes after warming up and beginning to trust) are delighted to talk about their work. It is normally very important to them. To have someone seriously listening to their concerns and excitement about their work can be a relief, even a therapy for them. It is fairly common for people not to be given such an opportunity in the normal course of their work. Consultancy can be such an opening. The consultant offers undivided, serious attention to the consultor as they talk about their work. The concentration is on how it is for the consultor. Others may listen to the consultor talking about their work but will have an eye on their own interest as well. This quality of attention leads to a particular intimacy on a number of levels – emotional, intellectual, creative, spiritual, task-focused, conflict handling, vocational and theological. At first, the intimacy is in sharing straightforward data, facts, stories and feelings, but, as the process continues, patterns

What the consultor knows	A Opportunity or threat	D Intimate enlightenment
What the consultor doesn't know	B Undiscovered country	C Resource or conflict
	What the consultant doesn't know	*What the consultant knows*

Figure 4.1 Shared knowledge in consultancy

may be identified, analyses developed and conclusions reached. Frameworks and models may be applied from theology, psychology, sociology or organizational studies in a particular mix that comes from the interaction of the consultor and consultant systems under these special conditions.

This process, if successful, accompanies the expansion of knowledge for both parties, but especially on the part of the consultor, both in terms of basic data and in terms of analysis and solutions. Using a classic consultant four-box model format (akin to the *Johari Window* in Luft and Ingham 1955), it is possible to dissect this process (see Figure 4.1).

Box A The consultor has significant information, feelings and opinions about the issue under investigation and can share as much of this as they feel comfortable with. It is likely that any information they hold back that is relevant could become a threat to the success of the consultancy process as such data might have a significant impact on the analysis and any solutions.

Box B There may be information that neither consultor nor consultant knows that might be of help in understanding the situation. Exploration into this by whatever means could deliver useful extra input to the work.

Box C The consultant may have useful tools, methods and analytical frameworks that will help to handle the consultor's information. The consultant may have knowledge as an expert in the area being discussed that could support the discussion. However, it may disable the consultor as an equal partner in the consultation. In organizations like churches, there is, also, always the possibility that, unknown to the consultor, the consultant is aware of details of the consultor or their situation. This can lead to a conflict of interest.

Box D This is the major creative space in a consultancy where the data is shared and both parties' analyses, hunches and conclusions are held in common in order to make progress with the issue.

Boxer and Palmer (1994) use a similar approach to examine what they call *consultancy positions*, with the consultant seen as a fool in Box B, a guru in Box C and a bird in Box D.

The natural process of a productive consultancy over time will lead to the reduction in size of boxes A, B and C. Individual and shared reflection on whether this is actually happening can help to identify whether the consultancy is proving as productive as it can be and whether there are dynamics that indicate a lack of trust or a misunderstanding of role, method or authority. It may be that Box A gets larger at the same time as Box D gets larger, as the consultor becomes more insightful about their situation. This is in line with the purpose of consultancy. It is not an objective of a consultancy to enlarge Box C, although this might be a useful additional result in terms of the consultant's reflective practice and development.

Being the creative space, Box D, Intimate Enlightenment, represents the place where it is most easy to experience working in Christ. Here is a setting for the liberation and deployment of the skills of both consultant and consultor to build positive, mission-centred options for the future. New understandings are opened up and new realities built. Here it is possible to work at the Kingdom-based task of identifying what stifles life and what promotes abundance. Work is central to people's self-esteem. Consultancy concerns itself with identifying, addressing and resolving what is twisting a church worker away from being able to achieve their vocational potential or a church community from engaged ministry in their setting. Theological processes such as salvation and redemption can be discerned as the consultancy contributes to the ability of the consultor to express themselves authentically in their full humanity in community. This is not to say that what goes on in this space is not regularly painful and difficult. Uncovering, naming and resolving structural and individual sin, where the possibility of community, vocation, just structures and respectful relationships are suppressed, carries with it considerable heartache and challenge. Even where they have been identified, the constraints can feel so immovable that the result is frustration, disappointment and loss of faith.

The intimate, constructive relationships built over the length of a consultancy can be supported and informed by the models of self-giving and receiving Christianity offers. Talking about the trinitarian model available for understanding the consultancy relationship, Lovell says:

> Critical features of the model can be seen clearly in the ways in which God, Jesus and the Holy Spirit give themselves and their resources freely and without condescension, pomp, fuss or ceremony. Each member of the Trinitarian God comes with great humility. They do not impose themselves: they allow us to ignore and exclude them, and we do. They come to engage with us, to confront and challenge, but they display great respect for all people and reverence for life. They come to accompany us, not to take us over. Omnipotent as they are, they depend upon human responses to their overtures to form loving and creative relationships.
>
> (2000, p. 126)

Consultancy as a collaborative activity

Once the decision is made to embark on some sort of consultancy, the only way that the work can proceed effectively is to recognize that it has to be based on collaboration. In content/expert consultancy, the consultant needs to have access to all the relevant information that describes the context surrounding the issue being tackled so that they can give sound, useful advice. It is up to the consultor to provide that access. The consultant may have to help the consultor in understanding what is needed, for example exactly which information, where to get it and who to talk to. The consultant may need to check the consultor's understanding. When the work is finished and the advice, for example in the form of report or a presentation, is ready, collaboration demands that the advice is heard and taken seriously. The consultor does not have to follow the advice to the letter or at all. It is advice but its quality and usefulness will have been helped if the quality of the collaboration has been appropriate.

In a process type of consultancy, with which this book is more concerned and on which this chapter will concentrate, the issues around collaboration become even more acute. Consider the case of Joe and Mark. (This is a case in which I had some involvement, but at a distance, knowing both the team and the two consultants. Again, names and other details have been changed to protect confidentiality.)

Joe and Mark

Joe was a member of a ministerial team. The team got together once a month for a staff meeting – in the evening so the self-supporting ministers could join the group. It was important that they were involved. They had crucial insights being involved in the world of work and were members of the congregations before going into accredited ministry of various kinds. The team had big issues to deal with, such as a drastic reduction in full-time, paid clergy and developing a shared mission plan, given the tensions between the different churches represented. All the same, the team worked reasonably well together and were all more or less committed to a common future. The team leader, Angela, persuaded the team to have a team consultant. The last one, Anne, came to one meeting in three for a couple of years and ran an away day. She used tools and activities that seemed to help the sessions go well. Joe thought the meetings were quite fun when she ran them. However, she had left the area and they now had another consultant, Mark, who came highly recommended. Angela had been using him to help her talk through her own work issues and thought he was really good. But he was very different from Anne. He sat at the back of the room, outside the circle. He said very little. From time to time he threw in a mysterious comment such as, 'There seems to be an issue that people here are dancing around. It's like a precious glass vase which people here are too frightened to handle in case it breaks.' Then he said no more. Joe was, by background, an engineer who had come into full-time ministry in his early thirties and found this all a bit like mumbo jumbo. He wondered what this man was being paid for and had no idea how to operate when Mark was there. When Joe expressed puzzlement at what was going on, Mark seemed to get even more inscrutable.

In this case both Joe and Mark wanted to get the greatest benefit out of working together to achieve the team's aims for these meetings. As it stands, it does not look as if that was likely. Problems could be:

1 Joe did not know how to operate as a consultor in the way that Mark was working.

2 Mark had not explained what he was doing, how it helps and how Joe could work with him.

3 There was the possibility that Mark was seen as Angela's consultant; so Joe might have speculated that his strange behaviour was part of some secret deal between the team leader and the consultant. Was there a hidden agenda Joe didn't know about?

4 Joe did not seem to have any authority to challenge or change what was happening or even simply to understand what was going on.

There is no question about the competence of the consultant in this case, but the fact that the consultor did not understand how he worked may have had serious consequences on the success of the work they were supposed to do together.

Options open to Joe are to stick with it in as good a spirit as he can, to create considerable fuss until he gets what he needs as a consultor, to opt out and find any excuse not to be there, or to display his sense of being excluded by misbehaving in the meetings. However, if the roles are clear, the method, process and the way of interacting are explicit and the authority any participant has in the process understood, Joe, as a consultor, is much more likely to get productively involved in the meetings when Mark is there. Effectiveness within the process itself is the first benefit of clear, shared understanding of roles, work and authority. The second benefit is greater likelihood of successful implementation of any outcomes. If, for the participants in a consultation, roles, work and authorities are unclear, the risk is that the consultant will be seen as the expert who is imposing their own solution, thus reducing any consultor's commitment to and ownership of the decisions and plans the team decides on. If the consultors are enabled to see themselves as adult partners in the consultancy process and function as such, they are more likely to see the decisions as their own. The team leader and the consultant need to take some time to explain to Joe the principles of what is going on. They need to negotiate roles, working style and authorities, and check at regular intervals that the process continues to allow Joe to contribute as he gets more skilled and confident in this approach. Just as Mark needs to be a skilled consultant, attention needs to be paid to ensuring Joe is a skilled consultor.

The role of consultant

The role of consultant needs to be understood in terms of a range of factors. What is it that they are supposed to do? What capability should they have? What authority do they need if they are to work productively with the consultor? Are there advantages to there being more than one consultant and how might that work?

How a consultant can help

The following is an extract from a letter I wrote as a self-supporting ordained minister and a commercial consultant, when I was in the early days of learning how to be a consultant.

I find it interesting in the team where I help out as an associate priest that I am being increasingly used as a process facilitator for the stipendiary clergy and the Wardens and the church councils. The help they need is how to arrive at decisions efficiently, quickly, and inclusively, with a sense of being able to own the decisions and feel accountable for them and with minimal loss of tempers. It's not that they don't know the answers; they just need help with the process to get them out. I contribute next to nothing to the content although it is important that I am theologically and ecclesiastically literate so as to frame the questions and the process appropriately and to analyse and reflect back what people contribute.

The role of consultant: the work

The fundamental task of a consultant is to work alongside a consultor in solving their problems, as Lippitt and Lippitt put it, 'collaborating with the client in all of the perceptual, cognitive, emotional, and action processes needed to solve the problem' (1986, p. 66). This does not mean that the consultant's work and the consultor's work are the same. The consultant has to work hard to make sure that the process is as effective as possible. Lovell suggests that consultants are responsible for:

- introducing effective consultancy processes
- seeing that respective and joint responsibilities of consultants and consultors are clarified and agreed
- making realistic assessments of what can be achieved in the time available so that unrealistic expectations are not aroused
- working to the consultor and his/her purposes, priorities, beliefs and situations
- helping consultors to be effective consultors
- building up the confidence of the consultor

- ensuring that whenever possible/necessary, the consultor has got the agreement and understanding about the consultancy of any with whom he/she is working so that the consultancy is seen for what it is and not a threat
- enhancing the relationships between consultors and those with whom they work
- their own learning and its implications.

(2000, p. 50)

Lovell's emphasis is very strongly on setting up the conditions, the approach, the working relationship and the organizational context that will make the consultancy fruitful and collaborative. Lippitt and Lippitt, in one of their descriptions of the types of consultancy intervention, build the next level of the consultant's work.

The consultant as joint problem solver

Under the right circumstances the consultant in this role brings to a client and to a situation important resources through the ability to

- perceive the situation accurately
- provide a wider perspective of the situation by testing assumptions
- define goals clearly
- express and test alternatives
- provide a sense of reality
- confront sensitive areas
- save client time and resources
- reinforce commitments
- link existing resources to other resources
- catalyze action
- divide the problem into manageable parts; and
- use and expand client resources.

(Lippitt and Lippitt, 1986, pp. 66–7)

The consultant can only work with what has been revealed in the consultancy and in any preparatory material, submissions or reports the consultor has offered. In order for the consultant to get as accurate a picture as possible, they will need to employ a range of tools, questioning techniques, listening skills, and analytical frameworks from an integrated range of disciplines to get the consultor to open up with clarity.

It may be that the very process of laying out the situation in a clear way and framing it in terms of models and patterns from those disciplines will unlock the problem sufficiently in itself. Very often it can be a matter of just getting a consultor to see where their day-to-day decisions and behaviours are dangerously inconsistent with the direction they are claiming to travel. For example, in many churches a pastoral team has been set up and trained to visit people who are sick. It is fairly common in my experience for the minister to do the visiting of the 'important' members of the congregation when they are ill. Surely, that is what a minister is supposed to do for an elder, a steward, the treasurer, the leader of the Mothers' Union. It is, however, absolutely predictable that such behaviour will lead to the demise of the pastoral team, as they and church members see that they are not the real pastoral visitors. It can be immensely valuable for the minister consultor if their consultant reflects that behaviour, the message it symbolizes and communicates so powerfully and its consequences. The consultor will then have to work on how they deal with their own feelings and their key people's feeling that the minister should come to see them. It becomes a matter of long-term culture change, education, continuing reflection on personal behaviour and the coherent consistency of the messages and symbols that are sent out by systems, actions and policy.

An issue for some who are providing consultancy help in churches is that they work for the organization as, for example, a regional officer or a diocesan advisor. There is, therefore, an additional dynamic to the network of relationships referred to above. The consultant may be representative, actually or symbolically, of the hierarchy or the consultant may be anxious to prove their worth as the continuation of their job or department depends on the local church seeing them as worth their cost. A detailed discussion of the role of the internal consultant will be found in Chapter 8, but it is important to say here that it is part of the consultant's work to recognize the conflict, analyse its consequences and manage it.

It is frustrating when recommendations that a consultant makes or plans that a consultant and consultor forge together are not put into practice properly or at all. This often feels like failure. The answer to this is to be clear about the work a consultant has to do. Peter Block says:

If I –
    know my area of expertise (a given),
    behave authentically with the client,

tend to and complete the business of each consulting phase, and act to build capacity for the client to solve the next problem on their own –

I can legitimately say I have consulted flawlessly.

(2000, p. 49)

The result, he says, if the consultancy has not delivered the desired change or if the consultant is dismissed, will not be a happy consultation but it is the best the consultant can do.

The role of consultant: capability

An effective consultant needs a certain mix of capability. Using a framework from Macdonald *et al.* (2006, pp. 45–52), the critical elements of individual capability can be categorized as:

- *Knowledge* – knowing all or part of a body of knowledge such as Biblical Studies, Psychology, Church Law or Group Work Theory. An individual will also have heuristic knowledge, that is, a self-generated body of knowledge that crosses disciplinary boundaries such as knowledge of establishing a new church or doing a funeral or about people with psychiatric illness.
- *Technical skills* – proficiency in the use of knowledge – often learned routines that we see as skills. I may have read books about group dynamics but can I run a meeting?
- *Social process skills* – the ability to interact productively with other people in various settings. This is not about being nice and may indeed involve challenge and confrontation. These skills make the individual able to read social situations, to understand the underlying processes and to influence those processes to a useful end.
- *Mental processing ability* – the way a person absorbs information, sorts it, senses patterns in it, makes judgements about it and reaches conclusions. As this ability increases, the individual can deal with and make relationships between greater variables and interaction of variables, in all their uncertainty, complexity and chaos. This determines the level of difficulty of problems an individual can handle.
- *Application* – the effort and energy that an individual puts into applying the other elements of their capability to getting work done. Often terms like drive, determination, energy, stickability or conation are used. It is the person's ability to act to get results in an efficient, effective and timely manner.

In terms of *knowledge*, consultants, as has already been said, should be able to draw on and integrate an appropriate range of fields and disciplines – theology, ecclesiology, missiology, organizational behaviour, psychology, group work, theories of change and consultancy theory, to name but a few. Consultants need to know what they think and believe about God, God in the world, organizations, Church and churches, mission, human nature, work, leadership, strategy and personality, not so that they can impose their idea of what the right answer is but so that they understand the questions that need to be addressed in helping the consultor build a rigorous analysis of his or her situation. The mixture will depend on the kind of service they offer and the settings they operate in. As was said in Chapter 1, consultants need enough knowledge to resource their being reflective practitioners and practical theologians themselves. Clear understanding of ethical and professional practice as a consultant goes some way to ensuring that what they do is safe and sustainable. Consultancy is an interpersonal process, whether with individuals or groups. There are certain bodies of knowledge around the dynamics of people working together in pairs or in a large group that inform the way a consultant can facilitate the process. This demands, for example, a toolkit of techniques to get consultors talking and interacting, and an understanding of the difference between an open, directed, closed or paraphrasing question. (For more on questions, see Chapter 7.) It helps to be familiar with ways of constructing the flow of a team's planning day that takes account of, say, emotional rhythms, learning styles and gender differences. The heuristic process means that, by means of their reflection on practice, each consultant will develop a personal treasury of knowledge that informs the way they work. Success in employing the knowledge will reinforce confidence in its technical value and encourage further study in the same area. Reflection will also reveal gaps both as a result of pondering on the consultant's own practice and watching other consultants do things well. This will identify areas of technical knowledge that the consultant will see as worth investigating. There is a nurturing, reflexive dialogue between the knowledge and success in deploying the knowledge in which knowledge becomes more secure when it is affirmed by experience.

The *technical skills* of a consultant often have to be developed by observation, safe practice and apprenticeship. Knowing the theory does not necessarily indicate any ability to apply it successfully. A consultant has to learn the ability to access the right set or mixture of theoretical models and apply them live. Being able to watch a highly skilled consultant at work can show how powerful this ability to apply learned knowledge can be. This concerns not only knowledge about the content of technical issues but also knowledge about effective process. Kubr says that a consultant needs an 'ability to listen, a facility in oral and written communication, and an ability to share knowledge, teach and train people' (2002, p. 785). A particular judgement that a consultant has to make in this area is whether they have both the basic knowledge and the skill to apply that knowledge. The disciplines of personal re-flection on practice, feedback and supervision are essential in this. In terms of knowledge and having the skill to apply it, it is very tempting for a consultant to say they can help when in fact they are in an area beyond their capability. They may be trying to look good, to help out a consultor in distress or grasping at work. In the same list of consultant qualities Kubr points to consultants needing to be able to 'recognize the limitations of [their] competence' and 'to admit mistakes and learn from failure'. Ethics are essential.

Awareness of and reflection on personality, learning styles and tem-perament are also helpful in a consultant. This does not mean that a consultant should come from a narrow set of personality types. It does, however, mean that consideration is given to whether the way a con-sultant is coming across is getting the best results. Rendle and Mann, in *Holy Conversations* (2003), talk about the difference between extra-verts and introverts where extraverts tend to do their thinking on the outside, verbally letting the listener in on how they are reaching their conclusions. Introverts classically listen, process internally and come out with a conclusion. The listener may not know how they got there and, indeed, neither may the introvert. Rendle and Mann suggest that a strategic intervention group such as a planning team needs to 'ex-travert its work – to work out loud' (2003, p. 41). Communication involves not just conclusions but also the dilemmas, insights, questions and planning process in getting to their conclusions. The consultant doing this sort of work needs to consider, however introverted they might be, whether they are extraverting their thinking process enough for the consultor, individual or group. If this is not the case, there is the likelihood of resistance to even the best plans, recommendations or solutions because people cannot see how they have been reached. The consultant who is an extravert will need to remember that feed-back means 'talking and listening. Information must travel both ways' (Rendle and Mann, 2003, p. 42).

In this example, it can be seen that *social process* is not just the prov-ince of those with exactly the right sort of demeanour from birth. It draws on understanding how collaborative working happens between people, for example from the study of personality types or learning styles. Effective social process does depend, though, on the ability to read interpersonal interactions well in order to assess which is the best mode of interaction or tool to use.

In order to build up the mutual trust, which creates the environment needed for effective consultancy, Lovell (2000, pp. 36–46) identifies seven aspects of this interpersonal behaviour:

- assurance of confidentiality
  A significant proportion [of church workers] … have suffered through breach of confidence in the church.
- paying attention: genuine interest, single-minded concentration and professional curiosity
  Engender feelings of peace (shalom) and fulfilment. Such absorption is pregnant with creativity when it is shared by consultors and consultants … foster and facilitate disciplined thinking, rigorous analysis and a businesslike approach … give consultants and consultors access to each other's subjective world.
- empathic relating
  Relating to consultors with warmth, empathy, genuineness, rigour and love, not … with austerity and supposedly cold clinical correctness … seeing what the situation might look like through the consultor's eyes.
- controlled emotional involvement
  Whatever the expression of my feelings might have done for me, it has had serious adverse effects upon the consultancy process.
- openness and privacy
  Consultors and consultants need to feel that the consultation has been a wholesome experience, that precious areas of privacy remain inviolate, that confidences will be kept, that they have discussed others in an honourable way.
- securing the freedom of consultors to be their own person in interdependent relationships
  Consultations are least effective when consultors become unhealthily dependent upon consultants, a danger greatest when consultations produce telling insights and workable ideas.
- the need for consultants and consultors to be respectful and humble in creative reflective engagement
  Consultants are allowed the great privilege of a guided tour of work that is a person's personal God-given vocation: they tread on holy ground; they need to take their shoes off.

In the list already referred to, Kubr (2002, p. 785) offers a menu of the behaviours by which effective social process would be evident

- ability to understand people and work with them
  respect for other people; tolerance
  ability to anticipate and evaluate human reactions
  easy human contacts
  ability to gain trust and respect
  courtesy and good manners
- ability to communicate, persuade and motivate
  ability to listen
  facility in oral and written communication
  ability to share knowledge, teach and train people
  ability to persuade and motivate
- intellectual and emotional maturity
  stability of behaviour and action
  independence in drawing unbiased conclusions
  ability to withstand pressures, and live with frustration and uncertainties
  ability to act with poise, in a calm and objective manner
  self-control in all situations
  flexibility and adaptability to changed conditions.

These lists are ideal and aspirational. The fact that most of us will fall short from time to time reinforces the importance of reflection, supervision and learning.

In terms of *mental processing ability*, the basic question is whether the consultant has the cognitive ability to encompass the complexity of the issues being discussed. If they have not, no amount of support from a more capable consultor, experience, training, hard work or social process skill will ensure that all the variables and impacts from and on the context will be taken into account. The analysis and the solution are likely to be undercooked and ineffective. This is clearly a matter where the consultant's self-knowledge is key, built on reflection on practice and attention to feedback. Addressing it realistically depends on honesty, courage and professional ethics.

Kubr (2002, p. 785) talks about a set of qualities around personal drive and initiative, including 'the right degree of self-confidence, healthy ambition, entrepreneurial spirit and courage, initiative and perseverance in action'. Being engaged in consultancy in churches can be frustrating. Church structures can be cumbersome, decision-making processes slow, resources thin on the ground, members and ministers cautious. Because of this, good levels of *application,* as a feature of a consultant's capability, can be the only way to ensure that a project gets to the end. A supportive feature of consultancy is that often the work consultancy session becomes some form of accountability for the consultor. In one session, the consultor may come up with a solution and commit to a plan for implementing it. The fact that the next work consultancy session is looming encourages the consultor to try to action what was promised. Words like drive or enthusiasm, which are often used in this area, paint a picture of massive energetic, if not frantic dynamism. It can be very helpful, particularly when dealing with groups, to communicate an energy and urgency. However, getting the end achieved just as often results from small, low-level, well thought through incremental activity. Application is being able to see the work through, often in church consultancies, against mighty and numerous obstacles in the form of systems, tradition, culture or fear. The process of change was once described to me in Canada as gentle pressure relentlessly applied. This incremental work may have to deal with intermittent meetings spaced apart over the year. The consultant without a miraculous memory will need careful note-taking after each session so that the next session starts from where the last left off. Effective, applied social process over time will demand maintaining considerable courage in respectfully challenging inconsistency or avoidance of difficult decisions. How application manifests itself is a matter of judgement. If the consultancy concerns a short-term project, the need may be for great energy, speed and hoopla, carefully designed to maintain the participatory collaboration to get the work done in the time available.

The role of consultant: authority

In reality, the consultant has very little authority. As has already been said a number of times, the consultor holds the authority to decide whether to follow and implement any plans or advice which the consultancy relationship generates. The consultor – in discussion with the consultant – decides even the process of the consultation, the methods used and the issues addressed. The only precondition that a consultant needs to make is that they are given as much of the background and contextual information to the issue as is possible and that they be listened to seriously. Without these conditions, authority to understand the context and to be heard, there is no point in embarking on consultancy, as the basis for a productive working partnership does not exist.

If it becomes apparent that these are not in operation, the consultancy is likely to cease or to be less effective than it should be. These are the consultant's role-based authorities. This lack of automatic authority means that the consultant has to possess, above all, a high level of skill in social process to make progress.

In addition, there may be earned authority. The consultor may accept advice, challenge, recommendations, process styles and tools because they trust the consultant. This may be based on the consultant's perceived experience. The consultor may be, for example, a rural minister or starting up a Fresh Expressions form of church on a housing estate and they might be more likely to accept help from someone who has had experience of such roles sometime in their work life. Earned authority might also come from the recommendation of a trusted source – someone they know who has worked with this consultant or a regional church officer who can attest to the quality of their work. As someone who has operated as a consultant in the secular and commercial sectors, I am often given an authority based on the fact that I have been able to earn a living over many years working in the business world.

The issue of authority becomes complicated when the consultant is an internal advisor of some kind. People with titles such as Diocesan Missioner, District Development Enabler, Regional Evangelism Officer, Parish Development Advisor or Development Support Officer are often explicitly appointed to be consultants on behalf of the larger church to work with local ministers, congregations and projects. Hierarchically, they are typically in close, regular contact with figures like bishops, District Chairs, Moderators, Divisional Commanders and the like. They are involved in the flow of information back and forth from the local to headquarters. The investment in their existence is a token of the desire by the larger church to make sure that what happens locally is as effective as possible. Thus, the perception can be that they are sent in as the hierarchy's storm troops or inspectors. They can be seen as a symptom that the organization thinks the local minister or congregation is failing. Trust can be difficult to build when there is a suspicion that reports are going back to the decision-makers about how feeble and unfaithful a certain minister or congregation is compared with other flourishing churches not far away. It is, therefore, crucial that, in the contracting phases at the start of an intervention, these issues are discussed and clarified. Unspoken assumptions, conspiracy theories and fears can ruin a consultancy project. Vagueness about confidentiality, for example, can provoke anxiety. What happens to information about what we are doing with this representative of headquarters? Being realistic and clear about what sort of reports will go back to those who have encouraged the local church to work with the consultant is better than pretending that it is all going to be kept secret. This will be a matter for negotiation, not only between the consultant and the consultor but also between the consultant and the church leaders to whom they report. It will then be a judgement for the consultant to make as to whether it is possible to work successfully as a consultant with the local minister or congregation under the conditions set, as similarly for the consultor. (There is a longer discussion of the internal consultant in Chapter 8.)

The role of consultant: what if there is more than one consultant?

In some cases it can be useful to work in a team of two or more consultants. This is often the case in organizational reviews, church audits or large-scale change initiatives. Sometimes it is just a matter of having enough people to cover the work that is needed. Working with other consultants can have the advantage of complementary skills, knowledge and approaches. As a consultant, having someone who has another kind of insight into the issues being presented and the plans and designs being built allows for healthy checking and calibration as well as benefiting from the synergy that comes from working on issues with more than one brain. It may also be possible to enhance the credibility of the consultant team by providing a more inclusive resource in terms of, for example, gender, ethnicity or denomination. It will be evident that having more than one consultant adds to the complexity of the working method. So, it is important that roles, contributions, authorities, timings, tasks, and relationships with the consultor are all carefully and explicitly negotiated initially, then monitored and renegotiated as necessary along the way. There is a danger that a consultancy team or pair can appear to exclude the consultor(s). So, care needs to be taken to address this up front and to continue to reflect on how the collaborative partnership is faring.

Running a session with a group, which is designed to encourage participation, elicit opinions and generate options, is a tall order for a lone consultant as it demands concentration on good, responsive group process and on the content of the data raised and conclusions reached. One consultant running the process while the other checks on coverage of issues, monitors the timing, records what is said and gives feedback on the social process can sharpen the effectiveness of the meeting. It may be possible also to play tag with a partner consultant, with one dealing with one section of the process, and then handing over to the other for the next section. In a long interview designed to draw out information from a member of an organization it can help to have a lead consultant with another watching, taking notes and with the agreement that they may interrupt when a point has been missed, is unclear or needs further investigation.

The role of consultor

Traditionally consultancy is seen as recruiting a consultant to do some problem-solving or design work. The difference from the general approach here is that it is the consultor who does this work. They are the expert in the situation and can ground the discussion in the complex reality they inhabit. The consultant is present to support the consultor in analysing the issue and coming up with a strategy. The consultant brings in expertise about the process and techniques of analysis and design. In this, they help the consultor develop their consultor skills and nurture their ability to be a consultant to themselves. Consultancies will work much more effectively if the consultor is well versed in the processes of consultancy. A skilled consultor helps the consultant do their job. So, as well as the consultant helping develop the consultor, it is an aim of the consultor to become a skilful consultor. Lovell (2000, p. 24) comments how helpful it would be if theological colleges taught trainee ministers how to be consultors, just as it would be helpful if they were taught how to be supervisees.

The role of consultor: the work

With whatever help from the consultant is necessary, the consultor is the one who defines the issues to be addressed in the consultancy and specifies the desired outcomes. From the first meeting, through the contracting stage, and into the ongoing process the consultor needs to be skilled at articulating the focus of the consultancy and explaining the context. Consultors stipulate the boundaries and the no-go areas. In the course of the consultancy they play a fully collaborative, partnership role with the consultant offering as much information, insight and skill as they can, treating the consultant with the same care for confidentiality and respect for what the consultant is giving as is to be expected in the other direction. They have input into the monitoring of the progress of the consultancy, question the process and suggest alternative ways of working. They evaluate the output of the consultancy and decide whether any plans should be implemented. They review the consultancy and give feedback to the consultant.

By being prepared for the consultancy a consultor adds to the effectiveness of the session. Sending a short preparatory note a couple of days beforehand in an email to the consultant with a catch-up on what has happened since last time, with any new information or reflections and with some thoughts as to exactly what is to be examined gives the session a flying start. It affords the consultant a chance to think around the issues and ponder on approaches, questions and hypotheses. It is notoriously difficult to get ministers and church workers to do this, as they tend to rush from meeting to meeting. However, as consultors will often travel some distance to see their work consultant, the time in the car or on the train can provide space to put some thoughts in order.

The specification of the focus of the consultancy can be tricky. Many church workers find themselves frustrated by the general state of the church and of their local situation. They often feel trapped by systems and structures that make their work difficult, but over which they have no authority. It can be helpful for the consultant to look at the issue in terms of what they can control, what they can influence and those areas in which they have no chance of changing anything. This can be shown in a diagram as below (see Figure 4.2), where the consultor sits in the area close around them, *control*, where they can arrange things as they like and need them to be. Around this is an area where the consultor has some *influence* over the way things happen, though it might take some negotiation, persuasion or adept social process. The outer area offers no opportunity to make a difference, *impotence*. If consultancy is going to be of use, energy is best directed at areas where the consultor has some chance of affecting what goes on. Spending significant amounts of time and energy working on the Impotence area is only going to end in frustration. It will be helpful to express the feelings and impacts on the consultor's ability to carry out their tasks that originate in that area. It may be that part of the consultancy should address how to cope with those inevitable frustrations. However, it is much more fruitful to focus on the areas of Control and Influence. A good aim for consultancy is to work on expanding those areas, if at all possible, adopting some of the area of Influence into the area of Control and some of the Impotence area into the Influence area.

The role of consultor: capability

The consultor and their situation are the basic material for the consultancy. They bring the capability they have. This is used to generate designs and plans. As has just been said, a major part of a consultancy

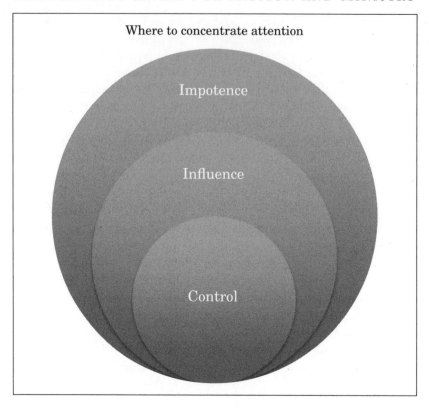

Figure 4.2 Control, influence and impotence

can be enhancing the skills of the consultor as consultor. This requires
the consultor to be open and reflective not just about their daily work,
but also about the way they work in the consultancy. A skilled consultor is more likely to get the best out of a consultancy. Self-knowledge
and self-awareness contribute constructively if a consultor understands
their own personality, their own intellectual ability, likes and dislikes,
their best styles of working. Some consultants find diagrams helpful,
while others gain little from the use of a flipchart, much preferring to
work through stories. This is a matter of both knowledge and reflection, and of acquiring the social process skills, for example of how to
tell the consultant that their approach just is not working. The consultor, therefore, is being asked to work on two levels at the same time
– dealing with the issue under discussion and reflecting on and evaluat-
ing how the process is working for them.

In terms of the mental processing ability, if the consultor does not
have the basic capacity to handle the problems and challenges of their

role there is a significant question as to whether they should continue in that role. In terms of organizational design, churches and church organizations, concentrate the vast majority of workers in direct delivery roles. Compared with other organizations there are relatively few managers, advisors and senior leaders. Most accredited workers will have titles like circuit minister, vicar, parish priest and church pastor. The complexity of these roles can vary wildly from a straightforward single church set-up to a multi-church rural group, a city-centre church with housing projects, cafes and dozens of staff, or a multidisciplinary chaplaincy. If the challenge is too great, the consultor may need to use the consultant to help contain the work suitably according to their capability until such time as the structural mismatch can be resolved.

The basic capability that the consultor needs to bring or develop is to be open to look at their work in a way that sees the interactions, meanings and consequences against a wide range of factors and theoretical models. Ongoing success in consultancy depends on the consultor's willingness and capacity to address their sense of vocation, their feelings, their spirituality, their ways of working and their relationships in the light of a network of theological and organizational understandings.

The role of consultor: authority

The consultancy relationship should be based on the assumption that most of the authority lies with the consultor. Consultors determine what is talked about and what not, how often meetings happen, what conclusions are reached, what plans are made and whether they are implemented. They assent to or decline consultancy methods and tools suggested by the consultant. By the very act of embarking on a consultancy, they are assigning authority to the consultant to have access to their work as far as they will admit them and to offer suggestions about process, analysis and design.

Sometimes consultancy is entered into because the consultor's superior has identified a need for help. For example, ministerial reviews by their nature identify developmental needs in ministers and other workers. Requiring, suggesting or paying for consultancy for a worker can be experienced as compromising the consultor's authority as described above. The worker's superior may ask for a report as to how the consultancy has progressed and there may be a feeling that they, not the consultor, have determined the agenda of the consultancy. In this case, the consultor and the consultant need to ensure an absolute clarity about authority over issues such as content, reporting and confidentiality with the sponsoring body.

The role of consultor: what if there is more than one consultor?

A later chapter deals with consultancy with organizations and groups but, at this point it is important to recognize that there are pitfalls to avoid by being aware of critical issues in working with more than one consultor in the same organization. Perhaps the most common example is to be working with the leader of a church community as an individual while being involved in a change process that requires the participation of the whole church or the leadership group. It is possible to assume that a consultant who is work consultant to, for example, the minister, would then be working alongside them when dealing with the church group as a whole. Careful attention needs to be given to developing a new, satisfactory relationship with the group with clarity around the difference and overlap with the relationship with the minister. I was once very surprised, when I turned up to facilitate an away day designed to look at the shape, nature and mission of a church, to find I was on my own running the day. The minister sat in the front row and let it all happen. I had been told to expect perhaps 25 people but it turned out to be 70. Looking at the future entailed dealing with bereavement over a treasured past, and surfaced tensions and sensitivities. The process for identifying and examining the issues produced tears, distress and considerable tension, all tokens of the work that needed to be done for this community to move on to the next phase. I had been working with the minister on his own over a few sessions and had assumed mistakenly that he was my partner in handling the process with the membership. By the end of the day, I was exhausted and unsure whether the day had been useful. I soon concluded that clarifying consultor and consultant roles, relationships and tasks is essential when dealing with complex consultancy relationships such as this.

The role of observer

Consultancy is difficult work. It can be useful to have help during sessions. One such aid is having an observer sit in on a session. An observer can both enhance participants' all-round learning from co-consultancy and enrich the quality of the consultancy itself by watching for things going on which the consultant might miss or undervalue. A slight distance and outsiderness allows a better overall view of the meeting, 'seeing the big picture' as the cliché goes.

The role of observer: the work

Normally observers remain slightly outside the group or consultancy pair and do not enter the discussion unless requested. They observe the overall event, looking at both content and process. They will be watching for what is said and not said, for the dynamic between the consultor and consultant over time. They may notice significant non-verbal messages, a silence, body language, the way the shape and feel of the interaction changes when the conversation hits a tender spot. They try to make patterns out of what is happening. What is the consultant doing – talking too much, using good question forms, paraphrasing, avoiding difficult areas under unspoken pressure from the consultor? Being typically consultants themselves, they are drawn to reflect on how the consultant works. Would they have asked that question? Would they have got the consultor to draw a diagram then? Would they have connected what has just been said to a couple of things that were said ten minutes before, the connection indicating a repeated pattern of behaviour or a strong feeling? Would they have tested out that hunch that occurred when relating all the incidents that the consultor has just recounted? With a good system for taking notes that allows remarks on a range of aspects such as timing, content, process and non-verbal behaviour, observers can give feedback on content and process, what went well and what could have been done differently.

In terms of capability, observers will benefit from having the same range of technical skills, knowledge, social process skill, application and mental processing ability as a consultant, as laid out above. The role of observer is a useful role in the training and continuing development of consultants. Initially consultants in training underrate the role of observer but then quite quickly realize how useful it is for the consultancy they are watching and how helpful it is for their own practice as consultants. Having observed consultancies in action encourages that observer, when acting as consultant, to keep checking on the big picture and on aspects of both content and process that they habitually miss.

The role of observer: authority

The observer's authorities have to be negotiated at the start of a consultancy. They need to be negotiated both with the consultant and with the consultor. A consultor may be uncomfortable if their work consultant simply arrives with an observer and tells them what the observer is there for. The consultor may not be happy with an extra person sitting there saying nothing, or may want to know what the observer thinks as the session progresses. The range of authorities that can be negotiated may include timekeeping, providing feedback at the end, intervening if something has been glossed over or missed, keeping notes, recording on the flipchart or advising the consultant.

Consultor, consultant and observer in creative engagement

In covering at length the nature of the different roles in a consultation, the aim is to ensure that the conditions for successful interaction are, as far as possible, in place. The specification of work, authorities and capability should focus on addressing the work issues of the consultor. Being clear about who does what and how they are qualified to do that ensures that a creative mutuality is progressively built in a safe and productive partnership. It promotes openness, the use of rigorous process and theory and inclusivity where people who think and believe differently can work together. This attention to process and working conditions is demanding and challenging but clarity means that the approach will enable people of all abilities to tackle their problems and ambitions. Because the focus is on the consultor's work, reducing the consultor's anxiety and enabling the consultor to be as skilled and in control as possible, consultancy can be both a strength, a sanity check and a support in the ups and downs of ministry, and a joyful, productive framework for progress in mission.

5

The Process of Consultancy

The journey is a central image in Christian spirituality as well as in history and literature. Whether it is on a day's journey on the road to Emmaus or over Abraham's many nomadic years, insights are gained as companions travel alongside each other, looking for the right path, each bringing their personality and hinterland into the conversation. As the pilgrims meet the journey's challenges, conflicts and joys, they face discoveries about themselves. The spiritual transformation of the mediaeval pilgrim to Canterbury or Rome happens at a depth that can rarely be delivered by a bus trip to Kent or a budget airline flight to Fiumicino. This happens both on the journey and because of the journey. In the Bible's biggest journey story, the exodus from Egypt, simply leaving Egypt is a lengthy struggle. After that, the journey and the learning take 40 years, so that the meaning of liberation can be made concrete in a new society and relationship with God. However, transformation and learning are achieved. This chapter suggests that consultancy can similarly be seen as a transformative journey.

Unless the consultor, organization or individual seriously travels the journey themselves, they are unlikely to commit to the plans and solutions developed in a way that will allow significant change to take root. Indeed, it is because the consultor needs to take this journey themselves for the change to embed that this chapter concentrates on process in consultancy. It is quite common to find an organization or an individual repeatedly using consultants with no beneficial effect. Often, in this case, it is not that the solution offered by the different consultants is any better. Indeed, it is often much the same. Frequently the significant factor in enabling a consultor to own a solution is not the proposed solution itself but the quality of the process undertaken. The likelihood of change in the way an organization runs or the way a leader leads depends on the personal and cultural changes that happen on the journey that is the consultancy process. Through the development of a careful, respectful trajectory, a consultancy can reveal possibilities where the situation had looked hopeless. It can build the consultor's confidence that they have a range of appropriate skills. These may already exist unrecognized or they may be developed with support. Lovell describes the consultancy process (not the outcomes) as incarnational, salvatory, revelatory, resurrectional, creational and sacramental (2000, p. 129–33). The extent to which consultor and consultant, working together, allow this to happen depends not only on clarity around what consultancy is for and the roles within it but also on careful management of beginnings, middles and endings, as well as the cycles and loops the journey will necessarily pass through on the way.

The stages of that journey as an overarching whole are the focus of this chapter. So, in this chapter, the phases of the consultancy process will be examined by looking at

- social process issues
- boundaries
- the stages or phases of a consultancy
- the beginning of a consultancy
    entry issues
    contracting
- the middle of a consultancy
    analysis and design
- ending a consultancy.

The phases of a consultancy

In many a consultancy book or manual there will be a description of the phases or stages of a consultancy. A typical pattern would be Lippitt and Lippitt's six major phases:

1 Engaging in initial contract and entry
2 Formulating a contract and establishing a helping relationship
3 Identifying problems through diagnostic analysis
4 Setting goals and planning for action
5 Taking action and cycling feedback; and
6 Completing the contract (continuity, support and termination).

(1986, p. 11)

This has an evident logic and a helpful, linear structure. Giving a clear basic structure, such a list helps the consultant and consultor check where they are and what they are and should be doing at any point. It works where the consultancy can be seen as a distinct, limited, even if lengthy project. Examples might be where the consultant has been invited in to tackle the reorganization and restructuring of a group of parishes, to help a minister over six sessions with their organizational and management skills, or to support the evaluation of a three-year-old cafe church in a rural town.

The Baptist Union of Great Britain has a process, which it calls *Mission Consultancy*. The definition of consultancy, on which it is based, is 'a partnership between church and consultants in discerning the call of God to a particular church in its context at a particular time and in taking steps forward in that mission' (2005, p. 2). This Mission Consultancy is seen at its heart as listening to the Holy Spirit regarding the church's spiritual journey, the consultant being there 'to help the church make its own journey' (2005, p. 2). It is a process designed for use when a big change or strategic decision is about to be made. Undertaking Mission Consultancy is normally an expectation when a church is looking for a new minister. There is an established, recommended sequence for the Mission Consultancy, set out as

a   promotion
b   regional minister approval
c   establish partnership
d   church preparation
e   consultants' preparation
f   questionnaire
g   consultants face to face with leaders
h   consultants face to face with congregation
i   consultants draw up findings
j   communicating findings to church
k   helping church to develop an action plan
l   helping church to implement the action plan
m   disengagement/celebration
n   review.

(2005, p. 4)

It is easy to see how the Lippitts' stages map onto this sequence. Although consultants and churches might deviate from this pattern given a particular context, it is laid out as a useful and workable basic model of consultancy for Baptist churches, which has been carefully designed (with an accompanying, constructive series of activities) to gather both commitment and data as well as to encourage members of the local church to develop their understanding of what mission means for them in their setting. A standard, tested procedure like this not only raises the likelihood of a process that will result in success but also means that, across a denomination, members will come to trust a method they know has worked elsewhere.

However, Lippitt and Lippitt's straightforward list does not cater for the whole range of church consultancy interventions and relationships. The framework fits a single consultancy project. Not all consultancies are discrete, single or sequential projects: a minister may have a work consultant whom they see every two or three months over the whole of their ministry; a team may have, as a regular feature, a consultant who sits in and comments on their process at one staff meeting in three; a church social services agency may have a team of consultants who work with them not just coaching individuals, but also running team-work training and supporting their systems design and strategy work. However, whatever the long-term nature of a one-to-one consultancy or a project's varied components, the same process factors need to be addressed to make sure that the intervention is as productive as possible. Whether consultor and consultant are following an established pattern or designing a bespoke method, the quality of the contracting at the start and re-contracting along the way, the regularity and conscious depth of monitoring and review as the work proceeds and a realistic evaluation at the end are well worth both parties' focus and energy. The phases of the work should be clearly identifiable, preferably using formats such as Lippitt and Lippitt's above, so that what is done at each stage is useful and appropriate.

Being clear about where you are in terms of analysis and design, two classic steps in a consultancy process, is crucial.

Analysis and design

Analysis: the phase where the issue, challenge or opportunity is examined, dissected and understood as deeply as possible.
Design: the phase where a plan or solution is developed to address the issue raised.

It is a consultancy cliché that taking a problem apart often reveals the obvious solution without necessarily having to proceed to think very hard about answers and plans. However, it is important to be clear about what exactly is happening. If a solution offers itself too early in the analysis phase, the temptation is to pursue it. Yet, it might be that the issue has not been examined to the depth required. Some knotty little problem may have been missed. The result can be that the solution does not address all the interacting variables and so fails. Thus, using the labels in lists like the Lippitts' helps to check exactly what is happening when. It is very healthy to hear a consultant or consultor ask, 'Can I just check something with you? It feels like we are designing a solution here. I am not sure we have looked at all the issues yet.'

The beginning – entry issues

Work comes to the consultant along many routes, for example, when

- an internal consultant is expected to keep in regular touch with the workers and churches in their area to identify where help is needed
- a minister cries out for help at an annual review, and a consultant on the denomination's books is identified as just the one for the job
- a bishop has seen someone struggling and suggests that a particular consultant work with them
- the synod has decided that the church in this area needs reorganizing or orienting towards mission and sends in a team
- a local minister who is struggling knows a consultant by reputation or has visited their website and asks for help.

From these examples it can be seen that the initiative may come from the potential consultor who senses a problem and looks for help, from the potential consultant who can see the consultor or their organization having a problem and suggests that help might be beneficial, or from a third party who sees the need and brings the consultor and consultant together.

The consultant, in particular, needs to reflect consciously on the nature of this first contact, as it can have a significant impact on the effectiveness of the consultancy. How the initial contact, the phone call or email, is handled sets the tone. The individuals concerned may have worked with consultants before; they may have just heard that using a work consultant is a good thing; they may have been forced to get themselves a work consultant. From the beginning the quality of the consultancy relationship starts to form. The aim is for trust, collaboration and a sense of safety to grow.

If a consultor has been told they need to see a work consultant by a senior figure in their church, the consultor system with which the consultant interacts may be unbalanced by the influence of other agents.

The question needs to be asked, 'Who is the consultor? Is it the person sitting with the consultant or is it their boss?' There is the risk of a triangular contract, either in fact or in the consultant or consultor's fantasy, which will destabilize the work as it proceeds. The consultant may detect a sense of coercion or unwillingness on the consultor's part as a result of this. The set-up may, however, be perfectly acceptable to the consultor, but the issue will need to be explicitly addressed in the contracting phase and monitored as the work continues. It may be that the looming presence of the hierarchy hampers the ability to address the real issues. Discussions about roles, confidentiality, reporting back and desired outcomes need to take place, therefore, between the three stakeholders concerned, consultor, consultant and the third party.

The beginning – contracting

Journeying at what Kosuke Koyama in *Three Mile an Hour God* calls the speed the love of God walks, priorities become more balanced, perspectives adjusted and a clearer understanding of what is really important is reached. It is sometimes a bit puzzling for a new consultor when the consultant they are proposing to work with does apparently no consulting in the first meeting. The importance of the work at this stage, *contracting*, cannot be overemphasized. The first meeting between consultor and consultant is essentially about working out whether it is possible for the two parties to work together productively. It is important that this first meeting is seen as an exploration for both people without any pre-existing commitment. Consultants who charge a fee will probably not charge for the first session, so there is no pressure to have any result or output other than a clear idea of whether to go forward and, if so, how that is going to happen and under what conditions.

The contracting meeting is an opportunity to understand not just the issue that the consultor would like to tackle but also to see whether the consultor and consultant and their personalities, capabilities, theologies and other approaches are likely to fit together in a constructive collaboration. This does not necessarily mean that they have to match exactly. Often consultancy prospers when the characters are quite different. Such difference, if in a framework of respect, courage and honesty, can lead to very useful challenge and new perspectives. In the case of an internal consultant, the consultor may have no choice. They have to work with their church's local advisor, officer or enabler. The constraint this represents should figure in the contracting conversation.

There may be no other option and so how well the relationship continues to work is a healthy part of ongoing review.

Some large consultancies have standard contracts covering many pages. Consultancy manuals and schemes will sometimes offer contracting templates, but contracting is an interpersonal event with a subtlety based on a unique interaction between the consultor and consultant systems. Guidelines and checklists can be very helpful in making sure all areas are covered and possible pitfalls identified. A written summary shared and agreed after the first meeting is useful. Sometimes the work proceeds based on an implicit contract, but getting both parties' assumptions and expectations about process and outcomes clearly out in the open and, if possible, written down can avoid risky misunderstandings later on. Strong contracting not only helps the consultancy progress constructively but also provides a good example of the benefits of clarity in working relationships in organizations like churches where misunderstanding and resentment often build over years on the back of mismatched expectations and unexpressed assumptions.

When consultants are desperate for work, contracting can be rushed in the anxiety to secure the work. A measured approach to contracting means that the consultant can ensure that the conditions are in place to make the work as successful as possible. In my commercial consulting a basic principle is that, if we do not have the tangible, conscious commitment to the change process from the head of the organization or that part of the organization, our work will struggle and probably fail in time. The results have always been patchy, disappointing and difficult to sustain when we have ignored this principle. The questions examined at the contracting stage may also raise significant professional issues for the consultant. If the conditions are not appropriate and are not likely to become so, is it ethical to accept the work even though there might be financial or organizational pressures to do so? Contracting can feel like paperwork and procedure for the sake of procedure, but in reality sets up the conditions for life-enhancing work. As Lovell puts it, 'Contract making is a sensitive interpersonal activity that explores the detail to get at the fundamentals of an agreement that will enable and sustain everyone concerned as they attempt to do the work that needs to be done' (2000, p. 120).

Just as contracting needs to be undertaken explicitly and consciously at the start of a consultation, the need for continuing monitoring needs to be built into any contract. As a project proceeds, needs may change or consultor and consultant may discover new features of the process or the issue. They may discover gifts and gaps in each other that mean that it would be useful to rethink the contract. The outcomes of a project and progress towards them are naturally the subject of ongoing review but evaluation of the process along the journey should also be explicitly part of the agreement.

John Gawne-Cain, a work consultant in the Oxford Diocese of the Church of England, produced the set of ground rules below for contracting for work consultants as part of his MA dissertation, a reflection on his years as a consultant. The principles draw on gestalt therapy and the work of Peter Block. For a fuller treatment of contracting than is possible here, Block's *Flawless Consulting* (2000) provides a readable, in-depth and thoughtful resource.

Ground rules for contracting

1 The responsibility for every relationship is 50/50. There are two sides to every story. There must be a symmetry or the relationship will collapse.
2 The contract should be freely entered.
3 You can't get something for nothing. There must be consideration from both sides (even in a boss/subordinate relationship).
4 You can say 'no' to what others want from you. Even clients.
5 You don't always get what you want, although you will survive.
6 You can contract for behaviour, but you cannot contract for the other person to change their feelings.
7 You can't ask for something the other person doesn't have.
8 You can't promise something you cannot deliver.
9 You can't contract with people who aren't in the room.
10 Write down contracts when you can – they are often broken out of neglect not intent.
11 Contracts are renegotiable – be grateful if a client tells you that they wish to renegotiate a contract midstream rather than doing it without a word.
12 Contracts require specific time deadlines or duration.
13 Good contracts require good faith.

John Gawne-Cain

In the first contact and the first formal contracting meeting a range of topics can be covered but the basic objective is to see whether the consultancy will deliver what the consultor is looking for. By a rigorous interrogation of the factors that need to be in place for a workable contract to be agreed, the consultant will help the consultor understand whether what is on offer will help. If the consultor has never been involved in consultancy before or has been involved in a different type of consultancy (an expert type rather than a non-directive type, for example), part of the work of this first session will be to explain the model and the process to the consultor so they can make an informed choice about whether to proceed or not. In the case of the consultancy being with a group, a team or a church council, the contracting may have to take place over a series of sessions, going from first contact to meeting with the leader(s) and then with the group. When, as is often the case, a consultant is brought in by the leader and starts immediately to work on the content of the issue with the group, the consultant and the leader will need to be sensitive to resistance, unspoken assumptions and unachievable expectations generated within that group. If such an approach is seen as necessary or desirable, taking some time to lay the contract out to the group can avoid considerable problems further down the road.

Exactly what is covered in the contracting phase will vary according to the type of consultancy. If it is a Mission Consultancy of the Baptist Union type discussed above, there will be issues to examine regarding access to data gathering, interviewing and information handling, which will not be relevant to work consultancy with an individual minister over a series of monthly sessions. See Appendix A for suggestions as to the range of areas to look at in the contracting phase.

It often happens that this first meeting involves doing some work on the issue concerned. Some of this will be diagnostic – helping the consultor to identify the issue to be tackled with a clear focus. Some of this will enable the consultor to see how the consultant works and what approaches and tools they bring, so they can make an informed decision about whether to engage the consultant. The contracting phase may also need more than one session. The consultor may need to go away and do further thinking about what they want and need. The consultant may go away and produce a proposal or a contract with a specification for the consultancy that integrates the various themes from the first meeting and offers a possible approach. The prospective consultor can then react to that written proposal, agreeing, amending or declining as appropriate. This, however, may not be the end of the contracting. There is always the possibility, as has been said, that the contract will need to be revisited and revised, possibly torn up and a new one agreed, as the relationship develops and the project's needs shift.

> ## Contracting and re-contracting for the real issue
>
> Starting to talk to people and looking round the organization, church or team can reveal a much bigger problem than the one originally identified. One example is a consultancy where I was asked in by a denomination to help with problems about staff managing their work in a very busy department. Having interviewed all the staff, it was quickly obvious to me that there certainly was a problem with managing the work, but that was nothing to do with overload. It was much more to do with distinctly unhealthy working relationships which needed to be addressed urgently. I wrote a report as soon as I could. As a result, a meeting with the church officers to whom the department was accountable was convened, which I was asked to attend. The real issue and the work that needed to be done were identified. The focus of the consultancy was renegotiated and a new contract drawn up. In such cases, there is always the risk that the consultor or the third party who has asked the consultant to intervene may refuse to tackle the issue that has been discovered, the real issue. The consultant may lose the work or be asked to continue with, in this example, the workload issue without addressing the underlying problem. In this case, I was asked to help in dealing with the core issue of the working relationships. To have continued with the originally contracted piece of work would have been ineffective and unethical, as it would have dealt merely with a symptom, with little prospect of a lasting solution to the issue, and conspired in letting an unjust, unproductive situation persist. I would have refused the work.

Leach and Paterson, in their book on *Pastoral Supervision*, take up Pohly's description of an agreement like this as a covenant. Although this seems to stretch the idea of a contract (clarifying purpose, method, outcomes, boundaries, roles and accountability) too far by comparing it with the complex, salvific relationship of a people with God over thousands of years, it does recall, as they say, 'the triadic nature of any relationship within the body of Christ, which not only recalls us to our common humanity and discipleship before the one who calls and sends us, but allows us to let the other be Christ's representative to us in this time and for this purpose' (Leach and Paterson, 2010, p. 16). The context for this work is the vocation of individuals and groups to mission and ministry as part of the Church.

Yet, it is interesting how often the use of the Bible or especially prayer as part of the process can be an awkward topic or simply unmentioned, particularly at the contracting stage. Working with consultancy students over the years, this is an area that regularly provokes heated debate and disagreement. This can be another example of the management of symbols, as the approach to prayer can be such a strong symbol of a person or a community's culture, theological approach and understanding of church. Some people assume it is natural for Christians working together to pray together. For many it would be very strange not to commit the session to God for support, inspiration and guidance. Others see the potential for manipulation and the imposition of what might be seen as the right answers. It has happened to me more than once at the beginning of a potentially tricky meeting where, for example, plans were to be made for which churches would get a minister and which not, the senior member of the clergy present introduced the evening with a prayer. The Holy Spirit was asked to guide the participants in harmony and unity to seek his will. My need as the consultant was for those attending to share fully and frankly their diverse demands and their anger, fear and hurt. Only then would it be possible to reach a workable plan. The prayer had already told the meeting that disharmony was not going to be acceptable. My constant fear after such introductory prayers was either the suppression of the desired input or its intemperate expression, or both. Finding the right approach demands sensitivity and flexibility.

Another issue that needs thought and discussion is the venue for the consultancy. Should the meetings be held in the consultor's vicarage or manse, in the office of the consultant or in some neutral space? There is no single answer. A number of factors will be taken into account. Often a minister will enjoy confidential space away from their ministerial setting. As has been said, the journey in the car or on the train can be a good time for the consultor to get thoughts in order about what the upcoming session is addressing. It may be that it is useful for the consultant to see the physical setting of the consultor's work. If the consultancy is working with a group, it is much more normal and convenient for the consultant to go to the group's setting. All the same, there are benefits in taking a group away for an extended session of clear thinking without the temptations of local interruptions. An issue for a consultant may be that for a 90-minute session, travelling an hour each way does not make financial or time management sense when two or three sessions could occupy the same time at home. The physical setting needs to be helpful to the consultancy process. Thus, considerations should be given to the kind of chairs, how they face each other, their respective heights, the use of a table, providing and placing paper, pens, a flipchart or a computer to work on, environmental noise, heat, air and lighting and refreshment. Mixed up in this question is the Christian tradition of hospitality, welcoming the stranger in. With consultancy being a collaborative activity between two competent parties with different skills and knowledge, the ambivalent nature of the Latin root for hospitality, *hospes*, can come into play. *Hospes* can mean both host and guest. The question of my house, your house or someone else's can support the notion that collaboration in consultancy involves serving and being served, taking the initiative and letting the other lead, as appropriate.

The middle – analysis and design

Analysis and design as stages in the consultancy journey will be examined in a later chapter in some detail, with suggestions for methods and tools. The aim of this section is to locate these stages in the overall process, to map out the general terrain to be covered and to look at some of the pitfalls to be aware of. The same principles apply to these stages whether the issue is being dealt with in a single session or over months or years. The need is, first, to understand the situation as it is in as much depth and detail as is useful; second, to understand what the desired state is, what needs to change and how; and, third, to work out how that is going to happen. Different techniques and bodies of knowledge will help at different points in this process.

The first stage, understanding the situation in its present and desired state, involves listening to the consultor, using good questions, gathering data with rigour and discipline, and exploring the networks and origins of influences and factors that underlie the intricacy of the issue. As consultancy is concerned with change, the issue will involve dissatisfaction with the fact that the situation is not as the consultor wants it to be. To get as clear an idea as possible of what the present situation is and how that differs from the desired goal underlies the success of the consultancy process. The aim of any plan or solution is to cross the gap from what is now to what is hoped for; or, in some circumstances, to help someone renegotiate their relationship to something hoped for which cannot realistically be reached. Describing both states with clarity, precision and complexity will enable any plan to deal with the present obstacles and to achieve the anticipated change as far as possible.

It is not just seeing the picture from the consultant's viewpoint with a certain objectivity but understanding what it looks and feels like from the consultor's perspective. However complex a consultant's analysis and impressive the solution they offer, if the diagnosis does not take into account what it is really like for the consultor, the plan is unlikely to succeed. This does not mean that the consultant should not offer ways of understanding the situation that have never occurred to the consultor. Through the cyclical process of questioning and listening, the consultant gains an intense understanding of the situation with a view from outside the situation. Working with the range of data offered by the consultor, the consultant helps the consultor see patterns and connections, causes and consequences. In reflecting back, summarizing and paraphrasing they may offer or stimulate tentative hypotheses based on their ability to integrate the data with the range of fields of knowledge talked about in previous chapters. This constitutes an invitation to the consultor to travel with the hypotheses for a while to see whether they shed light on the issue at hand. The inside/outside placing of the consultant means that this can be a really helpful pathway through a problem. The desired outcome is to come to a helpful, accurate and shared understanding of what is at issue.

The consultant will be asked to make judgements, as far as possible justified by data, but judgements all the same, in which the consultant's well-informed but subjective choices will determine the comparative weight of different types of input. Effective process will also demand working respectfully with the consultor's emotions. Feelings and emotions are just as much data as any statistics or records. The visceral reaction, anger at an injustice, pleasure at creativity, or a gut feeling that a structure is just wrong are important factors and merit exploration. Emotions will be a factor when reporting and feeding back what has been discovered in the early stages of a consultancy whether by wide-ranging research or individual sessions with one person. Conclusions, hypotheses and sometimes just the plain facts gathered can be disturbing and challenging when fed back to the consultor. In a consultancy session linking a series of behaviours as displaying a possible pattern or forming a theory based on a series of interviews with members of the church contains the possibility of shocking a consultor deeply, especially if the pattern or theory reveals uncomfortable truths. The consultant needs to be able to predict and handle the emotional response from the consultor as well as to manage their own emotions. Otherwise, they may end up sugar-coating the bad news in a collusive way or launching it at the consultor in an aggressive way.

While it is important to reinforce what is good and productive, the journey entails addressing difficult feedback constructively, especially bad news about the consultor's personal style, behaviour or capability. Block suggests that the key in this is to be as neutral and descriptive as possible. Although the consultant is called on to make judgements, their role is not to judge the consultor. Feedback, he says, should be 'descriptive, focused, specific, brief and simple' rather than 'judge-mental, global, stereotyped, lengthy and complicated' (2000, p. 223). The key aim is to describe what is and why, rather than declare what ought to be. Getting confirmation of and commitment to that analysis is an essential step before moving on to a third stage where plans and designs are made that deliver the desired outcome. It is worth delaying the journey for a while here to make sure there is a shared, accurate picture of the situation and why it is the case. Rendle and Mann use the image of Moses guiding the people through the desert to show that the journey may have to be quite slow for the conversations to have suffi-cient time for proper discernment (2003, p. xvi). If Moses had had satel-lite navigation and a direct route, there would not have been enough time for the Spirit to move through the interactions and conversations among the Israelites when faced with the data about themselves the journey was raising. As Rendle and Mann say, 'a congregation (or a system) cannot learn faster than it can learn' (2003, p. xvii). If this time is not taken, there is a danger that the consultant will be seen as the expert advice-giver who stands outside the organization. The consult-ant can be ignored or scapegoated. Schein's description of the work of the process consultant as one who 'attempts to involve the organization in self-diagnosis and enables the organization to give itself good advice' (2000, p. 192) assumes space in the process to foster such growth.

Reflecting on the data gathered, whether that is the description of the present situation or hopes for the future, needs to be given sufficient time. The consultant and the consultor as leader in their organization, therefore, require tools to get this to happen. In Macdonald *et al.*'s Systems Leadership Theory, a central, analytical tool is the *critical is-sue*: '*a critical issue is something that threatens the purpose*. People have described them as "show-stoppers". We describe them as "what-ifs" or "how-tos"' (2006, p. 351).

Identifying critical issues

In a project in Western Australia, in order to provide mission and ministry leadership in the widespread communities of the Gold-fields, the Anglican Diocese of Perth developed a new vision of priestly leadership. In his publication 'A New Vision for our Church', Bishop Brian Farran says that the stipendiary priest will be 'a very important resource person in each congregation that develops a team of leaders ... develops aspects of training and supervision in the leadership of the congregation. It means in many cases a change of leadership style and practice' (1994, p. 59). The key critical issues that were identified in getting to this state were:

- What should priestly leadership look like now?
- How do we change our programme so that we form priests who will model the new way of being priest?
- What about priests trained 20 years ago?
- How do we train lay leaders so that they also work in teams?
- We have several training programmes – how do we make them compatible?

In the example above from Australia, the importance of identifying the key critical issues early in the process can be seen when thinking about what the consequences would be if any were missed. For example, if the issue of those trained some years ago was neglected, assuming that they will just fall into line in time, the transformation of the leadership culture could be hampered or even blocked by experienced clergy who feel they have been treated disrespectfully. 'That's not what *we* understand as priestly leadership.' It is not just about identifying the critical issues but about identifying as many as possible early on and seeing how they interact or interfere with each other.

It may not be possible to identify them all. Sometimes unpredicted critical issues will present themselves as a plan is formed or even as it is implemented. If this is the case, it is important to stop and consider whether the critical issue is a showstopper, and therefore demands a radical departure from the plan or a simple tweak. Sometimes, in order to see if unforeseen critical issues will crop up, a plan will have a testing or piloting stage when the solution is tried out in conditions where there will be little or no damage if it does not work. It is too easy to see the analysis/design sequence as linear, but any such process is likely to demand loops back into the analysis phase when the designs or the implementation unveil problems. It takes some courage to abandon a carefully thought through plan, particularly when stakeholders are waiting for a result.

Lovell's Eight Thinking Stages (1994)can provide a helpful structure to the phases of this analysis and design stage of the journey, starting with understanding the situation as it is and as it is understood, then what the consultor desires as the future state and setting that in a physical, organizational and philosophical context (see Figure 5.1). An examination and articulation of the purposes, aims and values that form points of reference for the consultor in their present and future context provides data on the motives and drivers behind the desired change. The work then moves on to forming integrated pictures, patterns, concepts and hypotheses by drawing all the material together. This should describe the issue as fully as possible, by doing so, laying out all the important contributory factors, perceptions and influences. This opens up possibilities for constructing operable solutions. As the stages move into designing these solutions, Lovell puts a wholesome emphasis on plans having not just the description of what the desired state will be but how any plan is going to be implemented and measured. Often a spectacular plan stumbles because consultant and consultor do not pay enough attention to questions such as who is going to do what, when it is going to be done, how we are going to know when it is right, what we should be looking for along the way to ensure we are making good progress towards our goal, and how we manage all the different stakeholders. These questions are properly part of the design.

There are many tools, techniques and theoretical models to help the consultant and consultor negotiate the middle phases of a consultancy. This will be the subject of the next two chapters.

Endings

The ending of a consultancy is an important phase of the journey. Lance Lindon suggests five reasons for the journey to finish:

1 The needs of the client, as determined by the contract up front, are met (the client has solved the problem satisfactorily).
2 When it is clear that the client has taken control of his or her own destiny and no longer needs help.
3 When the client decides to stop (whether or not progress is being made).

Stage 1	Depicting situations, backgrounds, contexts, and how the consultors see and feel about them	Studying things as they are
Stage 2	Depicting things, as consultors would like them to be	
Stage 3	Establishing points of reference such as purposes	
Stage 4	Conceptualizing, analysing, diagnosing, forming hypotheses and synthesizing	
Stage 5	Drawing up development agendas	Defining what needs to be done
Stage 6	Designing work programmes and means of evaluating them	Working out how to do things
Stage 7	Planning ways of putting designs to work and of evaluating them	
Stage 8	Deciding, contracting and commissioning	

Figure 5.1 Lovell's Eight Thinking Stages (1994, p. 114)

4 When the consultant feels unable to continue to help the client.
5 When it becomes clear to either client or consultant that the costs of helping are outweighing the gains.

(1995, p. 26)

Ending the process can be the initiative of either party. It may be that the work is complete or that it is not seen as fruitful to continue the process. The initial or modified contract can be a helpful framework for any review. In either case, there is a variety of work to be done in the final phase without which the process would be less effective than it could be. These include

- checking whether the outcome has addressed the identified issue
- learning lessons from what went well and what could have been done differently in the process

- celebrating and recognizing what has been achieved
- checking the implementation will be sustainable
- clarifying any continuing relationship.

Some of this ending work may have been done earlier in the process. For example, the quality of the implementation plan, training for the change, resourcing, staffing, monitoring and times for review should have been part of the plan in a large project. In working with an individual, this may have been less the case and so the final session may be a good time to ensure that the consultor will have the support and systems necessary to sustain the new behaviour. Checking whether the outcome has delivered what was expected, whether the solution is fit for purpose, may be a matter of reviewing the work done and the plans made. It may, in addition, involve other players. Does the new Messy Church get the seal of approval of the children and carers who will attend, or the new visiting scheme of those who will be visited? The final session may be a review of a new structure that has been operating for some time six months later. Is it working as it should? Are there any unexpected consequences? Does it need any adjustment? How are people reacting to it?

Learning lessons from what has happened can be done on a number of levels. It may look at the quality of the end product, for example whether the new way of dealing with managing cafe staff has reduced absenteeism and complaints, or whether the street pastor scheme has produced young people who tell stories of feeling less excluded and marginalized. On another level, it is helpful if review includes some reflection on how the process has gone for both consultor and consultant. What have they learnt about the process of consultancy in their roles? What has worked and what not? What will they do the same or differently on the next journey? Care has to be taken in learning from the past. Some cultures, particularly the British, when asked what went well, seem to go straight for what went badly. Learning from what has not gone well is useful, but often mistakes stand out disproportionately in the memory. So, it is worth sticking with the positives for some time before moving on to the areas where the process struggled. In dealing with the negatives, it is often helpful to see them as opportunities for improvement by asking what, in reality, we can do differently so this does not happen on a future occasion. This is particularly helpful when the consultant and consultor are going to work together on a future project or are in a regular, continuing work consultancy.

One of the benefits of a courageous, clear appreciation of what has gone well is that it enables a healthy acknowledgement of the consultor's and the consultant's contributions. Consultancy can be hard work, its output important, and the personal transformation and skill development remarkable. Taking a little time to recognize that and give thanks for it makes people feel justifiably proud and builds confidence, even if the steps have been few and small. It reminds the participants that the journey of discovery and growth is solidly and practically part of their divinely granted creativity in support of God's mission in the world.

Consultants can be an anxious group of people. Feedback on what they have done well and less well is both essential to their development and soothing of their anxiety. However, once a consultant has finished their work with a consultor, individual or church group, a common experience is that they hear nothing more. Even if the consultant has a formal system for getting feedback such as a questionnaire sent a week or so afterwards, response rates are typically low. The consultant, therefore, has to develop ways of gathering bits and pieces of qualitative data to help assess what they have done. Having a good supervisor with whom to assess projects and individual consultancies confidentially assists in mining the experience for improvement and reinforcement. Personal systems such as journalling, the notes that the consultant keeps about each consultancy, and reflective review meetings with the other consultants, if there is a team, all help.

The key in the ending stage is to maintain the integrative nature of the consultancy. Do the espoused principles behind the desire for change match what has been decided and what we will do? Has the experience of travelling along this process modified my beliefs, my practice, my fields of knowledge, my sense of self, and my need for further development? What have I discovered about the operation of God in the many aspects of what we have just been through? Is what we have built something that will further the Kingdom here? This is key work for consultant, consultor and their organizations. However, in the rush to get on with the next important piece of work, they may not devote serious time and energy to reviewing what they have just done. In this, there is both the danger that they will continue to do unhelpful work and to work in a way that repeats the same mistakes or ends up reinventing ways of doing the same things over and over again. Thus, review as part of the phases of the consultancy journey is not just good for the consultancy but offers a pattern of reflective practice for daily work.

Social process issues

Journeys are risky endeavours. The consultor may feel they have fallen among thieves like the traveller in the parable of the Good Samaritan, left at the roadside battered and bleeding. Like Paul on the road to Damascus, the consultor may feel blinded and dazed by the new learning and need to be gently walked through what the revelation might mean. Like the downcast disciples on the road to Emmaus, sense is made and meaning and direction discovered as the patterns and connections become apparent on the way. Consultor and consultant walk alongside each other in tackling the situation and revel in discovering the quality of analysis they can achieve together. Charles Margerison paints a picture of a mutually supportive, collaborative journey with his notion of 'arm in arm consulting'.

> The consultant establishes a relationship which can best be summarized as 'let us work on this together'. This signals a relationship where the process of doing the assignment will be as important as the content. During an 'arm in arm' consultation, the client and consultant will work together to identify the issue, the methods, the data, the analysis and the action required. There may never be a final report; if there is, it will be difficult to tell who contributed what ... 'Arm in arm' consulting needs considerable trust and confidence.
>
> (2001, p. 23)

The benefits of addressing problems courageously and patiently unfold on the way, and new skills and insights reveal themselves. Privileged information is divulged and trust is built. However, there are some recurring issues which can trip the consultant up like boulders on the pathway or seduce the consultant and consultor down smooth, green pathways when the right route is somewhat narrower and more rugged. These issues include careful observing of boundaries, the potential for hostility, defensiveness and resistance, the danger of collusion and getting into infantile relationships. All of these have the potential to derail a consultancy and reduce its effectiveness. It is on these that this next section focuses.

During the first steps of the consultancy journey particularly, the consultant will need access to a range of social process skills to reinforce the trust little by little. Sometimes, however, the consultant may start to experience hostility from the consultor, or defensiveness and anger, often suppressed and unexpressed, but nevertheless readily perceived. This might result from the consultor's sense of not being able to change their behaviour or an unwillingness to reveal all the facts. The consultor may lack confidence that they can carry through what they have discovered and be tempted to return to what is familiar and safe, even if less effective. In order to handle this, the consultant and, increasingly, the consultor need to work with both the content and the process of the consultancy.

Resistance is a typical feature of consultancy. Think back to the difficulty the exodus Israelites had in merely departing from Egypt. It took massive persuasion on Moses' part and ten plagues. Some consultors will find it very difficult to give up what they are familiar with. In *Flawless Consulting* (2000), Peter Block suggests that consultants frequently respond by trying to overcome the resistance, normally by using facts, data, argument and logic. This merely reinforces the resistance, as resistance is an emotional response. It is an indirect expression of a reservation of some kind on the consultor's part. Block suggests the key is for the consultant to express what they are experiencing in terms of the resistance, in order to get the consultor to articulate their reservations, focusing on the concerns of the consultor rather than the strength of the consultant's argument. He offers three steps:

Step 1: Identify in your own mind what form the resistance is taking. The skill is to pick up cues from [the consultor] and then, in your head, to put some words on what you see happening.

Step 2: State, in a neutral, nonpunishing way, the form the resistance is taking. This is called 'naming the resistance'. The skill is to find the neutral language.

Step 3: Be quiet. Let the [consultor] respond to your statement about the resistance.

(2000, p. 163)

Non-verbal messages are important cues. If the consultor is constantly shifting away from the consultant, tied up in knots or pointing a finger and clenching a fist, shaking their head when the consultant is speaking or bent over towards the consultant like some sort of slave, the consultant needs to check out whether the consultor is uneasy or unhappy. The consultant's own non-verbal behaviour, such as feeling angry, bored or sleepy, might indicate they are experiencing resistance. The consultor repeating the same idea or question several times could be a sign of resistance as they think their point is not getting across. Block suggests that repeated use of phrases like 'you have to understand that ...' or 'let me explain something to you ...' might indicate they feel they are not being heard.

Finding neutral ways to express what a consultant sees happening takes some skill, but good questions or phrases can be built up as part of a consultant's toolkit. For example, if every response from the consultor is little more than a single word, the consultant might say, 'All your comments are very short. Could you tell me a bit more?' If just describing what has happened is not uncovering the resistance, the consultant might find it useful to express how they are feeling about how the consultor is behaving: for example, 'I am feeling quite frustrated because you keep giving me just a yes or a no or a single word every time you answer a question of mine.' If the consultor remains silent or monosyllabic, the consultant should be happy staying with the quiet and waiting for the consultor to be forthcoming. It is likely that such challenges to the resistance are touching important areas for the consultor. That is why the tension can rise. The emotions touched can leave the consultor confused, needing time and quiet to formulate some sort of response to what they hear and feel. Yet, they still need to fulfil their role as consultor by engaging in analytical conversation. By continuing to talk, filling the gap for the consultor, the consultant is allowing the consultor to escape the work they have to do as part of a collaborative consultancy. The consultor is allowed to slip out of their accountability for their behaviour in the session. At this point consultors, Block suggests, can seem like stones, but continues, 'there aren't that many real stones out there. If the surface of the client is that hard, the stuff inside must be equally soft' (2000, p. 171).

In her guidebook to working non-directively with groups, *Meetings that Work* (2000), Catherine Widdicombe underlines the importance of the consultor preparing carefully before embarking on a session with a hostile group. She suggests the consultant look at why the group is hostile and how the consultant might be involved in the causation. Writing down their feelings of, say, anger that the group excites in the consultant can help develop objectivity and a non-defensive posture during the session. Pointing out that, at least, in contrast to many church groups, a hostile group is 'energized and active' (2000, p. 141), a planned approach to criticism and anger can turn the meeting into a constructive event. In common with Block, Widdicombe recommends an objective statement of the situation, a request that the group explore what this hostility might mean. Considerable skill and alertness is needed to notice and draw out indicators of fruitful routes forward from the hostility. It is important the consultant recognize what hard work this can be given the levels of emotion and possibly distress. One of the skills is to recognize when it is wisest to take a short or a long break.

> If conflict erupts unexpectedly, it may be wiser to work it through there and then or to avoid, de-fuse or try to postpone it. You may feel there is more likelihood of making matters worse if feelings are running high, time is short or you lack the needed confidence or ability. You could suggest, 'I think perhaps we should give ourselves time to think or calm down rather than continue now.'
>
> (2000, p. 143)

If a consultancy is tackling significant obstacles to progress in mission on a personal or systemic level, the social dynamic will frequently be accompanied by strong, uncomfortable emotions and reactions, an understandable response to the cognitive dissonance the consultor is feeling. This is culturally quite difficult for many Christians: Christians are supposed to be nice. Being angry certainly is not nice. Conflict feels like failure rather than a natural consequence of movement, transformation and learning. Churches are supposed to be models of peace and unity. Often niceness seems to replace love. In their work across a range of industrial, commercial and not-for-profit organizations, Macdonald *et al.* consistently recommend seeing whether a leader's, a worker's or a system's impact on another worker is loving or unloving (2006, pp. 19–25). Often this means challenging poor behaviour, dishonesty, cruelty or unfairness. In churches, it can involve taking the risk of naming demeaning behaviour as exactly that. How often in a church meeting are people allowed to behave badly because everyone else is too nice to address the unfairness of that attack on the minister? Savage and Boyd-Macmillan illustrate how

> women, in particular, have felt the force of these norms. Nice Christian women do not get angry. Nice, Christian women do not argue, disagree, cause problems, or get into disputes ... When a woman starts to disagree and others start to squirm, the trump card includes a quiet cough, and 'Don't forget I Timothy 2'. End of discussion. The conflict goes underground and the learning opportunities are squelched.
>
> (2007, p. 57)

Consultants and skilled consultors need to be able to handle, work with and learn through fierce emotion and conflict. Often the disclosure moment is when the consultant plucks up the courage to ask a very challenging question, knocking the consultor back in their chair and risking a hostile reception. Handling anger and disagreement depends significantly on high-quality listening; what is often called active listening – listening more than talking, attentive, full of verbal and non-verbal response, empathetic, reflecting, paraphrasing, exploratory, staying with silence, checking and challenging.

One of the delights of the analysis and design phases is how often they are accompanied by laughter. As consultor and consultant explore together the roots of the issue under investigation and ways to work with it, pennies will drop and lights will go on, as half-understood patterns are discerned and hopeful possibilities discovered. This is no longer the slightly tense, anxious laughter of the entry stages but recognition of progress and growing trust built on the clarity of early phases such as contracting. It is also a trust built on the experience of journeying safely and constructively through the anxiety, hostility and resistance that naturally arise. The consultancy sessions can become a place full of possibility where the attention paid to the consultor and the options opened up come as a great relief and blessing compared with some ministers' or leadership groups' experience of pressure, stress and unfair expectations.

As a safe, collaborative partnership develops, it is easy to see, then, that there is a danger that this will become a collusive relationship, us against them. Psychodynamic and systems approaches to consultancy (as will be explored in Chapter 6) can offer helpful insights about the dynamics that may occur between consultor and consultant in this. A useful way of looking at what can happen is to use Steve Karpman's famous Drama Triangle (the *Victim, Persecutor, Rescuer* model; see Figure 5.2). It is a model that has been used extensively in family therapy and taps into deep human stories and stereotypes such as the villain, damsel in distress, and the hero seen in fairy tales and black and white movies.

Ministers as consultors can often present themselves as under immense pressure. It may be the obligation to look after more and more churches, to raise a fading church from the dead, to fulfil the demands of myriad community and church groups, or to cope with what they feel are simultaneous, unfair expectations from superiors and family. Ministers in these situations can feel persecuted and play out the role of victim. The Drama Triangle suggests that we play different roles in life, which match our feelings of, for example, powerlessness. The roles describe how we behave to satisfy our conscious or unconscious needs

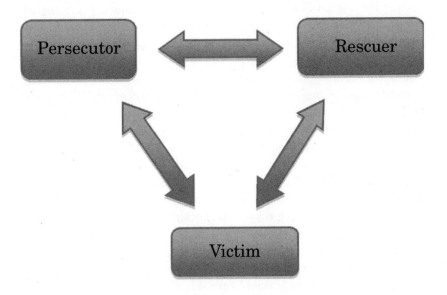

Figure 5.2 Karpman's Drama Triangle

Reproduced by kind permission of Stephen B. Karpman

in relationships. If a minister sees him- or herself as a victim (the damsel in distress), what they want is a rescuer (the hero) to save them from the persecutor (the villain). They long for an ally who understands how unfair their situation is and who will help them out. The rescuer may well feel flattered by this role. A consultant, whose livelihood depends on people needing to be helped, may encourage the victim to continue to need them as the rescuer. This will include reinforcing the idea that the consultor is indeed a victim and finding evidence that the persecutors are continuing to persecute. The situation will continue as long as the victim is prepared to keep being a victim. However, if the triangle is recognized for what it is, an infantile approach to working relationships, then adult solutions and relationships can be developed.

The aim of the consultant becomes to help the consultor out of being a victim by recognizing that they are adult. A typical way of doing this is to foster clarity between the different roles, negotiating expectations and assumptions. Are those who are persecuting the consultor clear that their minister is not available solely to them 24 hours a day or that they need to take on some of the work themselves? Is the consultor allowing the persecutors to see (behind the façade of the omni-competent pastor) the human being who is struggling with some aspects of their job and who would like to spend some time with their family? Sorting out such unhelpful relationships is often a matter of accepting that everyone involved is an ordinary person with typically mixed motives and limits on their understanding, abilities and insights. An important feature of this triangle is that it is possible to change roles. If one participant changes, the others change too.

In the example of the visiting scheme quoted in Chapter 4, the consultant who has helped design the pastoral visiting scheme could become the rescuer in helping the minister consultor understand how much he is the victim of the congregation's expectations that they will visit every member regularly. The consequent, confident assertion by the minister that clergy will be doing fewer visits may mean that the consultant now becomes the persecutor of the congregation. Some of the congregation will be angry that they will now not be visited with the same regularity, if at all. They may direct their anger at this interloper consultant. The consultant then feels victimized. If consultants are not careful, they can become scapegoats, the ones to blame for the change rather than the minister. Indeed, the congregation may ride in like the cavalry to rescue the minister. It was not the minister's fault. He was merely acting on the consultant's misleading advice. The minister then has to rescue the poor, misunderstood consultant. Thus, the triangle tumbles over and over. All the while, the actors can be avoiding their adult responsibility for what is happening. The tendency is to wallow in the roles and to avoid solving the problem, as that would mean abandoning the roles which are feeding a psychological need.

The aim of this section has been to point to the necessity of the consultant and, if possible, the consultor being sensitive to the quality of their interpersonal working relationship fostering constructive interdependence and watching out for collusion, defensiveness and parent–child interactions, among others. Regular, proficient supervision is an important resource in helping the consultant maintain a professional overview of these dynamics. Similarly, the effectiveness of the consultancy is enhanced by the monitoring of any conflict or inappropriate overlap in terms of role, content, knowledge or motive that is crossing boundaries that should not be crossed.

Boundaries

In consultancy, there are numerous boundaries that need to be clearly identified and monitored. Conflicts of interest can arise when both consultant and consultor know the same people or work for the same church. There are the boundaries between a non-directive approach and an expert approach, or between consultancy and counselling. There are limits set up by the scope of the consultancy. A well-known and dangerous feature of consultancy is scope-creep, where the focus of the consultancy broadens or shifts away from the original objective. There are understandings of confidentiality and role relationships. Thus, a vital element of the contracting that happens at the start of a consultancy relationship is the examination of boundaries and how to manage them.

Along the journey that constitutes the process of a consultancy, things change. For better or worse, consultor and consultant get to know each other well, get to know the issue better, learn more about themselves, and develop consulting skills, roles and relationships. Just as the growth of these relationships and skills can allow highly productive progress, there can also be a growth of inappropriate roles, relationships and behaviour. In reflecting on whether the development is healthy or dangerous, attention to boundaries can be of great help. Consciously considering how roles and relationships have developed can determine what might be healthy, corrective action to take if boundaries have been crossed or if boundaries have become defences. Using a diagram can help in checking that both work and roles are and remain within appropriate, agreed boundaries. Mapping out the consultancy as a system and its overlaps with the consultor's context and other systems can help to check on where the consultancy is located at any time. At any stage in the consultancy, where would the consultant place themselves? What are the overlapping elements? Has there been any movement? Is all of that appropriate and manageable?

Over time, boundaries can be crossed so that the consultant transforms from being an outside, non-directive support, collaborating with the consultor in thinking through issues, to a quasi-executive decision-maker for the consultor. The consultant may have become so helpful, such a beacon of light and possibility in the consultor's professional life, that the friendship between them is now something very different from a consultancy system. There may be collusion or dependency on either or both parts. In churches, especially in the case of internal consultants, the consultor and consultant may overlap not just when they meet in the consultancy sessions but they may be or have been part of the same church, district, agency or diocese. Even when the consultant was at first unknown to the consultor, it is quite common to find that the consultant already knows other actors in the consultor's system.

These connections need to be examined carefully to see whether the extra data they carry with them permit the consultancy to continue effectively. Normally this would involve a discussion with the consultor, but whether that is appropriate is a judgement initially for the consultant. The conflict of interests may mean that the consultancy has to stop. Boundaries exist between all the different systems and their overlaps. When they are crossed, the consequences need to be consciously examined.

Boundaries also exist between work consultancy and other types of helping support. Has what is happening moved from consultancy to counselling or spiritual direction? Has the content of the issue being worked on moved beyond the consultant's competence? Has the consultant moved from being a non-directive consultant to offering technical advice from their own experience, that is, become an expert consultant? In each case it may be a good idea to talk through the possibility that the consultancy has lost focus on its key matter and defining process, that the consultor should start to work with another helper who is competent in the disciplines now needed, or that the consultor needs to know they can take or leave the expert advice. These boundaries should be well established in the contracting phase and well monitored and maintained through the middle phase, even as they shift and transform along the journey. If so, it will continue to be possible to identify what is happening, whether it is happening in the right place, with the right assumptions, and what the consequences will be in terms either of continuing along the same path or finding another route.

Consultancy tourists or pilgrims

If the phases of a consultancy journey are well managed, it is rare that the benefit is merely for the project or issue concerned. Relevant analyses and insights will have been reached but, if the process has been through a healthy reflective process, the consultor(s) will understand that they have learnt new things about themselves, and will have gained new skills both in delivering the desired change and in undertaking analysis and design themselves. In addition, as their companion on the way, the consultant will also have learnt and grown. Doris Donnelly, in an article entitled 'Pilgrims and Tourists: Conflicting Metaphors for the Christian Journey to God' (1992), suggests that 'when the outward molds the inward, we become pilgrims, women and men *in via*, persons en route to some destination, toward some end'. She contrasts this with the modern notion of being a tourist, proposing the following distinctions:

> (1) pilgrims perceive an internal dimension to pilgrimage, while tourists are concerned with the external journey alone; (2) pilgrims invest themselves, while the tourists avoid personal commitment; (3) the focus for the pilgrim is to be affected by the pilgrimage, while the tourist seeks to be untouched by his/her experiences; (4) both the journey and arrival are of import for the pilgrim, while only the arrival matters for the tourist; and (5) community is formed for the pilgrim, and it is not a *desideratum* for the tourist.
>
> (1992, p. 20)

For the inward transformation to take root in terms of new skills, management of change and a developing sense of vocation, attention needs to be given to the quality of the journey. The tourist consultor led by the tour guide consultant is unlikely to be transformed inwardly in a way that convinces them that there is a realistic chance of succeeding with new ways of understanding situations and working in them.

This chapter has aimed to show the importance of being reflective on process in the consultancy journey. Without a clear, explicit management of beginnings, middles and endings, there is the risk that plans and behaviour changes will not sustain. Without clear contracts and continuing monitoring, review and adjustments, strategies are likely to be ineffective and the experience of consultancy unsatisfying. Handling the social process well, especially by understanding and avoiding the potential traps, is key not just for the process consultant but for the expert consultant as well. As in any model of practice, the hope is that this chapter has underlined the importance of attending to the process of the consultancy as a way of helping it be as productive as possible and to get better and better over time.

6

Models of Consultancy

'There are theories at the bottom of my jargon.'
Slogan from a badge, quoted by Olwen Haslam in
Letters page of the *Guardian*, 1 October 2010

As a profession (if to claim such a title is not too controversial), consultancy suffers from a lack of standard career paths and quality measures. Anyone can set themselves up as a consultant with little more than a website and a business card. Confidence in doing so is often based on the notion that they have already done the job they are intending to advise on. Thus, they are competent to act as a consultant in that area. They may have been on the odd course and seen consultants in action, from whom they have picked up a few tips and techniques. Without an integrating theory they will operate out of a smorgasbord of personal experience, half-understood processes and trendy, if obscure jargon. It is a contention of this book that professional consultants pay constant attention to the conscious, purposeful development of their consultancy model. The focus of this chapter, therefore, is to understand various factors that influence and constitute such a model and to examine some of the significant families of models that are in use in work with churches. The first two sections look at how to understand a consultancy model in general terms and how to understand your own:

- What is a consultancy model?
- What does my model look like?

The next section looks at various models of change. Consultancy is in essence helping with change. So, it is necessary to have some clear idea about how change is supposed to happen.

- Models of change
    Cognitive dissonance
    Force field analysis

Bereavement
Crazy time
Conversation
Prayer.

The third section of the chapter looks as some common families of theory and practice that are used in consultancy, what their main features are and how applicable they are to church settings:

- Non-directive church work consultancy
- Management consulting and organizational development
- Psychodynamic and systems psychodynamic approaches
- Appreciative inquiry
- Complexity and chaos approaches.

What is a consultancy model?

From an academic point of view, it is difficult to grasp what a consultancy model means, given the range of theoretical disciplines and applications of consultancy. Craig Lundberg, in an article called 'Toward a General Model of Consultancy', tries to construct a universal framework against which to judge such models. His initial stance is that there is little proper research into consultancy as a discipline and any literature is unsatisfying and discursive, probably because of the lack of theoretical frameworks and concepts. What does exist, he suggests, tends to be based on lists and classifications, which are too vague, prescriptive, or too infused with values to be objectively useful (Lundberg, 1997, p. 193).

He suggests that a generic consultancy model should demonstrate a rigorous and systematic attempt to describe the process underlying all forms of helping/change/improvement practice. It should deal with client systems and consultant systems of all shapes and sizes and be about change. Using existing ideas, it should be ideologically neutral, compatible with all of the dominant perspectives on organizations, cope with different approaches to reality, be future oriented and explicit about its theoretical purpose (1997, p. 194). He then develops a model based on the idea that a consultor is someone who needs help because they are feeling insecure and, therefore, experiencing anxiety. A client/consultor is a human system experiencing anxiety. Help happens when a human system perceives that its anxiety has been reduced. A consultant is a human system that responds and offers to provide help, that is, assistance in uncertainty reduction. Thus, the question a model needs to address is how the consultant is going to effect help (1997, p. 196).

As was discussed in an earlier chapter, Donald Schön, in a range of work but particularly in *The Reflective Practitioner* (1991), advances the notion of the reflective practitioner, the professional who solves the problems they face in their work by a mixture of 'knowing and doing' – what he calls 'theory in use', operant theory. This contrasts with the use of 'espoused theory', the book or classroom learning that is the typical approach to training of many professionals but that is the opposite of what they do in practice. The consultant needs to be living in a continuous iterative cycle of testing theory, using theory, and reflecting on what actually happens in a consultancy. Through the process of reflecting on action, they will be constantly refining the mixture of theory and implementation that makes up their developing praxis. Critics of Schön suggest that it is difficult to operate as a professional without any previous classroom learning but his work has helped to produce a balance between espoused theory and the natural way that we learn – by doing, reflecting on what we are doing and getting expert help, for example from a skilled apprentice guide. To be continuously improving, consultants need to see whatever they do as 'action research', a self-reflective process of investigation by people, operating in social/socio-religious settings. This process will inform and improve their understanding of what they are doing for the benefit of the people and organizations they are trying to help, and will improve their professional practice.

Using this dynamic, learning cycle, a model of consultancy can be defined as *a complex description of the integrating features of a consultant's theory and practice that shows how that consultant intends to help effectively in context.* Something like a consultant's brochure, it should enable a prospective consultor to understand how a consultant works and why, so that they can see whether that consultant might be of help.

What does my model look like?

In attempting to explore the nature of different consultancy approaches in his book *Consultancy Modes and Models* (2006), Lovell distinguishes between a consultancy mode and a consultancy model. A mode describes a distinctive but generic approach, which can support a number of models. A mode may be seen as the family to which a number of models belong. Lovell discusses six of these modes or families (systemic and systems thinking, development processes, organizational management,

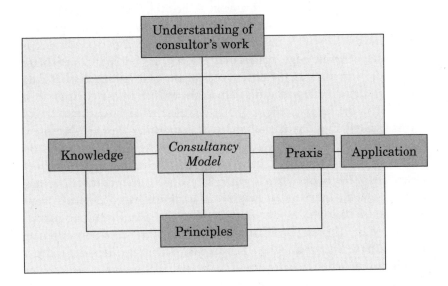

Figure 6.1 Lovell's Five Basic Elements of a Consultancy Model

Reproduced by kind permission, from *Consultancy Modes and Models* by George Lovell; Cliff College Publishing, 2005. ISBN 189836236X.

the non-directive approach to work, psychological process, and complexity and chaos theory). A consultancy model describes how the consultancy is actually done in a particular setting by a particular person or group. It lays out the basic theoretical assumptions expressed in an operational framework, process or system. Lovell sees a consultancy model as emerging from a particular combination of five basic elements, the relationship between which he lays out in Figure 6.1.

- *Knowledge* – concepts, theories and hypotheses underlying the particular model.
- *Principles* – fundamental truths, beliefs, values and assumptions, particularly for the consultant.
- *Understanding the consultor's work* – how to know enough about the consultor's work to be effective.
- *Praxis* – how the consultancy model is put to work, the practice and the theory of practice behind it (espoused and operant).
- *Application* – in which situations can the model be used successfully?

Whether or not you find this framework helpful, it underlines the crucial understanding for consultants and for those they are helping: every consultant works with a model that is made up of a personally developed range of knowledge, beliefs and practice. If they cannot articulate that model and the way the different elements of it influence what they are doing, there is a risk that the consultant will perform poorly or even abusively in the helping role.

It is unlikely that any consultant will be working with an absolutely pure model that is entirely out of one of Lovell's modes. Indeed, if the modes are seen as families, as is often the case in families, disagreements break out about what is right. Is this the pure approach? Is this new approach dangerous or helpful? The admixture of elements from other modes will be a matter of discussion and dispute among practitioners. Many church consultants, throughout their career in different jobs, will have been trained in a range of helping disciplines and models on which they will naturally draw. In the articulation and development of their models, reflective consultants will acknowledge what is major and minor in their models. They will take care, for example, that the theoretical bases of techniques or tools they use which come from a different mode or discipline do not contradict the fundamental assumptions of their substantive model.

Building on Lovell's framework, this book proposes the structure below for examining an individual consultant's or consultancy group's model (see Figure 6.2). This structure recognizes that the particular combination each church consultant brings is going to be nuanced according to their background, history and role. A healthy, professional model should always involve the dynamic of feedback and learning between constituent parts. Each element has an impact on the others and, if any of them change, for example after starting a new job, learning a new skill, meeting a new theory of organization or understanding a biblical insight in a fresh way, ripples will be felt in the other areas.

The structure is made up of four interconnected elements:

- *Fields of knowledge* – the bodies of theory from, for example, organizational studies and ecclesiology, consultancy theory, theology and mission, psychology, sociology, management and group work theory, which inform and shape the consultancy approach. In an expert model, this includes technical expertise and qualifications. It is important to be clear which are core fields and which are helpful but not of the essence of the model.
- *Skills and methods* – the techniques, methods and tools, and the skills

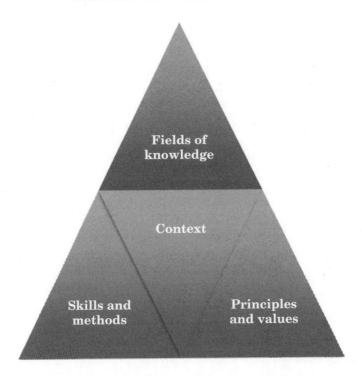

Figure 6.2 A structure for analysing a consultancy model

in using them, that a consultant will build up over the years, which support effective consultancy in their chosen model. This includes a rigorous, continuing dialogue with theories, especially from the fields of knowledge above, which ensures that the consultant knows how and why the skills and methods can be deployed productively.

- *Principles and values* – the complex of beliefs, values, assumptions and principles that drive, underpin and constrain the consultant's model of working with consultors. These may include what consultants believe about how God acts and is, what being human means, the nature of work, ministry or the purpose of mission, church and society. It may include ethical guidelines on what type of organizations or issues a consultant is happy to work with. It may include professional or commercial principles about fees, work–life balance, competition with other consultants or the optimum conditions for effective interventions.
- *Context* – an understanding of the consultant and consultor's backgrounds, stories and settings. Context sits at the heart of the structure as the determining factor of the integration of all four components.

As regards the consultant, context includes their experience and work life up to this point. It acknowledges their personality and formation, their preferences, strengths and weaknesses. Reflection on the purpose and setting of their role, for example, as an internal or external consultant or as a leader in the organization, assists in clarifying what they offer and expect. It also highlights any conflicts or boundary issues. For example, acknowledging the context may mean that, although the consultant's model might work well with groups, the consultant's preference for working with individuals and unease with group process means that the use of this particular model will be limited.

As regards the consultor, part of the work of the consultancy is for the consultant to build the depth of familiarity with the consultor (their setting, style of working, the way they see their work, purpose, organization and hopes for the future) that will enable relevant, valuable collaboration.

Two examples of consultancy models

About Vicky Cosstick

'When people ask me what I do, I say I am an independent consultant and change facilitator. I like to work with individuals, groups and organizations that are excited about and/or struggling with learning, change and development. My passion is tailor-making processes that help individuals, groups or teams, and organizations to be more effective, to change and to learn.'

Vicky Cosstick is a consultant, facilitator and coach who works primarily in the international aid and development sector, and with voluntary organizations. She has been working as a consultant and as a facilitator of small and large groups since 1980, specializing since 2002 in international development. She responds to client needs to design extremely practical and engaging processes to support and implement change and learning in organizations. Her technical expertise is in designing processes and agendas for teams with a wide range of country and technical programme experience. She has worked intensively on projects in HIV and AIDS, gender, sustainable agriculture, civil society, advocacy, sex and gender-based violence, and child rights, protection and participation. She has worked with groups and programmes in Kenya, Malawi, Rwanda, DRC, Uganda, Tamil Nadu, South India and Cambodia. Vicky has been influenced by a wide range of organizational practice and theory, including adult learning, gestalt and complexity theory. While her work is always flexible and creative, it is rooted in proven, well-established traditions of group dynamics and organizational development.

The OxCEPT approach

- We will work with rather than for you, your input into the consultancy process is as significant as ours.
- Once we have designed a process with you, we will be flexible about who does what. We realize if you are on a tight budget you may want to do more of the work.
- We will draw upon academic knowledge about theology, the church, the voluntary sector and social trends and ask if it seems relevant to your situation.
- We are sensitive to the connection between work and vocation for many of our clients.
- If, after an initial discussion, we feel we can't help you, we will say so.
- We only charge for the work we actually do.

In the box above are two examples of publicity materials for consultancies. The first is from Vicky Cosstick's website. Vicky, a Roman Catholic laywoman, has a history of work both in churches and in other not-for-profit organizations, particularly in the field of international development. The second is from the consultancy leaflet of the Oxford Centre for Ecclesiology and Practical Theology (OxCEPT), the research and consultancy arm of Ripon College, Cuddesdon, an Anglican theological college in England. Although both extracts are quite short, it is easy to start to see the mixture of fields of knowledge, skills and methods, principles and values, and context that make up their consultancy models.

Models of change

If it is about anything, consultancy is about supporting change. It may be a massive change such as shifting the way the church sees its purpose as mission instead of ministry, or a new regional structure and strategy. It may be something on a smaller scale, such as persuading the choir to accept the occasional modern worship song or getting the minister's paperwork in better order. It might be about accepting the death of a chapel and its dwindling congregation, or a team becoming more open, loving, honest and constructive together in staff meetings. Change is a central focus of Christian endeavour, hence the currency of words like conversion, repentance, transformation, formation, growth, discipleship, journey, forgiveness and sanctification. Consultancy responds to a perceived need for help, the recognition that the present situation is not as desired. It may be the anxiety that Lundberg talks about. This need is normally accompanied by some notion, however fuzzy, of how things should be. Part of the work of the consultancy may be the articulation of that desired state. As the consultancy is likely to focus on getting to that state, there needs to be a theory of how such a change, or change in general, might be achieved. What process will bridge the gap between the present state and what is desired, and build a future on solid, lasting foundations? Consultants should be able to explain, through their theories of change, why the things they do should produce the results they intend. So, what follows offers some approaches to change. It has to be recognized that among the change tools and theories that consultants use some are based on reputable research in academic disciplines such as sociology or psychology. Others have no such hinterland but are used because those who use them have found they work sufficiently successfully in terms of metaphor, image or rule of thumb.

Cognitive dissonance

An influential theory of change is based on the concept of cognitive dissonance originally proposed by Leon Festinger (1957) and colleagues in the 1950s. As human beings, we have difficulty coping with holding two contradictory ideas in our heads at the same time. The inconsistency makes us feel uncomfortable, experiencing dissonance. We need to resolve this dissonance. We can relieve it by changing our beliefs, attitudes and behaviour. We can also resolve it by denying the evidence that causes the dissonance or by rationalizing away what has happened, perhaps by blaming it on others.

Coping with dissonance

A self-supporting minister I know moved house, needed to find a new church locally and so went to the nearest church for five weeks. The congregation was mostly elderly, mostly female, and numbered between 20 and 30. The building was small with eight or nine rows of pews. The minister was male, in his thirties, confident in church and with a fairly loud singing voice, and so should have been

---

noticed. In all those five weeks no one in the congregation welcomed him or even spoke to him, apart from the priest who took the service, at the door on the way out. On advice from friends he decamped to another church. Later that year he came back to take a service. In the sermon he mentioned his experience – to audible intakes of breath, tokens of significant dissonance. At the end of the service he identified three reactions. One group, embarrassed, apologized profusely and said they would look at how they noticed and welcomed visitors. Having received information that challenged their view of their church as welcoming, they resolved to change their behaviour. A second group apologized and said they had not seen the stranger as the pew he was sitting in lay behind their pew. They denied the evidence in order to hold on to their beliefs. A third group blamed it on the minister. He should have tried harder to make himself known.

Under this theory, change is generated by creating dissonance that has to be resolved. Instead of persisting in Benjamin Franklin's definition of insanity, that is, continuing to do the same thing while expecting a different result, movement to the desired state is effected by offering contradictory evidence and then supporting those involved in travelling to beliefs and behaviours where there is no conflict between what they believe to be the case and what they experience. A common response to pressure to change is that 'people don't like change', especially in churches. However, many changes are welcome as long as people can see how it is an advantage to them. Installing efficient heating or toilets in a mediaeval church where there had been none is normally seen as a welcome change. Resistance to change comes when an individual or group cannot see how the change might benefit them and from a sense of helplessness. As Macdonald *et al.* say:

> In order for change to occur, a person:
> - must experience dissonance
> - must have a sense that the new behaviour will improve the situation (for the individual or social group)
> - must have a sense that he or she is an active player in the process, that he or she can influence the process.
>
> (2006, p. 27)

The task of the consultant is to help identify the factors that make those involved resist or support change and work with the consultor(s) in order to develop a change strategy.

Force field analysis

In a famous article in which he acknowledged the challenge of promoting change ('If you really want to understand something, try to change it!'), Kurt Lewin (1951) introduced his concept of field analysis. This involves understanding that any situation can be seen as a field populated by many co-existing factors. These factors are dynamically interdependent and all influence individuals' or groups' behavioural choices. In trying to effect change, these factors may support or obstruct the move to the desired state like opposing forces in physics. In order for change to happen, work needs to be done on identifying the driving and restraining forces and then forming an integrated plan to reinforce the former and counter the latter. This moves the equilibrium to the new desired state. Then work needs to be done on how to sustain that state. This is often known as the three-step process – unfreezing, changing and refreezing. The beauty of Lewin's model is that it is possible to do this analysis and planning diagrammatically using a layout like the one in Figure 6.3.

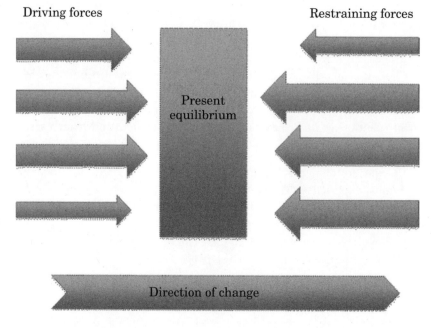

Figure 6.3 Lewin's force field analysis

Bereavement

The process of change involves leaving what people have been used to behind. Some people will be angry at having to move on. Even those who understand and welcome the change may be sad at letting go of an important part of their life. One way of understanding this is to see the change as akin to bereavement. A well-known analysis of the phases of bereavement was constructed by Elisabeth Kübler-Ross (1969). She talked to a large number of people dying of cancer and identified five stages: denial, anger, bargaining, depression and acceptance. William Worden (2009) uses these phases of bereavement to suggest that there are four tasks that the bereaved need to undertake to adapt successfully:

- Task 1 – accepting the reality of the loss
- Task 2 – working through the pain of grief
- Task 3 – adjusting to an environment in which the deceased is missing
- Task 4 – relocating the deceased emotionally and moving on with life.

In churches and religious groups, members' depth of attachment and commitment can make organizational change feel like bereavement. The suggestion from internal organizational consultants such as Mark Wakelin in the UK Methodist Church is that using these phases and tasks can help change embed more successfully and acceptably by supporting those affected through natural steps of grief.

Crazy time

To be in the middle of a change process can feel full of conflict. It is about travelling from one culture to another, culture meaning 'the ways of thinking, feeling and acting which are common to the members of the same organization' (Meier, 2010, p. 10). Some of the old assumptions, beliefs and behaviours are still prevalent. At the same time, the leadership and their supporters will be encouraging people to behave and believe according to the new culture. The individual is left in a quandary about whether to stick with the old ways, which are familiar, easy and make the world predictable, or to adopt the new ways, which feel risky and uncertain. One company president I worked with in the United States, Mark Kaminski, who taught me this model, called this 'crazy time'. What the individual in the middle of the 'crazy time' needs

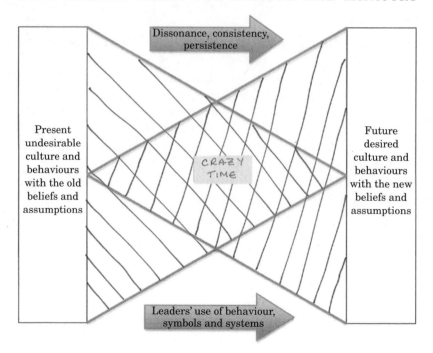

Figure 6.4 Crazy time model

is reassurance, holding and consistent, persistent reinforcement. The supportive message leading in the direction of the change via organizational symbols and systems and the behaviour of others, especially leaders, needs to confirm that the journey is beneficial or even inescapable. If the messages are not consistent and persistent in pointing the way to the future culture, it is too easy to revert to the old culture and rationalize away the need for change.

Conversation

In contrast to what are seen by some as mechanistic approaches to organizations, where you can plan change and predict behavioural reactions like some sort of chess game, organizational thinkers whose models are influenced by chaos, complexity and emergence theory insist that it is not possible to manage change in the ways suggested above. Critchley and Stuelten

> make a bold, yet simple claim based on the observable phenomena of human bodies in interaction, such as sweating, breathing, gesturing

towards, and mutually affecting one other. Our claim is that organizations are exactly that – human beings in an ongoing process of communicative interaction. In other words, organizations are not *things that can be worked on*, but *a participative process of interaction.*

(2008, p. 1)

With organizations seen not as entities but as processes in which people are interacting and constantly trying to make sense of their context, patterns emerge naturally through conversations, delivering unpredictable outcomes. Change becomes an issue of listening to those conversations and seeing the patterns in those social interactions. In their book on planning in churches, *Holy Conversations*, Rendle and Mann assert that change itself happens through conversation:

It is not the plan that will change people and give direction to the congregation. It is the conversation of the people one with another and with God – that is a part of the planning process – that changes people ... Margaret Wheatley states: 'there is no power equal to a community discovering what it cares about'. She then goes on to say 'it is always like this. Real change begins with the simple action of people talking about what they care about.'

(2003, p. xviii)

Consultants who use this approach can find it difficult when faced with members of churches who are accustomed, for example from their work backgrounds, to the positivist, so-called 'mechanistic' processes discussed earlier. What's the plan? What are the outcomes we are going to produce and when? As in any of these models of change, the theory should mould the way the consultant works. For a complexity-model consultant, the main task is to listen, notice, remain aware and reflect on the assumption that patterns, options and plans will emerge from structured and informal conversations between individuals and groups. They need to be wary of the external and internal pressure to be in control and to force outcomes, always sensitive to the impact their presence has on those conversations, while fulfilling the role of a critical partner in the conversation, ensuring the conversation opens up possibilities rather than reinforcing options that are unhelpfully constrained.

This is not an exhaustive list of workable models of change. You might want, for example, to look at John Kotter's work as an influential academic in the area of change in such books as *Leading Change*

(1996). He is an example of the organization-development tradition, which can be seen as assuming that change may be handled in a fairly mechanical, linear fashion, in his case in an eight-step model based on studies of a range of successful companies. The problem with this approach (and others like it) is that it is often taken as the answer to implementing change. However, it is a method rather than a theory. What is the theory about people that will ensure change happens? It is in danger of ignoring what one of the management websites (www. rapidbi.com) terms the three leadership rules about change:

> Rule #1 – People are different
> Rule #2 – People are different
> Rule #3 – People are different

Any change process needs to take into account that change is only going to be delivered by people changing their behaviour. Unless the plan takes into consideration the people factor, both people as individuals and the way people in social groupings such as organizations and churches respond, it is likely to fail. In a useful Grove booklet, *Leading Change in the Church*, Martyn Snow offers an equation:

$D \times V \times M$ must be $> P$

D = dissatisfaction with the status quo
V = vision of a better future
M = method or some practical first steps towards this future
P = pain or cost of change.

As he says, 'all change (and learning) involves pain, and because we want to avoid pain the motivational factors have to be very strong' (Snow, 2009, p. 18).

Prayer

In a faith-based context, a natural avenue in looking for change is to turn to prayer. As has already been said, prayer in consultancy is a controversial issue. Ministers and laypeople may well expect that individual consultancy and consultancy around a change project in a local church or larger organization will be accompanied by individual and group prayer. Different consultants and consultors will have different takes on what we are doing as Christians when we are praying for or concerning change, often depending on their understanding of how God acts in the world. Consider George Herbert's 1633 sonnet on prayer:

> Prayer the church's banquet, angel's age,
> God's breath in man returning to his birth,
> The soul in paraphrase, heart in pilgrimage,
> The Christian plummet sounding heav'n and earth
> Engine against th' Almighty, sinner's tow'r,
> Reversed thunder, Christ-side-piercing spear,
> The six-days world transposing in an hour,
> A kind of tune, which all things hear and fear;
> Softness, and peace, and joy, and love, and bliss,
> Exalted manna, gladness of the best,
> Heaven in ordinary, man well drest,
> The milky way, the bird of Paradise,
> Church-bells beyond the stars heard, the soul's blood,
> The land of spices; something understood.

His surprisingly vigorous, often violent, kaleidoscopic characterization of all that prayer can be suggests that prayer encompasses a wide range of intentions and effects. A consultant needs to have some ideas, however inclusive, particular or flexible, in their model of what, for example, a prayer group supporting a change process means. They also need to work with the consultor(s) to get them to articulate what is their expectation of prayer in terms of change. There should be, in the contracting phase, the possibility of working out if or how this forms part of the consultancy, for example if there are any expectations on the consultant to engage with worship or prayer groups.

Consultancy approaches

The aim of the following section is to introduce a range of what Lovell would call modes, general families of organizational and consultancy theory on which self-aware consultants can build their praxis models. The aim is to present the modes in as neutral a way as possible, but any author, particularly a practitioner author, will have prejudices for and against different ways of looking at organizations, workers and consultancy practice. For each model, some history and the basic principles and practice will be laid out. There will follow some discussion of its strengths and weaknesses. As the theoretical and practical base for these modes and models is often from a secular source, there will be some discussion about how well they apply in church settings. Hints on useful literature will be given at the end of each mode's section. As will be seen, the widely differing theoretical and practical nature of some of these modes means that it can be difficult to construct a framework that allows side-by-side comparison. It is probably the case that the best way to assess the usefulness of any mode or model is to talk to consultants and consultors who have experienced it. If you can get hold of it, Lovell's *Consultancy Modes and Models* (2005) provides more detailed introductions to a considerable number of models using his analytical structure seen earlier in this chapter.

A confusing term in trying to identify different modes, approaches and schools is the use of the word 'systems'. Some models, such as Macdonald *et al.*'s (2006) Systems Leadership Theory, use the term to underline the importance of systems, that is, the way work, money, people, resources, information and other elements flow in an organization in getting work done. Systems thinking as exemplified by Checkland and Scholes' *Soft Systems Methodology* (1990) or Seddon's *Systems Thinking in the Public Sector* (2008) encourage seeing the organization as a whole system, organized collections of process and activities, rather than individual elements or mechanical process. The need is to examine the interactions, feedback and impact from one part of the system to another. Psychodynamic systems approaches, such as Obholzer and Roberts' *The Unconscious at Work* (1994), take this further and investigate the importance of the unconscious processes of the organization as a system of interconnected people in roles and the dynamic impact their psychological needs, relationships and motivations will have on getting the work done. To heighten psychology's contribution to this confusion, insights from systemic therapy or family therapy are often applied to organizational behaviour, such as the Drama Triangle, the 'Victim–Persecutor–Rescuer' model mentioned in Chapter 5. A complexity approach will be using scientific theories about complex adaptive natural systems such as a colony of ants to understand a big organization. The breadth of use of the term 'systems' means that a consultant needs to be careful and clear when using or hearing the word. So here are five examples of consultancy approaches that are used in churches.

Non-directive church work consultancy

At the heart of the non-directive approach is the desire and the commitment to get people to think, decide and act for themselves in the light of as much information as they can handle. This involves

emphasizing the need to work with people as well as for them. Dr
T. R. Batten coined the phrase. For him non-directive workers aim to
help all kinds of people, separately and together, to think seriously,
deeply, analytically, imaginatively and purposefully about the sub-
stance of work, life and faith and to act upon their conclusions.

(Lovell, 1996, p. 10)

Non-directive work consultancy has its origins in the work of T. R.
(Reg) Batten. Batten was a teacher and educationalist who worked in
Nigeria and Uganda both in schools and as an administrator from 1927
to 1949. In supporting education as a central tool in enabling indig-
enous people to achieve a high quality of independence and effective
self-rule, he realized that working from European assumptions about
the way the world is was not enough. Recasting, for example, the study
of history so that it could be seen from an African viewpoint revealed
that working to promote change would only be successful if the world-
view of the people involved was the starting point for the analysis of the
present. Based on his belief in human equality and potential, and a rev-
erence for human freedom, Batten promoted the idea that improvement
and development issue from self-determination and self-help, principles
which he brought from the colonial sphere to the initial years of community development in Britain. It was from his academic base at the
Institute of Education in London with his wife, Madge, that he shared
his non-directive principles with a group of church people who were
dissatisfied with what they saw as the standard directive, paternalistic
and authoritarian style undertaken by those trying to promote change.
Both because it was theologically more attractive and seemed to offer
an approach that would be more likely to succeed, the group (including Lovell and Catherine Widdicombe) tested out Batten's approach in
church and community work.

There is an obvious connection in the counselling world of the time
with the coincidental development of the notion of *unconditional positive regard* for the client, put forward by the hugely influential American
psychologist, Carl Rogers (see Rogers, 1961). As a key component of his
client-centred therapy, unconditional positive regard demands un-
qualified acceptance of the client without judgement or criticism. This
acceptance of the unique worth of the client with all their foibles allows
increasing understanding of the client as the relationship between client
and therapist progresses. The parallel development of such a supportive concept in therapy and counselling provided fruitful fields (particularly among clergy and church workers) for a non-directive approach

to consultancy and community development to take root. The non-directive basis of the church work consultancy model involves not only an acceptance of consultors as they are but also a serious engagement with their work, its setting and personal background.

For nearly 20 years, this approach was communicated and taught through Avec, an ecumenical training and work consultancy agency in London. Through the provision of courses and consultancy services, large numbers of clergy, members of religious orders and lay people were encouraged to analyse their work, building skills in collaboration, egalitarian participation and reflection, and confidence in designing solutions to their own issues in terms of programmes and projects. Although Avec closed in 1994, its method and approach have continued to be influential through its former students and workers, through a series of books Lovell and Widdicombe produced and through courses such as the postgraduate programmes in consultancy at Cliff College and the York Institute for Community Theology in the United Kingdom.

In *Consultancy, Ministry and Mission* (2000), Lovell provides an abundance of tools to help consultors examine their work – the attributes, fields of knowledge and social or technical skills they need to fulfil it, and their understanding of it. Central to this is Lovell's concept of the *work-view*. Opening up a consultor's work-view involves examining in detail how the consultor sees their work revealing a complex mixture of theology and spirituality, emotion, knowledge and technical understanding, as well as what their work means to them in terms of vocation and connection with the world around and interactions with others' work-views. One very helpful emphasis in building the understanding of the consultor's work-view, whether the consultor is an individual or a group, comes from the tools Lovell provides around energy audit (2000, pp. 109–12). Both in the consultor's work and in the consultations, he suggests examining emotional, intellectual, moral and spiritual energy. Where does it come from, or from whom? What blocks, saps or renews it? What happens to the energy in different work settings and with different people or groups? What is the quality of the energy and what effect does it have? Individuals and groups are encouraged to keep energy journals to provide data on which to reflect. Awareness of levels of energy and managing the work being done at any time can influence the effectiveness of any meeting, consultation or the implementation of a task. An energy audit can illuminate why it is such a struggle for some groups to move on from one type of activity to another. How often do ministers get frustrated when church groups will happily discuss the details of who will make the tea and the cakes and spend as little time as possible on overall mission and purpose? Understanding why energy does and does not come can not only explain what is happening but also help in building a strategy which will deal with the energy-sapping aspects of the tasks people typically avoid.

The fundamental collaborative relationship between consultor and consultant enables a productive, creative interplay.

> Work consultancy in this model is not a series of mechanical procedures. It is a creative art, based on the insights of Christianity and the behavioural and social sciences performed in the glory and messiness of human spiritual life in the church and the world.
>
> (Lovell 2005, p. 156)

Seven interacting elements form the structure around which this creative process hinges:

1 roles
2 interpersonal behaviour
3 working relationships
4 work-views
5 thinking together
6 systemics and logistics (effective consultancy arrangements that fit in with the consultor's regular work routine)
7 beliefs, values and ethics.

When the creative process around the seven elements takes off, Lovell sees it possible for the consultant to work via virtual insidership, being able to stand in the consultor's shoes and see things through their eyes. He claims that, through successful use of work-views, the consultancy system can so closely correspond to the fullness of the consultor's reality that it provides a completely adequate basis for consultation, even though virtual.

In terms of the model's usefulness in churches, as distinct from most models of consultancy, church work consultancy has been developed within a church context. It is shot through with theological perspectives and principles. It has been used successfully in a wide range of church and community settings. Lovell and Widdicombe have taken great care to write up the theory in a series of books, papers and articles whose availability they are maintaining through the Avec Trust. Two factors seem to make it difficult to apply. The first is working out how to be non-directive while encouraging a rigorous, analytical process. The terms directive and non-directive can create some confusion when bud-ding consultants try to balance, for example, the absolute authority of the consultor to commit to designs and solutions of their own creation and the disconcerting challenge that a consultant needs to bring. The second is that the egalitarian, collaborative way of working is culturally alien for many used to the hierarchical culture of the churches. Not be-ing given an expert solution, having to work as a skilled consultor and having to take ownership of the solution that is developed through the consultancy may be a step too far for some.

Texts and Sources

T. R. Batten, 1967, *The Non-Directive Approach in Group and Com-munity Work*, London: Oxford University Press – *Batten's classic book on applying the non-directive approach to community development.*

G. Lovell, 2000, *Consultancy, Ministry and Mission: A Handbook for Practitioners and Work Consultants in Christian Organizations*, London: Burns & Oates – *a detailed description of the theory and method of the church work consultancy approach.*

C. Widdicombe, 2000, *Meetings that Work: A Practical Guide to Teamworking in Groups*, Cambridge: Lutterworth Press – *a practi-cal manual on how to use a non-directive approach to making meet-ings more effective.*

G. Lovell (ed.), 1996, *Telling Experiences*, London: Chester House – *accounts of the use of the Avec approach in a wide range of settings. Further information about Avec, its history, current publications and archives, can be found at www.avecresources.org.*

Management consulting and organizational development

Although historically arising from different beginnings management consultancy and organizational development overlap so consider-ably that they will be dealt with as a single approach for the purposes of this chapter. This is not to say that some may claim that their approaches have nothing to do with management consulting or that other approaches do not draw on the sources discussed in this section. Under Greiner and Metzger's definition, management consulting is an advisory service contracted for and provided to organizations by specially trained and qualified persons who assist, in an objective and independent manner, the client organization to identify management problems, analyze such problems, recommend solutions to these problems, and help, when requested, in the implementation of solutions.

(1983, p. 7)

Compare Beckhard's definition from his influential book, *Organization Development: Strategies and Models*, where he sees organizational development as

an effort, planned, organization-wide, and managed from the top, to increase organization effectiveness and health through planned interventions in the organization's processes, using behavioural science knowledge.

(1969, p. 9)

The emphasis in both definitions is on assisting in management issues. Although some management consultancy intervention can be seen in departments, sites or other subsets of an organization, any intervention is much more likely to succeed and be sustained if it understands the organizations as a whole unit, as a system with the leadership of the organization backing and driving any change. Although organizational development in the strictest terms issues from the work of social scientists we have already met, such as Lewin and Schein, it has been adopted by a wider range of managers and consultants as a whole-organization approach to increasing effectiveness. In promoting organizational development, these managers and consultants will combine insights from what is included under the broad banner of management studies, the classic components of an MBA. Each year, wave after wave of new approaches to improving effectiveness crash on the shores of organizational development. The list includes time and motion studies, business process re-engineering, lean manufacturing, total quality management, Just in Time, project management, flat organizations, Myers Briggs, customer satisfaction, the learning organization, knowledge management, visioning, emotional intelligence, empowerment, excellence and matrix management. In 1995, an American business consultant, Eileen Shapiro, produced a book called *Fad Surfing in the Boardroom*, in which she dissected with some humour the line of management fads that have held currency over the last few decades. Her advice to managers and consultants is to review, learn from and adapt the fads, using them if and where they help. Often pursuing a series of poorly implemented fads can be made to look as if change is happening. However, the work of the manager, even when assisted by a consultant, is to make the judgement to pursue only that which reinforces what is desirable and worth continuing and which discourages ineffective activity. Such is the range of theories and tools available in the world of organizational development and management consultancy that it is useful for a consultant to have recourse to handy summaries such as van Assen *et al.*'s *Key Management Models: The 60+ Models Every Manager Needs to Know* (2009), in order to understand the range of management models in use.

Staffan Canback (1998, p. 5) suggests that management consultancy has become a management technique itself. With the large numbers of consultants working across the world, it has become the means by which new tools, techniques and frameworks are rapidly spread through large organizations. In some areas their influence is even stronger. Canback argues that 'innovation in such areas as strategy is dominated by management consultants' (1998, p. 5). Management consultants, in promoting change and organizational development, will often bring in technical expertise, whether that is in finance, IT, production or human resources. They will also often combine this with a process consultation approach to offering help. Consider the following description of consulting offered by PricewaterhouseCoopers, whose origins lie in accountancy:

How a commercial consultancy sees consulting

We help organizations to work smarter and grow faster. Our work is always evolving to respond to industry trends and management focus, and we combine our deep technical skills in response to our clients' changing needs.

Over time, what we do remains closely linked with helping our clients improve the way they operate; innovate and grow; reduce costs; manage risks; leverage talent; and change the way they do business.

Our aim is to support you in designing, managing and executing lasting beneficial change.

(www.pwc.co.uk)

The offer is based on significant technical know-how but is clear that the consultor makes the judgements and decisions. Consulting is about support. Attention to context in terms of the changing environment means that the offer evolves, and there seems to be an underlying assumption that the working relationship between consultant and consultor will last for a long time, along the course of which lasting benefits will be achieved.

How useful then is management consulting in church settings? The fact that management consulting constantly draws on and encourages large quantities of new thinking, publishing and practice means that it has an innovative energy and dynamism to offer to the churches. Its use in commercial and public sectors where value for money, competition, accountability and continuous improvement are seen as key means, it offers a focused approach to delivery. It can also be attractive given that many church members who work in business or public service will recognize the tools and theories. This last consideration, among others, seems to have led to an assumption that it is possible simply to transfer secular organizational development and management techniques to church and community organizations. Great care is needed in this transfer to ensure that informed assumptions are made about the nature of churches as organizations and the relationships, aspirations and meanings carried within them. There may also be underpinning principles and theories that run counter to the values and principles on which churches are built. Stephen Pattison's *The Faith of the Managers: When Management becomes Religion* (1997) offers a healthy critique of the wholesale adoption of managerial principles in the churches. In his conclusion he says:

> Much that is useful and productive will probably emerge from the introduction of some managerial methods into religious communities. My own stance is not a Luddite one, and I hope it does not appear negative or alarmist. I am, nonetheless, very concerned that an insufficiently critical approach is being taken towards the introduction of the mantras of management into the overtly religious sphere. Part of the challenge of Christianity/religion to society is to promote a vision of human possibility, transcendence and mystery that stands over and against the closure and control represented by much management theory and practice.
>
> (1997, p. 166)

Texts and sources

The range of material available in the area of organizational development and management is so vast that it is difficult to recommend a small number of full texts. The following books provide summaries or readings from the most important and influential management thinking, from which it will be possible to explore further, when particular interest is piqued.

M. Kubr (ed.), 2002, *Management Consulting: A Guide to the Profession*, Geneva: ILO – *at 900 pages possibly the most comprehensive guide to management consulting, but divided into useful, digestible, practical chapters.*

J. M. Shafritz and J. S. Ott (eds), 2010, 9th edn, *Classics of Organization Theory*, Belmont, CA: Wadworth – *readings and excerpts from the most important writers on organizations and how they work and can change.*

G. Morgan, 2006, *Images of Organization*, Thousand Oaks, CA: Sage – *a remarkably rich range of images or metaphors of organizations.*

H. Mintzberg, B. Ahlstrad, and J. Lampel, 1998, *Strategy Safari: The Complete Guide through the Wilds of Strategic Management*, London: Prentice Hall – *a delightful ride through ten schools of how to do strategy in organizations.*

www.businessballs.com
– A free online learning resource providing, among much else, introductions to significant amounts of material on organizations, management and leadership. Treat as you would any online source.

Psychodynamic and systems psychodynamic approaches

Anton Obholzer's book, edited with Vega Zagier Roberts, *The Unconscious at Work: Individual and Organizational Stress in the Human Services*, first published in 1994, has been reprinted most years since. A series of essays contributed by current or former members of the Tavistock Clinic Consulting to Institutions Workshop, it has proved to be an important resource in understanding how organizations work and how consultants can be of use in working with them. The Tavistock Clinic was founded to help shell-shocked soldiers just after the First World War. With a culture of therapeutic practice, training and research, it developed not just its work with individuals but also with organizations. This meant applying their in-depth understanding of personal, psychological dynamics to what is happening in organizations, companies and institutions. Although there is no specific Tavistock model, the approach blends insights from psychoanalysis, for example from Freud and Melanie Klein, group relations from, for example, Bion, handling change from, for example, Winnicott, and organizational theory from, for example, Campbell and Huffington. The following quick sketch is aimed to point to a few of the key themes (among very many) in this approach that inform a psychodynamic consultant's work.

First, a central concern is what happens when people get anxious. From Klein comes the idea of paranoid-schizoid functioning, where the anxious individual will project the discomfort they are feeling on to others in the form of blame, scapegoating or making people goodies and baddies. They themselves may feel incompetent or powerless. If, however, the person is coping with their anxiety in a healthy way, they find what Klein calls a depressive state which is a constructive, balanced state to be in. As has already been shown, consultancy is typically about dealing with or generating change. Change is likely to cause anxiety and therefore to need containing. This, in a child's case, is normally provided by their mother. The holding environment she provides, the sense of safety and useful boundaries, allows the child to become ever more independent and accepting of the outside world in a way that allows him or her to function constructively. When working in an organization going through change, the organization should try to provide a safe holding or containment that the individual member can trust. Often the consultant can end up as the provider of that holding or as a component of its provision. A problem for an organization that employs or connects adults such as a church is that the ability of those adults to undergo change successfully, to trust the holding, depends on how successfully they have been through change situations from childhood on. If their experience has led them to believe that reliable holding is not normally available, the organization or the consultant will have to work very hard to have any chance of helping them through the change.

Second, with regard to the consultant's work, one of the characteristics of a consultant working from a psychodynamic perspective is that they will be constantly aware of the effect the unconscious has on what people say/don't say and do/don't do. The way consultors react, the words they use, what they avoid, whether they are late or prone to yawning, may offer insights into how they are affected by their work. The consultant will also be sensitive to transferences and counter-transferences happening during their interaction with the consultor. What do the consultant's feelings during or because of a session tell them about what is going on for the consultor(s)? Awareness of this and attention to professional distance is essential to avoid being drawn into unhelpful, collusive behaviour such as rescuing the consultor or allowing them to depend on you for solutions they can work out themselves, even if with some difficulty. (Some consultants find the insights of transactional analysis very helpful in this area. How it can help can be seen in the title of its founder Eric Berne's popular introduction to the field, *Games People Play* (1964).)

Third, with regard to people operating in groups, Wilfred Bion summed up in *Experiences in Groups* (1961) his understanding of how the unconscious processes in groups influence their effectiveness. Attention to the group's primary task, its work purpose for existing, can be overtaken by a second, which is to avoid attending to that primary task. This secondary task means that the group is demonstrating what Bion calls basic assumption behaviour (a group equivalent to Klein's paranoid-schizoid state) because it is too anxious or scared to face what they are supposed to do. Basic assumption behaviour can be seen in three types:

- *Dependency*. The fantasy is that the group members will have all their needs met by an omnipotent, omniscient leader. The members behave passively and offer no ideas of their own. They rely on the leader to provide direction because they see themselves as incompetent. Their resentment at their own impotence may lead them to depose the leader and find another one to idealize.
- *Fight–flight*. The fantasy is that the group must save itself whatever happens and they do this by running away or by hostile behaviour. Thus a group may be aggressive towards the leader and each other, chat, blame outside people or factors for everything that is going wrong, keep arriving late or just give up.
- *Pairing*. The fantasy is that the group has met to reproduce. It follows that two of the group will get together to produce the offspring, the messiah. This messiah may be a person, an idea or an action. The pair carry out the work of the group, generating ideas and plans, and nothing happens. The group give the pair great authority. However,

they need the pair to fail. If the pair succeed they have no need to keep hoping, and it is their hope that gives the group meaning. If the messiah is born, the messianic hope must disappear as it has been fulfilled. So, any actions or plans are likely to be scuppered before they reach fulfilment.

Understanding which of these is happening enables the leader or other member of the group to determine what they need to do to draw the group out of such behaviour.

Effective group functioning

According to Bion, the work group is that aspect of group functioning that has to do with the real task of the group. So, with a committee, PCC, home group, etc., which has come together for a particular purpose, the members of the work group co-operate as individuals and belong to it so the task can be accomplished. The leader is not the only one with leadership skills, and only leads when the situation needs this. The work group seeks for knowledge, learns from experience, constantly questions how to reach the goal, and it therefore results in growth and development, is in touch with reality and so on. Bion says that the characteristics of a work group are similar to the Freudian concept of the ego, which is that part of the mental apparatus that mediates between external reality and the rest of the self. How often have we been in groups like this?

Consultant Ian Fishwick, in an unpublished lecture
at York St John University, 2009

Fourth, with regard to organizations as systems, in work by the Tavistock and others, psychoanalytical and psychodynamic insights and frameworks have been developed into an understanding of organizations as systems, open to interact with the world in order to carry out their purpose. A psychodynamic systems approach focuses on the unconscious dynamics of the organization, on understanding what the deeper and hidden meaning might be of the behaviour demonstrated. It examines the interrelationships between key organizational features such as boundaries, roles, structure, leadership, authority and culture. By using psychodynamic concepts, the defences and anxieties and the resultant behaviours, patterns and structures that impede organizational effectiveness may be understood in a way that they can be managed.

Anton Obholzer says his favourite definition of consultancy is 'licensed stupidity' where the consultant can, 'as a non-member of the institution ... ask naïve questions' (Obholzer and Roberts, 1994, p. 210). When talking about the consultancy role, he says:

> The institution, therefore, is best served by a form of consultancy which does not have a preconceived idea of what the structure of the organization should be on the completion of the intervention, while giving the consultant opportunities to communicate ideas as they arise. A public process of striving towards understanding, instead, should determine the outcome ... The consultant, who offers a psychodynamic understanding of institutional process also brings a state of mind and a system of values that listens to people, encourages thought and takes anxieties and resistance into account.
>
> (1994, pp. 209–10)

In terms of this model's applicability in church contexts, the evidence is that it is widely used. Many ministers and lay workers have gone through groups at the Grubb Institute, and the popularity of books like Bruce Reed's *The Dynamics of Religion* (1978) attest to the model's impact. As complex, diverse groups that focus on what matters deeply to people but can be understood and articulated in hugely different ways, there is likely to be significant emotional content, both conscious and unconscious, in the way they behave as groups. Members and leaders invest intense, profound and lengthy commitment to what they perceive as the purpose of the churches and often interact with others in the group at an intimate level. The resultant aggression, dependency, leadership issues, transferences and so on may only be uncovered by a psychodynamic approach so that the church can move on healthily.

Texts and sources

A. Obholzer and V. Zagier Roberts (eds), 1994, *The Unconscious at Work: Individual and Organizational Stress in the Human Services*, London: Routledge – *a clear exposition (particularly in the first four chapters) of the issues in organizations that can impede its effective operation, especially in service organizations.*

W. Bion, 1961, *Experiences in Groups*, London: Routledge – *Bion's classic text on the unconscious processes in groups.*

D. Campbell and C. Huffington (eds), 2008, *Organizations Connected: A Handbook of Systemic Consultation*, London: Karnac – *essays from Tavistock consultants that lay out the systems approach to consulting.*

E. Nevis, 1987, *Organizational Consulting: A Gestalt Approach*, New York: Gardner Press – *the classic text on Gestalt consulting with its emphasis on understanding the whole (Gestalt) of a situation and all its interacting factors and how we try to make sense of our situations.*

Appreciative inquiry

Sometimes in working with churches and faith-based organizations the sense of struggle, past failure and impending slow death block any attempt to change, move forward and grow. A model of encouraging change that takes a distinctly positive approach is *appreciative inquiry*. This model was developed by organizational thinkers and practitioners in action research and was given a substantial, formal framework by David Cooperrider and colleagues in Ohio in the 1980s and 1990s. The basic premise of appreciative inquiry (often shortened to AI) is that, if you keep looking at the problems or difficulties you have got, then that is where you will remain. Indeed, you will find even more. If, however, your 'inquiry' is asking about what you do well, what is best about your organization and where you have had success, then that is what you will find. The desired change will happen because it will be based on what you are good at, what you know works. By understanding what is and has been the best you can be, being the best you can be in the future becomes more possible.

The key strength of AI is the way it asks questions to find and build on what is working well and turns that into a vision for the future.

Charles Elliott's description of AI's four process stages

- *Discovering periods of excellence and achievement*. Through interviews and storytelling, participants remember significant past achievements and periods of excellence. When was their organization or community functioning at its best? What happened to make those periods of excellence possible? By telling stories, people identify and analyze the unique factors – such as leadership, relationships, technologies, core processes, structures, values, learning processes, external relations, or planning methods – that contributed to peak experiences.

- *Dreaming an ideal organization or community*. In this step people use past achievements to envisage a desired future. This aspect of appreciative inquiry is different from other vision-creating or planning methodologies because the images of the community's future that emerge are grounded in history, and as such represent compelling possibilities. In this sense appreciative inquiry is both practical, in that it is based on the 'positive present,' and generative, in that it seeks to expand the potential of the organization or community.

- *Designing new structures and processes*. This stage is intended to be provocative – to develop, through consensus, concrete short- and long-term goals that will achieve the dream. Provocative propositions usually take the form of statements such as, 'This community will do whatever is necessary to build a school and have a full primary cycle within the next year.' Or, 'This company will champion innovation by creating new teams that integrate marketing and product development more effectively.' Or, 'This village will protect what remains of the local forest and will plant one thousand trees over the next two seasons to ensure the forest's survival for future generations.' Provocative propositions should stretch an organization or community, but they should also be achievable because they are based on past periods of excellence.

- *Delivering the dream*. In this stage, people act on their provocative propositions, establishing roles and responsibilities, developing strategies, forging institutional linkages and mobilizing resources to achieve their dream. New project plans will be developed and initiated, new relationships will be established and the group will proceed with vision and a renewed sense of purpose. As a result of the appreciative process, people will have a better understanding of the relevance of new initiatives to the long-term vision of the organization or community.

(Elliott, 1999, pp. 15–16)

Although AI was originally developed for use in commercial corporations, it has proved popular in voluntary and not-for-profit organizations, for example churches and international development work. Its use of imagination, memory and stories, and its positive demeanour mean that it offers a less gloomy way of delivering change than some other approaches' fixation with sorting out problems. As Gervase Bushe says, 'as a change process appreciative inquiry is a powerful "pull" strategy' rather than the exhausting pushing that can characterize many a change process (1998, p. 50). Theologically it focuses attention on God's generosity in gifting the Church and its people in so many ways. In particular, it helps churches look at where they can successfully make a difference instead of feeling that they have to deliver an unmanageable range of mission and pastoral activities, which was how their church appears in their fantasies about the past. It may be ironic to say this, but the problem with AI is that it can ignore or underestimate the ability of difficulties to obstruct the process of constructive change, especially if the process is applied in a shallow way.

Texts and sources

D. L. Cooperrider, D. Whitney, J. M. Stavros, 2008, *Appreciative Inquiry Handbook*, 2nd edn, Brunswick, OH: Crown Custom Publishing – *a solid introduction to the theory and techniques of AI by its creator among others.*

C. Elliott, 1999, *Locating the Energy for Change: An Introduction to Appreciative Inquiry*, Winnipeg, MB: International Institute for Sustainable Development – *a clear, passionate introduction to AI by a renowned Christian economist and expert in development issues. The whole book can be downloaded free at www.iisd.org/ai/locating. htm.*

Complexity and chaos approaches

One of the criticisms that is laid against traditional organizational and consultancy models is that they assume an ability to predict, control and direct what happens in an organization. The struggle that many leaders and consultants have in achieving results through what can be seen as a mechanistic, programmatic approach to human systems and change led some to speculate that such an approach was not just very difficult but possibly based on the wrong assumptions. By the 1980s the Santa Fe Institute in New Mexico had developed an approach to complex systems in sciences such as evolutionary biology, ecology, climate change and global economic patterns. In an interdisciplinary collaboration it provided a forum in which scientists from different subject areas could compare notes on what they were seeing in their research in terms of emergent, adaptive, co-evolving behaviours in complex systems. This became known as the *complexity sciences*. The chaotic and unpredictable nature of what seems to happen in organizations led organizational theorists to draw parallels between complex chaotic systems in science, such as our immune systems, the weather or a beehive, and human entities such as a big company or the health service. The characteristics of the systems in science, being both chaotic and stable at the same time or the way they evolve with emergent properties via complex responsive processes, were seen to offer potential insights into how complex human organizations operate and within them how to understand change.

Central principles in a complexity approach, particularly for the consultant, include:

- Change happens on the edge of chaos, the boundary between order and chaos. This means that there has to be an openness to being out of control in that creative place where it becomes possible, if the participants are aware, to see patterns emerging. This means we have to live with and handle anxiety and uncertainty. When the next stage is found, we also have to avoid the temptation to settle into an over-controlled place away from the edge as this is likely to be a place of slow stultification and death.
- Complex systems are always trying to self-organize. Feedback between the individuals acting on a local level with each other and with the environment indicates where there are spaces and possibilities to move into. Such feedback may be as a result of competition or collaboration or both.
- Like the famous flap of a butterfly's wing in South America 'causing' the hurricane in Siberia, small actions can have big effects.
- In human systems, conversation is a key tool in understanding organizational processes. Rather than imposing a plan or strategy, listening to what members of the organization are talking about in, for example, a coffee break will allow insight into what people think important and where development can be and is happening. The skill needed from leaders, the organization and consultants is to do what

complexity theorists refer to as sensemaking. By listening, questioning, facilitating conversation, reflecting, and coping with the lack of control, they need to identify the repeating patterns emerging that may well indicate the direction in which the organization should go.

- Any leadership or consultancy invention, even just listening, has an impact on the system. This may be large or small.
- There may be a small number of simple, epigenetic rules that determine the behaviour of a large group of individuals like the rules that keep a flock of geese in formation while in flight.

A complexity approach has significant attractions for the church consultant. Its close attention to what is going on at a local level and what is said and done by individuals values and respects every member of church and society. Its emphasis on living on the edge of chaos and waiting for self-ordering patterns to emerge rather than imposing plans resonates with the Spirit blowing where it wills and the dynamic, creative, trinitarian dance at the heart of God. As Christians we are called to live in a constant, possibly uncertain state of self-examination, open to conversion, renewal and transformation, looking for signs of suffering, redemption and resurrection.

Weaknesses in the complexity approach lie, first, in the question of whether it is possible to apply scientific models and theories to a social science topic. Terms like uncertainty, chaos, complexity and emergence have specific scientific definitions and applications. Is it possible to apply a scientific theory divorced from its context and the data that give it meaning to a social science setting? It may be that it becomes simply a metaphor being applied by people who are not in a position to understand the original science. Second, as has already been said in this chapter, a complexity approach consultant will often struggle to get people to understand how they are working. They may be confused by the lack of plan, clear schedule or any description of tangible outputs. This will especially be the case where members of a church group are used to more managerial approaches from their secular or previous church experience of consultancy and change processes.

Texts and sources

M. Wheatley, 2001, *Leadership and the New Science: Discovering Order in a Chaotic World*, 2nd edn, San Francisco: Berrett-Koehler – *a challenging, influential introduction to the application of modern scientific concepts to the world of organizations, strong on chaos theory.*

R. Lewin and B. Regine, 2000, *Weaving Complexity and Business: Engaging the Soul at Work*, New York: Texere – *a well-written introduction to complexity and its application in organizations.*

P. Shaw, 2002, *Changing Conversations in Organisations: A Complexity Approach to Change*, London: Routledge – *an account of how one consultant from the Hertfordshire University Complexity and Management Centre works constructively with the messiness of conversations in organizations.*

Information about the work, history and approach of the Santa Fe Institute may be found at www.santafe.edu.

Conclusion

The aim of this chapter has been to offer the consultant, potential or actual, pause for thought. How a consultant works with consultors should be based on carefully tested theory filtered through the consultant's reflective assessment of its effectiveness, impact and ethics. As has been seen, a consultant's praxis, their model in action, is not merely theory or skill or personality or theology, but a complicated, interactive, nurturing mixture of them all and more. The recommendation of this chapter is that it is a worthwhile and important part of a consultant's work to spend some time when starting up, as well as at regular intervals along the professional way, to check if and how their model coheres.

7

Analysis and Design

The aim of this chapter is to examine some of the issues concerning analysis and design based on one consultant's experience over a number of years and in particular situations. The areas to be covered involve working with individuals, groups and organizations, and in one-off interventions, over a series of sessions and in extended projects. Examples of models used and theories employed are given to illustrate how tools that consultants have grown to trust can be used. It is not the aim of this chapter to push a particular framework over and above all others but to encourage consultants to test out what works for them seriously in the situations they operate in.

It may seem that 80 per cent of the way through a book about consulting is a bit late to start to discuss the analysis of problems and the design of solutions and plans. However, it is the logic and contention of this book that a productive, reflective combination of all the areas that have been discussed up to this point is necessary in order for a consultant to be of use to the consultor. This is the basis of the learning and reflective cycles mentioned in Chapter 1, the practice of improving how we work by thinking about what we have done and holding that up to the light of tested theories and models. This stands at the heart of any consultant's professionalism. Furthermore, if you take the work of writers such as Albert Bandura seriously, our ability to perform successfully in situations, in his terms *self-efficacy* (Bandura, 1977), is most likely to improve if we reflect on occasions when we have performed well in similar situations.

Holding with Lovell's schema of eight stages in creative and imaginative thought for the process of a consultation (see Chapter 5), this chapter assumes the standard three phases within that are, as he puts it, 'studying things as they are; ... defining what needs to be done; working out how to do things' (Lovell 2000, p. 79). Thus, the first two phases can be seen as analysis and the third as design. Thorough analysis will in many cases not only provide a clear understanding of the issue from the consultor's point of view but also often reveal the design of what needs to be done about the issue. The design process entails building that discovery into a workable plan. However, in other cases, the solution is not so clear. Design may involve tackling the issue from a new angle or with completely different techniques and structures. Using a robust, integrative, organizational and ecclesiological model helps in this. It should provide both analysis (the understanding of the issues, its context, strengths, problems, the causal relationships behind its present deficiencies and consequent implications) and design (solutions and plans to deal with the presenting and discovered issues). In addition to this, robust models will have a predictive use. Often the analysis of a church issue will reveal that it is not possible to construct a perfect solution and plan. A good model will not only tell you what is needed for something to work well but will also tell you what will happen if it is not possible to create the ideal conditions you desire. This is typically an issue where consultors are tempted to apply business management models directly. For example, although ministers may see and want to treat church volunteers as serious, professional workers, they do not have the employment bureaucracy role relationships to enforce accountability and manage performance. The predictive ability of rigorous theories allows the design stage to foresee the difficulties they will have in managing volunteers. The predictions associated with what the model sees as ideal conditions in handling a team of workers mean that consultor and consultant will build elements into the plan to address the lack of managerial authority. If what is expected in a business setting is impossible, they will help the consultor recognize the limits of what they can do. It may be, alternatively, that models that function well in business settings are not appropriate for the churches, even if adapted, and other approaches which fit better should be used.

After some comments about an often underestimated tool of consultancy, how we use questions, the chapter looks at three types of consultancies that consultants are regularly asked to undertake: working with an individual, working on a single occasion with a group, and working on a long-term project to effect some major change. Sample approaches are discussed to indicate how the work might be undertaken with examinations of a number of critical features of each. There are three sections:

1 Working with an individual
  • Exploring the nature of a consultor's role and work
  • What is the right work?
  • What are the psychological issues?

- Handling a consultancy over many sessions
- Getting a one-sided picture.
2 One-off interventions with a group
3 Organizational studies and analyses
  - Critical issues – building trust and commitment
  - Critical issues – the nature and usefulness of the research
  - Moving into design
  - Systems design
  - Implementation and measurement.

Questions

An essential tool at each stage of a consultancy is questions. The consultant needs to understand the different types of questions and when the different types are best used. With experience, consultants will also build a stock of question formats that have proved useful. A colleague of mine refers to 'killer questions', questions that may shock or challenge, but that unblock the consultancy process and encourage an important, new insight. These are good ones to make note of.

Question types often used in encounters like consultancies, with some examples, are:

- *Open questions*: encouraging the consultor to talk widely, avoiding single-word or brief answers, and exploring how the consultor thinks and feels.

  What do you enjoy about your work?
  How do you feel your work is going?
  How would you describe your relationship with *Chris*?

- *Directed questions*: encouraging the consultor to prioritize by narrowing the field down.

  What are the three areas where you see most room to improve?
  How do you think your congregation feel when you turn up late?
  Where are the key areas that I could help you with?
  What would you like us to look at now?

- *Closed questions*: encouraging answers of few words which can elicit or check facts, clarify actions and reinforce commitment.

  Who compiles the rota?
  How long do you spend writing your sermon?
  When did you last have a day off?
  Exactly when will you start the change we have just agreed?

- *Reflective, paraphrasing or summarizing questions*: ensuring the consultant has understood both the content and feeling of what the consultor has said, validating what has been said and restating or organizing what has been said in a way that might enhance both parties' grasp of the issues.

    So are you saying ...?

    If I understand you correctly, that means ...?

    So your main issues are ...?

    So, you are feeling ...?

    What would you think if I said there might be a pattern here, in that every time you ...?

- *Hypothetical questions*: encouraging the consultor to explore specific, possible options or potential solutions.

    If you were to move your day off from Saturday to Monday, how would that work?

    How could you run that meeting so that it didn't take more than 90 minutes?

    How do you think the Women's Fellowship would feel if you didn't turn up every week and how would you deal with that?

The shape of a consultancy will often dictate the type of questions to be asked. A common trajectory is

1 exploratory, open questions at first to lay out the issues, with reflecting questions to check understanding;
2 then directed and hypothetical questions to open options and test practicalities;
3 finally, closed questions to ensure clarity, check dates and plan, and to assess commitment to taking action.

The reality will have more cycles and loops in it, but the sequence of questions should enable the flow of analysis and design. There are useful lists of questions in many of the resources available to consultants which will help in building this section of their toolkit, for example in Campbell and Huffington's *Organizations Connected: A Handbook of Systemic Consultation* (2008, p. 25ff), Hopkins and Hedley's *Coaching for Missional Leadership* (2008, Chapter 5 and p. 160), Widdicombe's *Meetings that Work* (2000, pp. 51ff.) and Shier-Jones' *Pioneer Ministry and Fresh Expressions of Church* (2009, pp. 60, 120). There are also some very useful tools scattered through Leach and Paterson's *Pastoral Supervision* (2010), especially in terms of getting consultors to talk about their work.

This may feel like basic listening skills and that is what it is. Yet, conscious reflection on what types of question a consultant is using when and why can support constructive consultancy process immensely. A consultant should be a skilled active listener, monitoring not just what is said but also non-verbal and body language. This means that all the messages the consultor is receiving reinforce each other consistently and that all the messages the consultor is giving out, spoken and unspoken, are heard. Some consultors benefit from aids in ensuring messages are well captured, validated and structured. A flipchart, a whiteboard or just pieces of paper shared by the consultor and consultant can be really helpful. Using paper or a flipchart means that alternative, descriptive methods, such as pictures, flow charts or diagrams, become a possibility. Care needs to be taken if the consultant is writing up or drawing what has been said on a flipchart in case it is seen as rephrasing in the consultant's terms. This can introduce tensions about whose meaning has priority. Interestingly, control of the marker pen can be important, as this may symbolize powerfully who is running the show. The value of these visual aids is seen in how often consultors are very keen to take the flipchart sheets away with them at the end of sessions. A general point is to ensure that the techniques, processes and tools take account of the way different people think and learn. What has worked for the consultant or has worked with past consultors may not be the best way of working with the present consultor. Having both a range of methods and the flexibility to adopt different strategies appropriate to the situation is important.

Working with an individual

The build-up of questions over time allows consultant and consultor to work though a whole range of factors that might impact on the issue being addressed. A common issue on which consultants are asked to work with ministers is the management and organization of their work. Often this will be expressed as needing to do some work on their time management. There are plenty of books and websites that provide effective solutions and advice around time management, and it may be that the consultor just needs to read and apply one of those. More commonly, though, the issue is a complex of personal, organizational, theological and contextual factors. This is where questioning demonstrates its effectiveness.

After the contracting meeting, a useful start is to get the consultor to lay out their situation briefly in writing, perhaps in an email sent to the consultant before their first meeting. The session starts with the first, open question: 'Will you tell me about the issue you want to work on in our sessions?' In the 'time management' case, the consultant's questions may uncover a picture of the minister's study, the way their diary looks, the setting in which they work, the number of churches and organizations, structures and role relationships, with the way they have dealt with demands from church members, their expectations of themselves as a minister and their skills in using a computer or chairing a meeting. Both consultant and consultor at this stage have to listen for clues in what is being said. For the consultor, just laying out their situation in the presence of an interested listener may reveal patterns and useful insights.

One helpful question tool, which I learnt from a colleague, Ian Macdonald, is *chasing the verb*. A minister recounting their busy work life will use verbs to describe what they do. 'I *lead* the worship', or 'I *run* the Pastoral Visiting Group'. Chasing the verb means asking what they mean by *run* or *lead*. *Leading the worship* might mean preparing the whole service, reading all the lessons, preaching the sermon, doing the prayers, opening the church, organizing the coffee rota and setting out the chairs and the books. Alternatively, it might mean enabling the worship group, training worship ministers of various kinds, developing systems that include as many people and talents as possible and encouraging a culture of every-member participation over a number of years. The work involved in these is quite different, demanding different capability and purpose. Such different ways of looking at the work of leading worship also betray very different operant and possibly espoused understandings of ministry, priesthood, leadership and ecclesiology. Each of the verbs in the descriptions of what *lead* means can then be interrogated to see what the work and the intention of the minister might be. Eventually, open and directed questions might give way to paraphrasing questions or ones that suggest hypotheses about what the action of the verbs might imply about the minister's approach and about tackling the problem they have brought.

Problems, cases and situations

A useful way into the presentation of consultancy issues is to make use of Lovell's distinction between problems, cases and situations (1994, pp. 29, *passim*). Whether this is a problem, a case or a situation will shift the approach to be taken appropriately in terms of tools used, factors taken into consideration and reasonable expectations of outcomes.

- A *problem* is a current, limited issue (not necessarily small) that is providing difficulties for the consultor (individual or group) at the moment. The work the consultor wants to do is to try and come up with a solution to the problem, which can help now or in the near future.
- A *case*, sometimes the subject of a case study, is an issue that has finished but that, usually but not always, did not finish satisfactorily. The work to be done is to examine the whole story of the case, particularly what the consultor did and did not do in order to learn from what happened.
- A *situation* is a very broad depiction of where a person or a group is at the moment, particularly at a stage when they feel they could be moving on to something different. The work in talking about a situation needs to range back into the past and the individual's journey so far, into the future with their hopes and ambitions, and sideways in all directions to look at the context, the work being done, the understanding of church, ministry and mission and how the consultor sits in the midst of all that in terms of feelings, effectiveness, energy levels, change, development and beliefs.

Exploring the nature of a consultor's role and work

For both consultor and consultant, effective questioning and drilling down into what is meant in practice and in the theory in the consultor's head can reveal a variety of important, relevant factors. These can deal with the individual's understanding of their church as an organization, with the understanding of what a role such as minister means and entails, and with the individual's assumptions and beliefs about their ability to function and fit effectively into the role and the organization.

The Grubb Institute has done considerable work on the three-way interaction of the individual, their role and their organization. One of the Institute's key insights is the notion of the 'organization in the mind'. The way people in roles in organizations conceive those organizations has a huge impact on the way they and the organization function. Jean Hutton, the Grubb Institute's former Managing Consultant, tells the following story:

I had a client, a Methodist minister in the United States, who was sent to a developing, up-market housing area to establish a new church. Together with a small group of residents they agreed that their aim was to grow a church. Two years on they had a very large congregation and an extensive programme of church activities. When he presented his situation to me he indicated that he was concerned that they had lost their way. After several sessions a hypothesis emerged to suggest why this had happened. Though they had applied the label 'church' to their institution, at an unconscious level their institution-in-the-mind was about being a *business*. The local lay people, who were themselves highly successful in their business and professional careers, were more familiar with a business culture and automatically applied it to their new institution, the church. Together with the minister they developed an organization-in-the-mind along the lines of running a business, a venture in which they succeeded. Somehow in the process the meaning of church was lost.

(2003, p. 1)

The first phase of consultancy, through questioning and consultors describing their understanding of their role, of themselves in role and of their organization, uncovers what they really think. For example, in this case, they see their church as a business. There are many helpful models, which provide frameworks for locating these constructs. For example, adapting the Grubb approach, useful discussion can follow from the description of the consultor's situation in terms of where the issue sits as an interaction of the three elements (person, role, organization) within their context. Setting it out visually can be very helpful (see Figure 7.1).

Getting the consultor to describe their understanding and mental construct of each element and the way they overlap allows the consultation to focus on areas where work is needed. It can also help to check if the issue is properly one for work consultancy. For example, if the issue is mostly in the person circle, it may be that counselling is the right sort of help. Work consultancy will generally operate in the overlap areas. This tool can also help to identify whether the work being done in the consultancy is addressing all the areas it should. Some consultants are more interested in the influence of personality on effectiveness and concentrate on that. This may have the consequence of giving too little attention to the organization structures or systems that make it difficult for the consultor to do their job.

Another useful three-element model to help understand where the source of problems might be is to examine the work and the role in terms of its people dimension, its programming dimension and its technical dimension (P, Pr and T – see Figure 7.2). The technical dimension

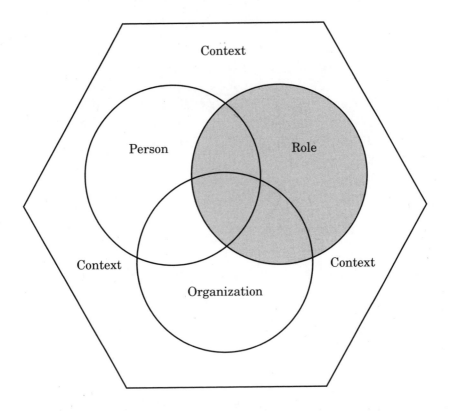

*Figure 7.1 The consultor's situation: person, role and
organization in context*

focuses on developing the technical knowledge and skill to achieve an
output. This might be theological or liturgical knowledge, skill in using
PowerPoint, or accountancy training. It might be knowledge of marriage law and systems or theories of change management. The programming dimension concerns organizing what needs to happen in terms
of planning, timing, scheduling and ensuring the sequence of activities
in series and parallel enables delivery on time. The people dimension
addresses the interaction with people that needs to be undertaken successfully in order for the work to get done. Different roles and tasks
have different combinations and proportions of the three components.
However, it is hard to imagine any role that does not make demands in
all three, however much the role-holder might feel most comfortable in
just one of them.

Many ordained roles have considerable freedom to define what they
do, when and how. Looking at what the role needs in terms of these

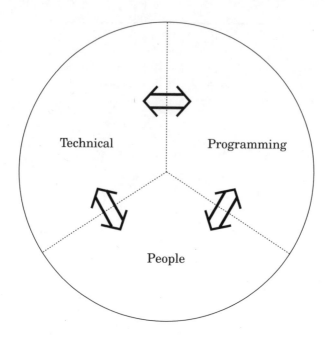

Figure 7.2 The dimensions of work (P, Pr and T)

three elements and at what the minister in that role is doing in practice may explain why they are feeling stressed. It should offer avenues to explore to relieve the stress so that the minister becomes more effective in role. In any organization, leadership roles are likely to have a larger proportion of the people and programming components. Although they will have accountability for a range of technical areas, they do not need to be, and cannot be, technical experts in all those areas. The people and programming components indicate that they need to have the right people in post in those technical areas at the right time and have the people skills to ensure that they give good advice and produce the desired work when and in the quality required. This model helps in identifying whether the minister is doing the right work. I remember once meeting my local minister coming out of a hole in the ground on the afternoon of Christmas Eve. The boiler in the church had broken down and needed to be fixed for the midnight service. He was down in the boiler room with his overalls on. I wondered whether this should have been his work on Christmas Eve. He was capable of it and loved fiddling about with mechanical things. Using the P, Pr and T model raises questions about what he was doing. Is there other work he should be doing? Is his personal interest in fixing things getting in the way of ensuring that the people who should be fixing the heating are doing their job? Are there role issues in organizational terms and theological terms about what a minister's role is and the structural, working relationships with lay members of the church? Is there a pattern of unbalanced focus here? Or is it just an emergency on a day when the heating needed to work to which he was responding when he had time and others were busy?

What is the right work?

The question of what the right work is and whether the minister is doing it comes up repeatedly in consultancy. Ministers and other workers feel frustrated that they seem to be constantly diverted from the work they want to do. This may be laid at the door of the demands put on them by the role and the local and regional church that is their setting. On the other hand, it may be a function of their personality and preferred style of working. A useful model for examining whether the right work is being done, from the world of management studies, is Stephen Covey's *Urgent/Important* matrix (1994, pp. 150–82; see Figure 7.3).

Covey's drive is to help workers be more effective by ensuring they understand what is important for them in their work. In Quadrant I are tasks that are important in achieving your purpose and have a pressing deadline. So, these must be attended to. In Quadrant II sits the range of activities that create the conditions for effectiveness. They are about planning, building relationships, research, training and development, looking for new ways to do things, building supportive systems and structures and preventing failures. Quadrant III houses activities that tempt and seduce the worker into devoting significant time and energy to them, but that contribute very little to making progress. Quadrant IV activities are a complete waste of time. The principle is to spend as much time and effort in Quadrant II as possible as this will sustain and

	Urgent	Not urgent
Important	Quadrant I	Quadrant II
Not important	Quadrant III	Quadrant IV

Figure 7.3 Covey's Urgent/Important matrix

improve the ability to be effective. It will also reduce the quantity of work done in Quadrant I as the conditions will increasingly be built where most things happen in an orderly, predictable, managed way and emergencies become rarer and rarer.

One minister I worked with, whom I shall call Jenny, came for consultancy on a problem that had been identified as time management. Using Covey's matrix we looked at the distribution of her time and energy in her role. Jenny saw that she spent a lot of time in Quadrant I dealing with urgent and important things like funerals or a pastoral problem. Yet some of the work there, what she saw as fire-fighting, could have been reduced if she and the churches' activities were better organized and planned. She also spent a lot of time in Quadrant III, often because she was not good at saying no to people who interrupted what she was doing and wanted a lot of her time immediately. She was surprised how much time she spent in Quadrant IV, surfing the web, checking for emails and having nice conversations with folk she liked for rather longer than necessary. She realized that she should be doing much more work in Quadrant II but spent hardly any time there at all. So, having done a detailed analysis of the types of activities that fitted in which quadrants, part of the commitment to action at the end of each session was a small but significant plan to reduce working in Quadrant IV, then III, then I, and to build up the time and energy spent in Quadrant II. Acknowledging that work in Quadrant II needs concentration, focus and protection, the plan included building support among the congregations for the new way in which their minister was going to be working and strategies to resist the tempting charms of Quadrants IV and III. The steps needed to be small at first, such as only answering emails in the first hour of the day when at her desk. The confidence Bandura talks about needed to be built on small successes before she tackled large-scale change.

Using analytical tools such as Covey's must sit alongside reference to theological models of church, mission, ministry (lay and ordained), community, collaboration and leadership. The consultant does not need to be an expert in all such different models from theological and management sources. The key work here is to examine the consistency of the consultor's espoused picture of their role and what they actually do. Reflecting, paraphrasing questions can be pertinent here as the consultor works out whether their everyday actions and decisions are contributing to achieving the model of church and community they espouse. It can be quite a shock for a consultor when they are faced with a range of Quadrant I behaviours that are undermining what they believe in deeply and are hoping to build.

A desirable state in any organization is that the right people are in the right roles doing the right work (Macdonald *et al.*, 2006, p. 60). Much of what has been said in the past few paragraphs deals with the right work. It is helpful to have a scheme that describes the nature of that work, such as that offered by Elliott Jaques' Requisite Organization theories (see, for example, his *A General Theory of Bureaucracy*, 1976). By understanding the different levels of complexity that are needed in order for organizations to work well, it enables that work to be allocated to both the right role in the organization (someone in a position to get that work done) and to someone with the capability to do the necessary problem-solving (someone who can do it). By describing the work complexity involved, a discussion can happen as to whether the minister has the capability to undertake the work. If that is not the case, the consultancy discussion might move to how to acquire that capability by the use of the congregation or external resources. It might ultimately lead to a discussion about whether the minister is the right person for the job. Does that mean redefining the role, the minister moving on, or examining different ways of working such as collaboration? (A readable introduction to Jaques can be found in Art Kleiner's article, 'Elliott Jaques Levels with You', which can be downloaded from various sites such as www.well.com/~art/s%2Bb12001cm.html/)

What are the psychological issues?

In describing her situation, Jenny expressed strong feelings of frustration and stress at what she found herself doing. She said she felt a clash between what she liked doing and felt she ought to be doing and what she was expected to do by her churches. She was surprised how tiring she found this job having worked in high-pressure business roles before ordination. The analysis done in the sessions of how she spent her time made sense in terms of the Myers Briggs personality tests she had done. She knew she needed more space to recover from social interactions than she was getting. No mealtime or sitting down to listen to *The Archers* seemed to be safe from a phone call or a knock at the door. In order to investigate why this might have been, she undertook an energy audit as laid out in Lovell's *Consultancy for Ministry and Mission* (2000, pp. 405–6). As her frustration was both in how she saw herself working and in the way that the churches' culture made people behave, Lovell's offer of a second energy audit – for the situation – offered the possibility of understanding more of her context as a person in role in an organization.

Lovell's energy audits

1 A personal energy audit
- From where and in what ways do you find the emotional, intellectual, physical, moral and spiritual energy to do your work?
- How do you draw upon them?
- What is the present quality of your energy here and now?
- What does 'energy' mean to you?
- What metaphors and concepts do you use to think about it?
- Do you experience positive or negative surges of energy? When? What causes them? What good and bad effects do they have upon you? And others?
- What consumes most energy? Why?
- What saps your energy? Why?
- What galvanizes you?
- What renews your energy? How?
- What restricts or blocks your energy? Why?

What are the implications of the observations you have made above?

2 A situational energy audit
- Who or what are the main sources of emotional, intellectual, physical, moral and spiritual energy in your working situation?
- How do individuals draw upon them?
- What is the quality of this energy? How is it renewed and developed?
- What importance do people attach to it?
- What metaphors and concepts do people use to describe the energy in the organization?
- Are there positive or negative surges of energy in the organization? When? What causes them? What good and bad effects do they have?
- What consumes most energy? Why?
- What saps energy? Why?
- What galvanizes people collectively?
- What renews the energy flow? How?
- What restricts or blocks the energy flow? Why?

What are the implications of the observations you have made above?

(Lovell, 2000, pp. 405–6)

Many church workers will be used to personality and personal style assessment tools such as Myers Briggs or the Enneagram. The energy audit can work well with workers who already understand what feeds them and what exhausts them. It becomes possible to see why some tasks are frustrating. Some of the tasks a worker finds exhausting or difficult, because they are counter to their natural preferences, might be productively handed over to others; some that they have to do themselves might benefit from developing approaches that limit how much time they absorb by planning carefully what the purpose of the activity is, how long it should take and what time of day or of the week would be a good time to undertake it. It is important to encourage the minister to understand that there is no ideal or single right personal profile to be a good minister. Francis and Robbins say:

> Different personality profiles equip individual pastors to exercise ministry in distinctive and predictable ways. Certain expectations of ministry, for example, are fulfilled most adequately by stable extraverts. Locating neurotic introverts into such posts runs the risk of disappointing the congregations which hold such expectations and harming the health of the pastor. There are other equally valuable areas of ministry in which the neurotic introvert would excel and where the stable extravert would experience and generate disappointment. The God who creates diversity in personality may also rejoice in diversity in ministry.
>
> (2004, p. 25)

Using tools such as the energy audit, the Covey Urgent/Important matrix and insights from the personality assessments will often reveal influential, psychological processes. If a minister is clear that they are doing work in Quadrant III that they do not think is important and that they do not like doing, it is worth investigating what is going on to make them feel guilt, anxiety and anger. Are there issues around established power relationships and culture? If consultor and consultant feel competent enough, work can be done together to identify projections and transferences and develop tactics to handle this, both in identifying the psychodynamic transfers and working out responses when they happen.

Handling a consultancy over many sessions

It is sometimes the case that a consultor is enthusiastic in consultancy sessions to talk about their work, to play with models and theories and to promise change by the next session. When the next session comes, the consultor may report successes or backsliding as if to a parent. The consultant can become a figure to whom a consultor feels accountable. If consultants have been careful to write up what happened in each session, they may have a clearer recall than the consultor. This can reinforce the parent–child relationship unless the consultant challenges what is happening. If the intention of a consultancy process is to enable a permanent, constructive change in the consultor's behaviour, consultants can become anxious (like a parent) about whether consultors will continue to behave in a consistent way or revert to their familiar, unhelpful patterns when the consultancy sessions finish. Insights from the psychodynamic approaches to consultancy are helpful here. Consultant and consultor need to talk about how the consultor might maintain the behaviours they have identified as useful. This could centre on creating and maintaining systems, support, supervision and regular checks. It might even include continuing to work with a work consultant, even if less frequently.

Getting a one-sided picture

One of the uncertainties in working on analysis with an individual on their own is how reliable their picture of any situation is. It is always the case that anyone's understanding of their situation is going to be more or less partial. In consultancy, this can be more extreme than usual as the reason for asking for help may arise out of painful breakdown, feelings of inadequacy, unfair expectations and unjust treatment. Given the confidential nature of what goes on in a consultancy, it is often difficult as well as inappropriate to validate what is said. All that can be relied on is the genuine desire of the consultor to deal with reality. They will want to test their own perspective through the ability of the consultancy process in all its variety to help the consultor home in on the truth. Often a fruitful, essential piece of work is to encourage the consultor to stand in the shoes of the other people involved in the situation, particularly those whose behaviour and apparent beliefs the consultor finds difficult to understand. The cultural gap between the consultor's world-view and the beliefs of antagonists in the situation in their church is indispensable material for the analysis. Without understanding and dealing with this gap, proposed solutions are likely to fail.

In working with an individual, opening up a simple-seeming topic such as poor time management can uncover a wide variety of issues from many disciplines. These may concern managing work and time, the effect personality has on how work gets done, understanding the work of the role, structurally and theologically, especially the role of a leader, recognizing psychological and cultural pressures in organizations, and managing change. This analysis forms the basis of the design phase. The gap between the ideal and the reality provides a template for designing the plan to address the issue. The models suggested here are not meant to be an exclusive set. There are many, including the ubiquitous three-element models (as triangles, overlapping circles or a circle divided into three like the Mercedes Benz logo) and 2x2 matrices, which experienced consultants will pick up to populate their toolkit.

It is becoming increasingly common for ministers to use a work consultant or a work consultancy group regularly throughout their ministry rather than just when they have a problem or a particular challenge, just as they use a spiritual director. Such an ongoing support is a sign of a healthy reflective approach to practice and can be a significant help in maintaining perspective and releasing pressure as well as problem-solving.

One-off interventions with a group

The role of an internal consultant or the need to encompass enough work to earn a living mean that consultants' portfolios will often include activities such as teaching, training and facilitation. A common request is a workshop, to run a day or a weekend session with a group. This may be expressed as 'team building', an away day or strategic planning. There are obvious constraints on what can be achieved in a day, so the preparation phase becomes immensely important. Contracting for such an event can be difficult but benefits from persistence. Getting a clear understanding of the reason for the day – why it is happening and what it is hoped will be achieved – is essential. If the consultors' grasp of the purpose and desired outcome of the day is cloudy, the consultant can help them focus their thoughts and encourage a sense of realism about how much it is possible to achieve in a day. It may be, on negotiation, that just laying the issue out clearly so that there is a shared appreciation of the present situation is enough. Part of the contracting will involve managing expectations round the event.

A crucial question is why they want an external person to come in when, in many churches, there are people perfectly competent to run such a day. Is it about having an independent view or allowing those who could run the day to take part as contributors? Is it that they hope an expert from the diocese or a fancy commercial consultant will have the answers? For a local church, an away day can be a significant investment of time, money and emotional energy for a significant number of people. This may be heightened if the day is seen as the key to moving on to the next stage, to finding the answer or to breaking a stalemate. This puts enormous pressure on the consultant to provide not just a process that helps but answers to their problems and plans for their dreams. Working with a group should not differ from working with an individual in the constant effort to ensure an adult–adult working partnership and the promotion of the group's skills as consultors. So the agreed process for the day should support the assumption that everyone is there to work and contribute; that it is for the church group to identify and take any decisions; and that the consultant is there to help them do the thinking. At every stage, the group should be clear about what is happening and why, with an overall picture of the day given at the start. In an example of a one-day session, participation can be encouraged by participants understanding how what is done first thing in the morning sets the tone for the working style for the whole day. Participants should be clear that the tools used to understand the problem and construct a shared picture will then build into the design in the afternoon. The methods used to involve all the participants need to address the fact that some people are comfortable talking in a big group and some not; some people think verbally, some in pictures, some quickly and some slowly.

Advice Centre volunteers reconnecting with their vision

A local Churches Together set up an advice centre in an English town, as there was no Citizens' Advice centre. Staffed by volunteers and open for a couple of sessions a week, it provides help with forms, advice about benefits, housing, employment, financial management and the like. Leading up to their annual rededication day, the Chair and Secretary identified a disconnection between the staff and the original aims of the Centre, and they wanted some help to reconnect. They asked me to lead the day. In consultation with the Secretary, I designed a process that would encourage the staff to talk to each other in a biblical context about their individual and group experience and their hopes about their work in the Centre. To shape the session and as a new way of thinking about their work in the context of their faith, I suggested using an incident from the Gospels in an imaginative, somewhat Ignatian way. This exercise in theological reflection involved using the story of the woman with the jar of ointment from Luke 7.36–50. They were told that the purpose was to focus on their work in the Centre in the town and how that work looks from the point of view of a range of people. This was to be done by inserting themselves into an event in the life of Jesus. One of the staff read the passage out loud. I then asked people to divide themselves into equal-sized groups to look at the story from the point of view of the woman, the Pharisee, Jesus, and the other guests respectively. In their groups, in character, they discussed what they thought and felt about what was happening in the story, about themselves and about the other participants. After 15 minutes or so, each group talked in plenary about how their characters felt, while the other groups listened. As each group talked, there was a lot of laughter and some sense of shock that, for example, the Pharisee's reaction was actually quite understandable, or that Jesus was probably quite angry. As the groups started to interact, respond to and argue with each other, what had been a one-dimensional story became much richer and relevant. New angles on the approach to their service users emerged. One expert advisor said that he could see what a problem it was for someone like him who had worked hard all his life to be advising someone who had never worked and did not seem to think that they should get out of bed in the morning to earn a living. He needed to think about what it was like to be that person. After making sure people were out of character, there was a coffee break, and then the Centre's Chair and I opened up a discussion about handling diversity in terms of the purpose of the Centre. This led to some rich insights and proposals for work over that year in terms of staff training.

Organizational studies and analyses

A regular request for consultants' help comes in the form of a wide-ranging study of a situation where a plan for the future is needed. Typical situations are when a local church or a group of churches has to make big decisions about how to cope with falling or rising numbers, inadequate income, issues with buildings or some major, significant change in their local context. It may be that an organization or a department has been asked to consider how it might best meet the demands of new priorities or a new vision for the structure of which they are part.

It might be about setting up a Fresh Expression of church. Again the three-part process applies well in these cases: 'studying things as they are; ... defining what needs to be done; working out how to do things' (Lovell, 2000, p. 79).

The difference in such cases is the increase in the level of management of the consultancy. Take, for example, a fairly typical example of a Church of England team ministry consisting of a group of parishes and churches with a team of ordained and lay ministers of various kinds. One of the team vicars has retired, and this is a good opportunity to look at the team in its setting to see what it should look like for the future. The diocese in the person of the Archdeacon has met the team council and suggested that outside help would be useful. The diocese has funding for a consultancy project. After initial meetings and investigation, it is likely that a series of interlocking critical issues will be identified. Such critical issues might be:

- How to be clear about what the team and diocese want out of this consultancy. Are there any unspoken expectations or constraints?
- How to cover the quantity and variety of the work in the time.
- What if people in the churches are used as part of the consultancy team?
- What if more than one consultant is used?
- How to ensure the timetable agreed is reasonable and takes into account the need for consultation and time to reflect and come to decisions within the normal rhythm of church meetings, seasons and holidays.
- How to ensure that the process and the consultants are trusted, that is, not just seen as the diocese's or the team rector's enforcers, and that decisions are likely to be supported.
- How to make sure that all the right people are interviewed, especially those who have difficulty being heard, both within the churches and in the community and the public services.
- How to get access to all the pertinent financial, legal, historical, sociological and political data.
- How to check that findings are as accurate and useful as possible.
- How to get all this done within the budget that the diocese has made available.

Any plan to tackle such a project will need these critical issues to be managed and solved in a complex way that involves careful sequencing, parallel activity, project management and monitoring. Responding to these critical issues also indicates that a range of data needs gathering and that a range of data-gathering methods needs to be employed. The first step is to make sure that the question or questions being asked are clear. Who do you need to talk to and about what? Some information will be collected by interviews with individuals and gathering people for meetings or focus groups. It may be necessary to reach larger numbers by written or web-based questionnaires. In order for the analysis to be as full as possible, though, it will be necessary to investigate other types of data. This will be important in understanding what effect developments like secularization, postmodern living, and a multifaith society is having in the area. Some of this will be documentary, such as:

- minutes and records of committees and councils
- financial records and reports
- legal information about the status of entities, ownership of buildings, nature of roles
- facts and figures about the local population, local issues and the geographical area from local government and other agencies
- local history
- facts and figures about the team and its parishes
- architects' reports and surveys on the condition of the buildings.

Some of the information needed for the analysis will be gathered by working with groups of people on their reactions to what the consultants discover, seeing how they respond to the facts and possibilities of their situation. An often forgotten source of data is what can be gathered by observation. Important conscious and unconscious messages are given out by physical symbols both in the churches and in their environment. The physical state of a church, its tidiness, its notice boards, the way it smells, the fact it has disabled access, effective heating or peeling paint and dirty toilets all communicate messages about what is important. The way people behave in church settings also gives clues about what matters – the way new people are welcomed, how fairly, courageously and respectfully people deal with each other at church meetings, or the treatment of young people and children. This is useful information about the match between church members' espoused and operant beliefs. A walk round the neighbourhood with a parishioner can provide considerable material for understanding the area and its mission issues. What is the housing like and in what condition? What can be seen in terms of local shops, services and businesses, employment opportunities and community facilities? What is happening on the streets? How do people interact? What does what can be seen reveal about the local community? Taking a camera with you as you walk round the area or visit church buildings and grounds can provide powerful evidence to help in the analysis. An outsider consultant who is attuned to looking for such symbols offers the chance for local people to recognize aspects of their context that they may no longer notice (in the manner of the boiling frog) and that might benefit from attention. The construction and management of symbols will also be an important feature of the design phase. What powerful symbols will be created that communicate the change and reinforce it on a non-verbal level?

In a project like this, logistics can be a difficult issue. If possible, it is a big help to find someone in the team with good administrative skills and good connections in and understanding of the area to act as a local support for external consultants. Through the whole process of the consultancy project they can provide contextual information. They can book appointments for visits and interviews with those whom the consultants and their key consultors see as useful to interview. These are likely to include church people and others such as community leaders, school heads, local government officials, groups that meet on church premises, the police and faith groups. It is important that the consultants ensure that such a support person is well briefed and happy with the amount of work expected, with how they are to work with the consultants and with the confidential nature of the role. In one such consultancy I was involved with, the local churches identified a retired local councillor who was a member of one the churches to be the support person. He was a good administrator, had the time, and knew all sorts of people and groups in the community. He had lived in the area for decades and had the sort of personality that smoothed entry into pertinent church and non-church settings. Finding the right person makes managing the project easier, more flexible and more likely to gather all the information needed, while providing easy access and a warm welcome to a range of people and bodies.

Practical advice to identify the sort of information to seek and interviews to hold can be found in such resources as Helen Cameron *et al.*'s *Studying Local Churches* (2005) and Cameron's *Resourcing Mission: Practical Theology for Changing Churches* (2010), Maggie Durran's *Regenerating Local Churches* (2006), Malcolm Duncan's *Kingdom Come: The Local Church as a Catalyst for Social Change* (2007) and at the Fresh Expressions website, www.sharetheguide.org ('how-to-do-it advice on starting, developing and sustaining fresh expressions of church based on shared experiences').

Critical issues – building trust and commitment

Surprisingly, of all the critical issues identified above, the one that can occupy most energy is how to build trust among the congregations. People who feel excluded, threatened or coerced by the consultancy process can wreck a project like this. Clumsy handling of mergers, closures and new initiatives over many years may have led some people to position themselves as opponents of change and advocates of how it was in the good old days. Most members of churches, good-hearted, faithful people, are likely to be keen to see their churches move on in mission and growth. At the same time, a number of individuals may have become fierce protectors of particular interests. The anticipation of possible closures, reduced numbers of ordained ministers and the loss of certain types of services at the time of the consultancy project may feed this anxiety and generate defensive behaviour. It is worth devoting considerable time and energy to designing a process that handles such people's defensiveness, particularly with the church councils where such people may exercise their influence.

A general process I have used successfully consists of a number of stages. First, church council meetings are held, jointly or separately as local leaders advise, to explain the consultancy process. The proposed process document should have already been distributed. Careful attention is given to contributions, suggestions and objections and the proposal adjusted to respond as fully as possible. The second, larger part of the first meetings revolves around various ways of getting people to tell the stories of their churches and mission and ministry in their area. Rather than staying in seats round a table, council members can be encouraged, in some cases, to use long pieces of lining paper to create a timeline that goes into the past as far as those there can remember and to speculate about the timeline they would like the churches to go through in the future. With others, storytelling might be used, again both about the past and the future. Storytelling is a recent development in the study of organizations. Denning says:

> Storytelling doesn't replace analytical thinking. It supplements it by enabling us to imagine new perspectives and is ideally suited to communicating change and stimulating innovation. Abstract analysis is easier to understand when seen through the lens of a well-chosen story and can of course be used to make explicit the implications of a story.
>
> (2005, p. 6)

Sometimes participants at such meetings prefer to show their stories and timelines in picture or diagram form. One method is the soft systems technique called rich pictures (see Checkland, 1981). The idea is to supplement or replace the standard meeting processes that tend to favour the educated, middle-class, masculine stereotypes. Engaging with the timelines and stories people offer, it becomes possible to see what models of church, mission, discipleship and community are current among the membership, as well as how people see the way the community has changed over the years and what that has meant for the churches' roles. As people listen to each other telling the stories that were important, salient and that helped make sense of the situation, others in the room may begin to see a richer, better informed, more historical picture of their context and what the future might look like. One of the key aims of these meetings, apart from gathering information, will be to develop a relationship of trust between parishioners and the consultants. Thus, consultants' positive behaviour – honesty, not giving an answer if they do not know, including everyone whatever their age or personality, treating everyone as adults, being seen as professional, fair, accessible and even charming – is crucial.

Then could follow a sequence of meetings for further stages of the project. Using similarly inclusive processes, the first takes place when the entire data gathering has been done and initial conclusions proposed. Reports are distributed before the meeting so that people have time to understand the documents. At these meetings, the findings are checked for factual accuracy and comments on the conclusions are invited. It is made clear that these are initial, if strong, recommendations but that it is the accountability of the team councils, the team staff and the diocese to work out what the future looks like. Even though recommendations may entail bad news for some churches in the team, the openness and pace of the consultation with members of the congregations should mean that they see what is in the report as fair, with some exciting possibilities and opportunities for the future. Subsequent meetings will finalize the recommendations and work out the next steps and exactly how their implementation will be carried out.

Another approach, using a complexity approach or Rendle and Mann's recommendations in *Holy Conversations* (2003), would be conversations. The consultants encourage conversations and listen in on conversations that are happening already. Handling the various elements of a project like this – getting church members and leaders talking about the issues, to each other and to the consultants, reaching out into the community to find out what is going on and what is needed locally, harvesting all the facts and figures to base decisions on – still need to be done. It takes a highly skilled complexity consultant to promote a process from listening in to conversations round the water cooler/coffee machine all the way to strategic plans, budgets and commitment from all the congregations. Rendle and Mann, however, still make use of some common management tools such as a *SWOT* analysis (2003, p. 69) where you look at the *strengths, weaknesses, opportunities* and *threats* in the situation.

Critical issues – the nature and usefulness of the research

There is a useful saying of Korzybski's that 'the map is not the territory' (1995, p. 58). A study can only provide a snapshot of the situation at the time. But it should be a fair and realistic snapshot. In studies like these, consultants should see themselves, as far as possible, as theologically astute, social science researchers. They ensure that there is, for example, a consistent, semi-structured questionnaire as the framework for interviews. Thus, data can be collated, hypotheses made and tested and conclusions drawn. They look at issues of bias, salience, sample size and validity in the people they talk to, the questions they ask and the nature of the responses. Although in most instances of consultancy studies, it is not possible to apply the rigour and depth that would produce articles for a peer reviewed academic journal, consultants still need to follow what they understand as the principles of decent quality research.

Action research is a highly successful and well-regarded method of combining the process and general expertise of the consultant with the authority, participation and expertise of the consultor and their organization in a collaborative partnership that is designed to bring about improvement. As can be seen from what Bob Dick says below, action research has the distinct aim of producing some sort of change or action through what is learnt in the organization being studied by the active participation of the consultant/researcher. He says:

Action research can be described as a family of research methodologies that pursue action (or change) and research (or understanding) at the same time. In most of its forms it does this by

1 using a cyclic or spiral process which alternates between action and critical reflection and
2 in the later cycles, continuously refining methods, data and interpretation in the light of the understanding developed in the earlier cycles.

It is thus an emergent process which takes shape as understanding increases; it is an iterative process which converges towards a better understanding of what happens.

In most of its forms it is also participative (among other reasons, change is usually easier to achieve when those affected by the change are involved) and qualitative.

(Dick, 1999)

The action research approach fits with non-directive, process consultation in its absolute respect for the members of the organization and for their skill, expertise and authority in sorting out their own issues. It also fits because its focus is not just studying an organization but studying an organization rigorously in order to support change. For an example of action research applied in a church context, Cameron *et al.*'s *Talking about God in Practice* (2010) describes a method that she and her colleagues call Theological Action Research, a method based on conversations with participants in church work projects of various kinds in their 'Action Research: Church and Society' (ARCS) project (for information, see www.heythrop.ac.uk/outreach/arcs-project.html). The constructive nature of action research is underlined by their emphasis on the dialogue between the four voices of theology: *espoused theology* (what people say they believe), *operant theology* (what they demonstrate by their behaviour), *normative theology* (beliefs expressed in creeds, the Scriptures, official church teaching and liturgies), and *formal theology* (academic theology, normally in dialogue with other academic disciplines). Conversations between church workers and theologians allow action to be taken not only to address the work of the organization but also to build the capacity of workers to reflect theologically on their activity. Those who are involved in expressing their faith in local communities have an opportunity to hear what formal and normative theology have to say to them while formal and normative theology have the opportunity to listen to (and be changed by) voices on the ground.

In the example of the team ministry just mentioned, useful work could be done through a series of conversations initiated with groups and individuals around their picture of church. The notion of pictures rather than models allows people to draw diagrams, images, words and dynamic, connecting symbols such as arrows and relationship lines to show what they understand by church as it has been, as it is and as they see it becoming, either out of necessity or in their dreams. In working with church members, consultants can draw on material such as the Alban Institute church life-cycle model, mission-shaped church material, and Dulles's images of church, as well as denominational reports and statements of principle about ecclesiological understanding and priorities. Thus, the conversation grows not just between the people in the room and across the whole project, but with formal and normative theologies.

Moving into design

A criticism that can be directed at what has been said so far in this chapter is that there is less detail on the design side of the consultancy process than on analysis. One response is that it is often the case in consultancy that a high-quality process of analysis makes the solution to the questions raised fairly clear. A second response is that the nature of the design will very much depend on the interaction between the consultor and the consultant. The consultant may have been engaged because they are an expert in a specific model of understanding and designing church work. They may have a reputation for helping emerging churches, or for financial and strategic planning. The model of consultancy they bring will determine the approach to building plans to address the issues. A capable consultant will have in their toolkit a theologically backed range of theories and methods that they trust. It is part of consultants' professional work to assess their offerings' integrity, usefulness and continuing rigour.

There are endless books and manuals of varying quality available about running churches. Add to these the range of material from secular sources and it becomes obvious that consultants need to undertake serious, reflective selection in order to resource their toolkit. In a seminar on design with a group of consultancy students at the York Institute for Community Theology, the following list of more or less useful design frameworks was produced:

- Robert Warren's *The Healthy Churches' Handbook* (2004)
- Natural Church Development
- Mission Action Planning
- Tearfund's Discovery Programme
- Hopewell's *Congregations: Stories and Structures* (1987)
- Rendle and Mann's *Holy Conversations* (2003)
- The Australian Churches' *National Church Life Survey* (www.ncls.org.au)

These were only those identified as reasonably useful by those in the room at the time. In recent years, much church material has majored on leadership, yet religious frameworks tend to be weak on how to build appropriate systems and structures that will enable the church organization to carry out its work effectively over time. Insights from secular frameworks, such as systems thinking in the already cited Campbell and Huffington systems approach, and Macdonald's Systems Leadership theory, provide carefully worked-out approaches to constructing what is needed. There is also a wealth of material from the voluntary sector, which is particularly strong on governance and volunteering.

Systems design

Given the large amount of material that has already been mentioned in this book about the nature and structure of organizations, it is easy to see how questions of shape and structure are more readily dealt with in the design of solutions to problems. What comes less naturally is attention to systems. This refers to the systems, processes and routines in an organization, 'specific methodologies for organizing activities in order to achieve a purpose'. Following this definition, Macdonald *et al.* (2006, p. 108) show that systems' function is to 'direct flows of work, information, money, people, materials and equipment'. The systems provide the frameworks for these flows to happen. Systems are a form of leadership in that they influence the way things are done around here. They drive behaviour. In churches there are systems operating at all levels, from big, national systems like choosing candidates for ministry or authorizing liturgy to local ones like worship rotas, how the money is counted and banked after Sunday services, or managing a network of fellowship/cell groups.

Systems are often characterized as mechanical and bureaucratic but their social impact can be immense. They affect people and their effect can make people feel bad or good, treated respectfully or marginalized. A recent example is the introduction of systems for checking volunteers' criminal records in order to prevent child abuse. This is a reasonable, advisable reaction to the perceived risks of adults working with children in church settings. However, the impact on many people was that they felt they were being accused of awful crimes or that they were no longer trusted, however long and faithful their service had been. As a consequence, churches lost Sunday school teachers and youth workers. What seems like a really well-designed system can founder if the impact on people has not been investigated and predicted in a way that contributes to the system's design. If this social process analysis is done well and influences the design and implementation of a new or changed system, the system is much more likely to achieve its purpose and contribute to a positive culture in the new set-up. Macdonald *et al.*'s *Systems Leadership* (2006) provides a very helpful guide to systems design. Its framework of 20 systems design questions can be found with short explanations in Appendix B.

Implementation and measurement

A brief word is necessary about implementation and measurement. Consultancy either with individuals or with whole churches or groups of churches involves considerable time, effort and cost. It is, therefore, helpful to be disciplined in working out whether any change has happened and how that might be identified and described, particularly the desired change in people's behaviour. This forms part of the initial contracting and should be a consideration in the design process. What is the world going to look like as a result of what we have been doing together? How will we know? When church projects are seeking money from public bodies for their work, they will nowadays often be asked to demonstrate measures of success in terms of outputs and outcomes. Outputs are seen as the direct product of an activity and normally are easily measured, for example quantitively. Outcomes tend to be long-term benefits which the outputs contribute to and which match the overall purpose of the change. They are more likely to be measured qualitatively. So, in the case of the minister and her time management problem, the outputs might be fewer, smaller piles of papers on Jenny's desk, respected, set times for dealing with emails and less frequent interruptions at mealtimes. The outcome would be that she felt she was doing the right level of work in a capable church where ministry happened on the basis of enabled people whom she is supporting in a relatively hands-off, systematic, organized way.

Measures of success or missing the mark are likely to include both quantitative and qualitative elements, for example numbers of people attending regularly in the different age groups and stories about the quality of relationships, confidence or spiritual growth. Although it seems easier because counting attendance feels objective and indisputable, the danger of quantitative measurement particularly is that it can become just a counting exercise. The measures can warp performance towards doing only what gets measured rather than working towards the overall purpose, as has sometimes been the case with school exam league tables or hospital emergency room waiting times. Nevertheless, the danger of not having a rigorous, explicit set of measurement criteria is that the change process or the consultancy itself can drift, as participants are too polite to address the fact that it is increasingly a waste of time. The key is to judge which measures and marks of achievement most effectively identify progress and support the purpose of the change, and to keep checking whether those measures continue to do so.

Final comments

Having recounted some examples of analysis and design and the tools that can be used, the expectation is not that a consultant, having read them, can pick up the particular approach described and run with it. The aim of hearing the stories is to encourage the consultant to begin to explore key features of consultancy in action. Consultancy is about process above all. However expert they might be in technical areas, if consultants' understanding and management of social process is poor, it will be difficult for any consultancy to be constructive. Consultancy relies on being able to access a variety of fields of knowledge and handle them in a supportive, interdisciplinary way. It depends on the serious application of reputable theories and models in a sensitive, reflective and responsive manner. Consultancy is a collaborative exercise where change is effected by enhancing the capability of the consultor(s) to contribute to the consultancy and to develop their ability to tackle their own issues. As Edgar Schein says (2000, pp. 192–4), the idea of consultancy is to help the organization give itself good advice.

8

Issues in the Provision of Consultancy in Churches

This chapter addresses issues in the provision of consultancy, how churches access consultants from outside or inside their organizations and how those consultants practise in a way that is safe, useful, ethical and always improving. Topics covered, therefore, are

- providing consultancy
- the internal consultant
- consultants in the hierarchy
- supervision
- ethics and codes of practice.

Providing consultancy

Although the notion and practice of church consultancy has been around for some time, its provision is patchy. There are independent consultants and consultancy companies who have church work as all or part of their portfolio. There are, as will be discussed later, advisors and officers in roles as internal consultants within the churches at various levels. National and international mission and development agencies also offer consultancy. However, in some areas of the church there is still an assumption that, if you want to benefit from the services of a consultant, you go to the commercial and public sector. In many congregations, there are competent consultants and secular managers who will provide helpful support. Yet, one of the central messages of this book is that churches should have the confidence to look to the talent that exists inside their own institutions. Many church workers and members, ordained and lay, have all the potential to make highly effective work consultants within their own church and more widely. Furthermore, many experienced ministers would find it a rewarding, validating and dignifying way to use their wisdom in both content and process. So not only is drawing on internal practitioners a way of increasing the job satisfaction of ministers and church workers, it can be a cost-effective way of providing an essential service. Churches need to set up systems to recruit, train and support such consultants. In Britain, some churches like the Anglican Oxford Diocese or the London Methodist District have run training courses to develop their own people as consultants. Others have taken advantage of training courses and degree programmes run by, for example, Avec, the York Institute for Community Theology, the Tavistock Institute, the Craighead Institute or Sarum College. Running through these courses is the rigour that the interdisciplinary, contextual and experiential nature of becoming a consultant demands. It is not just a matter of reading a book like this and assuming anyone can then offer consultancy. The courses provide access to well-proven theory and engender the habit of continuing reflective practice.

The growing experience of consultancy provision indicates that there is no one right way of doing it. Different churches provide consultancy variously through:

- specific, employed officers
- ministers who are trained to be consultants to each other in co-consultancy groups
- a sponsored network of qualified consultants, who may be ministers employed by the church, or lay people who give their time free or for a fee
- buying in consultants from the commercial sector

In terms of where consultancy fits within the churches' structures, in some situations it is part of continuing ministerial development/ education; in others it is located in the mission department. Alignment with the leadership of the organization has a major bearing on the effectiveness of work consultancy. It is important that work consultancy should have the informed backing of the individuals and councils that lead the church. Consultancy provision should integrate well with other systems such as ministerial review, mission and pastoral planning and development and training.

The internal consultant

The internal consultant is a common feature of churches. Often they will have titles that contain words like enabler, advisor or officer, combined with terms like development, evangelism, mission, social justice or youth and children's. Many of those who hold these roles will describe what they do in terms very like the consulting approaches laid out in this book. They may see themselves as non-directive or expert depending on the understanding of their role and their preferred style of work. The key issue is that the internal consultant is, as Peter Block puts it, 'at every moment embedded in some part of the hierarchy and the current politics of the organization. You have a boss you must satisfy (at least to some extent). Your own department has certain goals it must achieve' (2000, p. 130). Churches will devote precious resources in employing such consultants in order to support their organizational goals. It might be simply to help local churches and ministers to be more effective or it might be to drive some organizational culture and behaviour change based on the leadership's recently fashioned vision.

Internal consultants I have worked with often display a sense of being trapped or at least subject to conflicts. Do I do the right thing for my consultor or what gets me in my manager's good books? What if they are not the same thing? There are also pressures arising from how internal consultants are perceived. An internal consultant's purpose and agenda can be seen to push what the larger organization, the district, the territory, the region or the diocese, wants. If this is the case, will the local church or minister believe that the internal consultant is working with them with transparency and trustworthiness rather than forcing them into what they don't want? Will the consultants report back to the centre how poorly the local church or minister is performing in mission? There can be confusion as to who is the real customer of the consultant's work. Is it the local church where the work is being done or is it the larger organization represented by the consultant's manager? It can happen that the internal consultant, as a representative of the organization, might see part of their role as making sure that the consultor keeps to the church's rules and norms. This can be an issue when consulting in sensitive initiatives such as Fresh Expressions or emerging models of church. Even just asking the question as to whether what is proposed breaks or keeps to the rules may influence, manipulate or skew both the working relationship between consultant and consultor and the plans that are developed. Constant reflection is indispensable in a liminal role such as an internal consultant. Standing between two worlds, translating one to the other through understanding and being able to inhabit both cultures demands self-awareness, a particular capability and clarity in accountability relationships.

As with any consultancy process, a key element is the quality of the contracting conversation between the consultant and both parties to this perceived or actual conflict. As with any social process, if all the most supportive organizational conditions are in place, it will be a matter of the consultant's performance and behaviour over time building a level of trust and positive reputation that will enable them to operate effectively. News gets round churches very quickly about who is supportive and trustworthy and who not.

When internal and external consultants get together, one of the common complaints from the internals concerns choice. If they are the only person in that consultancy role in their organization, they have no choice about what they take on. They have to do it all. Consultors also have no choice. The said consultant is the only option whether you like them or not, whether you think they will be any use or not. A typical reaction from external consultants is jealousy that the internals have the opportunity to experience dilemmas about all this work thrown at them. The situation of the internal consultant benefits normally from too much work while having the disadvantage of some work they might not have chosen. The ethical issues about competence to do the work underline the need for regular, reflective analysis and conversations with colleagues and managers about whether the role's demands are reasonable.

Consultants in the hierarchy

In contrast to secular employment hierarchies, those who look like managers in churches rarely have the ability to function as secular managers. There are normally too few of them to have a workable span of control. It is not possible for a weekly or daily conversation to happen between an archdeacon and all the clergy in their archdeaconry. They will not have the authority that a secular manager typically has to require a minister, church worker or church to do as they say. Culturally, church leaders tend to prefer describing their work as enabling, standing alongside, persuading and encouraging. As such, they may see themselves as consultants to the local church or minister. There are risks in this approach, as the overlap between the hierarchical role and the role of a consultant is likely to be extensive. It may be helpful to think of such leaders as seriously using consultancy skills and approaches with discipline and integrity rather than being full-blown consultants. There will be times at which they will have no choice but to say, in their roles as leader, that a certain course of action is not permissible as it breaks their or the organization's rules. It is, however, certainly the case that consultancy training and methodology can be of great help to people in these roles.

Supervision

Work consultancy can be an isolated activity, particularly for the lone operator whether internal or external. This entails a number of risks. Working on one's own with individuals and groups runs the danger of deviating from appropriate standards and quality. It can become difficult to ensure that a consultant's assessment of how well or poorly they are carrying out their work is accurate, be it over-flattering or unhealthily negative. A consultant may become distressed or ineffective if the focus of dislike, aggression or scapegoating when they are closely identified with an unpopular change. Without reference to other consultants, a consultant might flounder in terms of developing new ways of approaching their work and tackling issues. There is the risk that the consultor is no longer safe, as the consultant has not noticed that professional boundaries have been crossed. One important response to these risks is that the consultants undertake regular supervision.

Supervision is used to designate a number of overseeing relationships. Some of these uses have a tendency to confuse the hearer because of the overlaps between the different activities in question. In many organizations, someone's direct manager is called their 'supervisor' and the management function 'supervision'. This is not what we are talking about in the supervision of work consultants. In the churches an activity that goes on between a newly ordained or probationer minister and their supervisor, for example their incumbent in Anglican terms or their superintendent in Methodist terms, is often called supervision. I suggest that this is the nearest ordained ministers get to a managerial relationship. The trainee and their supervising minister meet on a regular basis to talk about the trainee's work and how they are coping with the challenges of the role. In a secular bureaucracy, this is a function that would be covered by the mixture of training and coaching that the manager provides for the trainee. The aim is to develop the individual in their skill, competence and reflective ability in doing the job. As many ministers go on to work in situations where there is no managerial supervision of this type, there is a growing emphasis on making sure that ministers provide themselves with such supervision. Recent texts like Frances Ward's *Lifelong Learning: Theological Education and Supervision* (2005)and Leach and Paterson's *Pastoral Supervision* (2010) testify to the perceived value of what Leach and Paterson call a 'space in which [the supervisee's] wellbeing, growth and development are taken seriously … and a realistic point of accountability within the body of Christ for their work' (2010, p. 1). The focus is for those in ministry to be reflective on their practice in a conscious and disciplined way. This is equally true for the ministry of work consultants.

A helpful resource for understanding, receiving and delivering supervision is Hawkins and Shohet's *Supervision in the Helping Professions* (2000). They quote Hess's definition of supervision as 'a quintessential interpersonal interaction with the general goal that one person, the supervisor, meets with another, the supervisee, in an effort to make the latter more effective in helping people' (2000, p. 50). The focus of the work done in supervision is the interest of consultors, how to improve and enhance the service they receive. An adaptation of the clinical rhombus first used by Ekstein and Wallerstein (1972) in discussing the supervision of psychotherapists, demonstrates the multiple connections between the four stakeholders in the supervision of church work consultants (see Figure 8.1).

In supervision, the focus of the work to be done is the quality of service to the supervisee's consultors. So, the diagram shows the connection between them and the supervisor as well as with the supervisee. In the diagram, the organization may represent, for example, the church within which the supervisee is delivering work consultancy and to which they belong. The supervisor, therefore, has a connection with the organization, which relies on them to ensure it is getting decent work consultancy from the supervisee. The organization may also represent the professional body or consultancy company, department or partnership to which the supervisee as a consultant belongs. They will

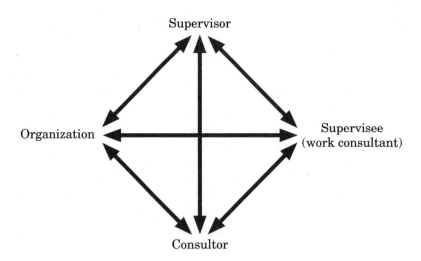

Figure 8.1 The work consultancy supervision rhomboid

be concerned to guarantee the quality of the supervisee's work in the interests of the consultor, with an eye on their continuing business and in terms of their reputation for professional standards. The nature of these connections will vary with the context, for example according to who employs the supervisor and the supervisee. In the contracting phase with which any supervisory relationship must start, the impact of these connections needs to be carefully explored and articulated.

Hawkins and Shohet (2000, pp. 50–2), using the work of Kadushin and Proctor, see supervision as having three functions:

- educative or formative
- supportive or restorative
- managerial or normative.

The *formative* function focuses on the skills, understanding and abilities of the supervisee, encouraging them to look at their content and process. This helps the supervisee understand their consultor better and investigate their own responses to the interactions and the accompanying dynamics. The formative function also studies how they worked and the consequences of that work. The supervisor may talk through alternative ways of dealing with the issue and provide new information. The *restorative* function recognizes that involvement in work like consultancy makes the supervisee vulnerable to anxiety, pain and emotional projections. It offers space and time for the supervisee to work these through with another person and to gain another person's perspective on what they are undergoing. The supervisee should receive validation and support both as a person and as a worker. The *normative* function allows quality control to happen both in terms of consultancy as a profession and with reference to the organization for which the work is being done. In this, there is particular concern for professional and ethical standards.

There is no one pattern of supervision provision. For internal consultants, supervision may best come from within their department, if there is one. Some choose and pay a supervisor outside their organization. Some networks of consultants do supervision in a group. This may follow an action learning set process with a skilled facilitator or a clinical model where the facilitator is an expert consultant. Some networks may offer one-to-one supervision on a peer level using other consultants in the network. In many consultancy companies more experienced consultants will offer supervision to the less experienced. As in work consultancy, contracting is important. Hawkins and Shohet (2000, pp. 56–8) suggest that the contract should contain five elements:

- practicalities – time, frequency, place, length, fees, missed sessions, etc.;
- boundaries – issues to be examined, confidentiality, what supervision is not (for example counselling);
- working alliance – mutual expectations, style, fears, hopes, features of successful supervision, reflection, learning and improvement, supervision model;
- the session format – typical session shape, how many consultors discussed, written presentations sent beforehand or not, record-keeping;
- the organizational and professional context – expectations of the organization and/or professional bodies.

Supervision may be seen as policing the consultant. Yet, its core is reflective practice, analysing work in order to ensure high-quality and improving provision for the consultor. In *Lifelong Learning*, Frances Ward underlines the essential nature of supervision as learning:

> The role of the supervisor … is to provide a facilitating environment which is both challenging and secure. To do this, a supervisor needs to be able to hold the space with some sense of oversight, and yet also to be able to enter into a learning agreement that is agreed together and mutually respectful. Supervision is seen as the opportunity for both supervisor and reflective practitioner to learn. How the supervisor models the quality of listening, challenging and dialogue contributes to the implicit learning of the reflective practitioner, so that good, rather than bad, habits are gained. The supervisor also needs a particular practical wisdom and oversight to hold the space of supervision so that the anxieties of new learning are not avoided through various strategies and games of resistance.
>
> (2005, p. 183)

Ethics and codes of practice

When I left working as a higher education chaplain to become a commercial consultant, I had an exit interview with the university's Secretary General. His reaction to what I was about to become was the old story that all a consultant does is steal your watch to tell you the time. There is a significant level of suspicion about consultants around in the organizations who use them and even more in those who don't. This can be a healthy warning for consultants to make sure that they uphold the highest possible standards in the work they provide over against the sort of consultants whose work is backed up by less than professional standards, suspect ethics and disreputable practice. A consultant's work, therefore, needs to be supported by an ethical and professional framework. Such a code of conduct allows the consultor to see what they are being offered in terms of behavioural expectations and encourages what Kubr calls the 'voluntary assumption ... of the obligation of self-discipline' (2002, p. 142) on the part of the consultant. Such codes will never cover all contingencies and are dependent on how well consultants follow them. As Lippitt and Lippitt say:

> The process of continually evaluating one's code of ethics and the application of those ethics must continue through one's professional life, with the use of trusted colleagues as testers and clarifiers. The acquisition of ethical competence reduces anxiety and increases effectiveness in the situational decision-making that is a constant in the consulting process.
>
> (quoted in Kubr, 2002, p. 142)

Any examination of the quality and professionalism of consultancy needs to address three areas:

- standard of service to the consultor
- independence, objectivity and integrity
- duty to the consultancy profession.

Each area can be broken down into a number of specific issues to address. Many of these will be self-evident from discussions earlier in this book, but it is useful to express them explicitly in the context of a code of ethics.

Standard of service to the consultor

A basic assumption behind accepting and carrying out work for any consultor is that the consultant has the consultor's best interests at heart and that what a consultant provides will be of the highest possible quality in meeting their needs.

Competence

Is the consultant capable of delivering what the consultor wants? A mark of an ethical and effective consultant is that they say no to work for which they are unsuited, however desperate they are for work either as an external or an internal consultant.

Clarity over output and fees

At the inception of a contract or a working relationship there should be clear understanding and agreement on what will be the outcome of the work, how long it will take, how much it will cost, the resources that will be consumed, etc. The consultant may be the expert on the methodology being proposed but should not use the possession of esoteric knowledge to confuse the consultor into buying more consultancy than they need. It may be that there will need to be amendments, extensions or even reductions, but it is easier to discuss this with the consultor when the need arises. The contract set up at the start of the work can have the possibility for this built in.

Clarity on the nature of the relationship with the consultor

Is it clear that the consultant gives advice, no more, to the consultor and their organization? The executive authority remains with the consultor. It is important to be clear as to who is the consultor. Is it the leader or the leadership group of the organization? Often the nature of the work means that consultants may be spending most of their time with a particular department, the training people or the development advisors. In this case, the consultor will need to review and clarify regularly who the consultor is. Sometimes there will be a number of consultants from different consultancies working on a project because of a need to integrate initiatives, say, on leadership, finance, architecture, IT and evangelism. Accountability for managing the interactions between the consultants has to remain with the consultor, however tempting it may be for the consultants to sort it out between themselves.

Due care

Any advice given should be based on as complete and objective an analysis of all the data available as possible. Any advice or recommendations should be delivered in such a way, for example with sufficient context, that the consultor and their organization can understand it and have a good chance of implementing it.

Confidentiality

Much information gathered while working with consultors will be pastorally or organizationally sensitive. Care needs to be taken as to the use of information gained from consultors while working with other consultors, within different parts of the same organization and with other consultants.

Feedback on progress

Care should be taken to give consultors regular information as to the progress of the work (process and output) and feedback should be sought from the consultor both during and after the work so that problems can be addressed and an accurate, final assessment made.

Transparency

The work of consultancy is normally an open, collaborative process. What consultants do is expert, particularly in process, but is not about black-box magic.

Respect

With their experience of a range of churches and faith-based organizations, there may be a tendency to become cynical, dismissive and over-familiar with the holy. A consultant's work is informed by an absolute respect for the consultor and their organization's employees or members.

Independence, objectivity and integrity

In order to be effective consultants, that is, assistance from outside brought in to help solve problems, consultants need to maintain an independence, objectivity and integrity that allows them to give advice and offer analysis that is in the consultor's long-term best interest as far as they can tell. To do this, consultants need to be able to identify critical issues that may compromise that objectivity, independence and integrity and act to deal with them.

Privileged information

One of the reasons consultors use recognized church work consultants is for their expertise in particular areas, say, in pastoral reorganization or people systems. This expertise is built on work with other organizations. As above, the understanding must be that information gathered elsewhere is confidential. Consultants must be sure that there is not a significant conflict of interests, for example if they work with the bishop's staff team of a diocese and a group of parishes who are challenging the bishop's decisions. It may be that the conflict is so serious that the only ethical way forward is for the consultant to withdraw from the work. It is very easy for consultants to use such insider information inappropriately to their own advantage, particularly in organizations that enjoy gossip as much as churches.

Objectivity – short- vs long-term

Whatever the consultor may want to hear, consultants' advice normally concerns what is in the long-term best interest of the consultor. If the consultant is being asked to help produce solutions that they see as unhealthily short-term, they have to consider whether they continue to do the work. If they see their work or the theoretical material on which it is based being used in a way that compromises the material or that may damage the long-term interests of the consultant, their organization or their members, then they need to raise that clearly with the consultor and respond to the consultor's answer appropriately.

Delivering different feedback appropriately

Consultants may discover things going on in an organization the consultor does not want to hear about. They may identify behaviours demonstrated by the consultor that are putting the organization in jeopardy that the consultor will not face. There is a skill in social process demanded of the consultant in giving feedback to the consultor about this in such a way that the message will be heard and acted on. A consultant will need to develop this skill, as this is an unavoidable part of the work.

Stakeholders and vulnerability

Consultants need to reflect not just on the long-term effects of a decision but also on its wide-ranging effects. The concept of stakeholders helps in this. There may be people inside or outside the organization, features of the environment, elements of the local community, or other parts of the church, who will be adversely affected by what the consultant is helping the organization to do. A good question to ask is who is at risk as a result of the action that is being proposed.

Consistency with purpose, policy, beliefs

It is very helpful for consultants to develop a clearly articulated purpose, policies and belief statements about their work. In order to earn a living or to keep their job, there may be pressure to accept any work that comes their way. However, there are moral and practical questions about undertaking certain types of work for certain types of organizations. It helps to know what work a consultant would turn down and why – a weak, unsustained commitment to change; the initiative for the work coming from too low down in the organization; little likelihood that the work will be done in a collaborative fashion; no long-term strategic view; little chance of sustained implementation given the consultant's experience of them. Can the consultant stomach the consultors' views, what they see as mission, how they interact, their view of equal opportunities, their understanding of leadership? (Margerison has an interesting discussion of what he calls the ethics of accepting or rejecting assignments (2001, pp. 93–5).)

Inducements

Care needs to be taken around things like hospitality and gifts both received from consultors and potential consultors or offered to them. Is the basis on which such gifts are given and received clear, understood and respectable?

Duty to the consultancy profession

As has already been said, many people hold consultants in some suspicion. How consultants operate should enhance the reputation of consultancy and demonstrate that consultants can be professional, ethical and worth using.

Continuing professional development

It is important that consultants keep developing their knowledge and practice. Supervision helps in this, as does feedback from fellow consultants on how they are operating. Learning from one another is particularly important   All this is reinforced by reading and study, attending conferences, writing papers, delivering talks, developing new ways of working, and membership of professional bodies.

Respect for other consultants

Even in the churches, consultants find themselves competing with a range of consultants with a range of professional ethics and practice. It is important to show respect for others' skill, qualifications and obligations. It is rarely seen as dignifying to denigrate other consultants.

However, it is not good to be seen as cowardly or dishonest in not informing consultors of the risks and consequences of using consultants whose effectiveness is suspect. The UK Institute of Management Consultants' Code puts it nicely: 'When asked by a client to review the work of another professional, a member will exercise the objectivity, integrity and sensitivity required in all technical and advisory conclusions communicated to the client.'

Use of others' material

Consultants are always likely to be using a heady mixture of material from a range of sources – books they have read, courses they have been on, consultors or consultants they have worked with, education they have undergone. It is a matter of professional and academic etiquette as well as legal protection to acknowledge sources as far as is humanly possible in written material, on slides and in what is said, as well as ensuring that any fees or commissions due are paid to the appropriate person. It is simple dishonesty if consultants apparently claim someone else's material as their own or benefit from other's material financially or otherwise without giving them proper recognition, again financially or otherwise.

Reasonable fees

Good consultants are by definition good at what they do and deserve a decent reward for it. Judging what is the right daily rate is a sensitive piece of work, especially in churches. This involves judging the value of what is offered, what the consultor can afford, calibrating fees with comparable consultants, and considering if the relationship with the consultor will result in work over the long term. Often consultants are seen as charging exorbitant fees and it is an embarrassing but necessary part of the social process with the consultor to ensure they understand what they are paying for. In working with not-for-profit organizations, especially voluntary organizations, there is an assumption that consultants should work for nothing or nearly nothing. Those who earn their living by consultancy are entitled to charge rates that constitute a decent living. If work consultants are already paid ministers in the church, it would be reasonable to assume they would not charge for their time. This depends on the nature of the role and the culture of the church they are employed by. Consultants may charge nothing or little for work with churches and charities but must realize that they are setting up an unfair competitive environment for consultants whose living depends on that sort of work and those sorts of organizations. There also appears to be a correlation between people paying for consultancy, valuing it and implementing it.

Factual, relevant, truthful publicity

Consultants' publicity, for example in brochures or on websites, should not be dishonest or misleading. It should be factual, relevant and accurate. Some consultants append a great list of organizations they have worked for. The impression is of massive amounts of work over many years when it may have been just a day's workshop three years ago.

Running your own network, department or business

Consultancy organizations, departments and businesses should be run ethically, professionally and legally. This ranges across providing any employees, partners and associates with a fair, safe, challenging and rewarding work environment, being properly insured and running financial systems and paying taxes according to best practice.

Many consultancy organizations will publish their code of conduct on their website as it is a key professional tool as well as an assurance of good practice for the prospective consultor. There are also useful discussions on such codes and consulting ethics in standard consultancy texts such as Lippitt and Lippitt (1986, pp. 77–98), Lovell (2000, pp. 143–5) and Block (2000, pp. 307–26).

Professionalism

Although there is some debate as to whether consultancy can be seen as a profession, this chapter has promoted the idea that consultants should strive to demonstrate professionalism. That is, all they do should be aimed towards the best interests of the consultor, even if that means delivering unwelcome news or turning work down. The online source Business Dictionary defines professionalism as the 'meticulous adherence to undeviating courtesy, honesty, and responsibility in one's dealings with customers and associates, plus a level of excellence that goes over and above the commercial considerations and legal requirements'. Even in church work consultancy, this does not happen automatically, simply because the people involved are Christian. Such professionalism is produced when practitioners think carefully about their work and the way it is supported.

9

The Consultancy Journey

Becoming and operating as a consultant is an enormous privilege. To be allowed in to others' situations when they call out for help, support and collaboration is both rewarding and supportive of mission and ministry. It is not easy work but can be seen as what Vincent Donovan termed 'an adventure, a journey of the mind and of the soul, a disconcerting, disturbing, shattering humbling journey' (2001, pp. 1–2). Unless consulting is such a journey, full of challenge, creativity, community and mutual learning, it may be that God's hope for the work of the Church will not reach its rich and faithful potential. The possibility of learning and growth is central to the effective ministry of a church consultant. A useful model of uncertain origin, often quoted in learning and development, is the *Conscious Competence* model (see Figure 9.1). It shows the process we go through when learning something new.

The process of learning how to run a consultation reveals all sorts of gaps in our understanding of the disciplines behind it: theology, organizations, social process, psychology, consultancy models and the rest. As consultants learn from experience, become more practised and handle the interaction of all those disciplines appropriately, they become increasingly effective in helping consultors. It is sometimes assumed that the aim is to move to the fourth stage, Unconscious Competence, in our practice. The danger, in terms of this model, of getting to and remaining in this final stage, is that the consultant runs all the risks of growing ineffectiveness as a result of unidentified, habitual, counterproductive behaviour. A colleague of mine suggests that a good place to be is somewhere around the third step. While it is right that a consultor expects a consultant to be capable, this allows for the option of realizing that the consultant may be suddenly faced with something that they do not know how to deal with. Though disconcerting, this is an opportunity for learning and creativity in a collaborative process.

When discussing the general ethos of his church work consultancy model, George Lovell talks about this constant openness to learning, formation and mutual giving:

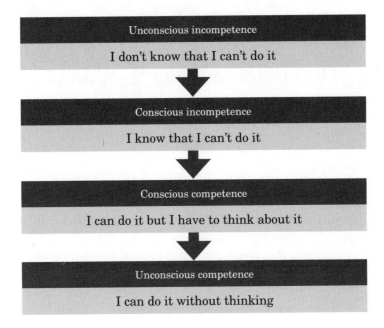

Figure 9.1 The Conscious Competence model

It is characterized by receptivity, affective as well as intellectual responses, waiting or attentiveness and the acceptance of pain as in-
trinsic to the bringing forth of life. It constrains people to stop and
think, stimulates them to go and act and deters them from being
quietists or activists. It is a spirituality of being and doing. The atmosphere is that which goes with reflective, creative activity – people
discovering and learning together and from each other how to do or
to make something of importance to them and to their God. It is the
ethos of healthy people at work rather than sick people at therapy. It
is a learning atmosphere.

(2000, p. 146)

It is in this spirit that this book is offered. It is a contribution to the
development of reflective practitioners. The intention of this book is to
offer a survey of the factors that need to be taken into account in offering consultancy for the support of mission and ministry with a number
of useful frameworks, effective tools and helpful hints as to where to go
for further information, support and professional development.

Appendix A

The contract: topics to address

1 **The change**
   (a) What is the issue to be addressed?
   (b) Why is this issue important?
   (c) What is/are the expected outcome(s) or deliverable(s)?
   (d) How will a successful outcome be recognized?
   (e) If the person commissioning and/or paying for the consultancy is not the consultor, what are their expectations in terms of authority, accountability, feedback and outcomes?
   (f) What can the process realistically deliver?

2 **Logistics**
   (g) Schedule.
       (i) When does the outcome need to be delivered?
       (ii) How much time is available to work on this between now and then?
       (iii) How often will a consultant and consultor/group meet and for how long?
   (h) What are the boundaries of the investigation and analysis?
       (i) Where and how will data be gathered?
       (ii) Are there any no-go areas?
   (i) Venue for any sessions.
   (j) How will what is happening be communicated to the stakeholders or church members concerned?
   (k) Is there someone to help with organizing interviews, visits and access to buildings and documents?
   (l) Payment and expenses.
       (i) Fee – by the day, hour or project
       (ii) Travel and accommodation
       (iii) Office expenses and support
       (iv) When and how to be invoiced and paid?

3 The consultant(s)

(m) What is the consultant's role and method?

(n) Who will do what if there is a team of consultants?

(o) How to handle the interaction with other agencies or consultants working with the consultor at the same time?

4 Behavioural expectations

(p) What support and involvement does the consultant look for from the consultor (and their organization, if appropriate)?

(q) What support and involvement is the consultor willing to give?

(r) Confidentiality.

    (i) Keeping individual discussions in confidence.

    (ii) Keeping data and people anonymous/generic.

    (iii) Confidentiality expectations on consultor as well as consultant.

(s) How to handle conflict and disputes.

(t) How to end the consultancy.

(u) Review.

    (i) Regular monitoring, updates, and feedback during the process.

    (ii) Evaluation and feedback at the end.

Appendix B

Systems design: 21 questions

These design criteria have been adapted from Macdonald *et al.* (2006).

1 **Why has the system been chosen?**
   Is there a need for a new system or to redesign the old system? Might the proposed system be a way of avoiding addressing poor behaviour directly? How does the new system fit into our strategy?

2 **Who is/should be the owner?**
   Who has the role, the authority and the overview to authorize the new system? Often this is mistakenly left to a specialist rather than the person who can see all the possible consequences of the new system in operation.

3 **Who is/should be the designer and the custodian?**
   The designer is the person or team with the right technical knowledge to work out the design of the system. This is complex work and relies on getting input from all the various groups of people who will be affected by the system. The custodian manages and checks how the system is being applied and reports on that to the system owner.

4 **What is the system's purpose?**
   It should be possible to state the purpose of a system in a clear, short, single-focus sentence. If the purpose is not clear or there are multiple purposes, the system is not likely to work well or it will do one thing well and not the others.

5 **Is it a system of equalization or differentiation?**
   Does the system treat people the same or differently? Systems in organizations may do either but which they do has to help get the organization's work done. If not, the system will be seen as unfair.

6 **What is the underlying theory?**
A system changes an input into an output? How is that supposed to happen?

7 **How is it to be measured?**
How will you check if the system is doing what it should? What are the key measures?

8 **How is it to be measured?**
Clear simple measures can be constructed that check whether the system is achieving its purpose. A clear purpose statement will show how success will be identified and communicated.

9 **What are the current benefits of the poor system?**
Who gains under the present arrangements and how will they react if the system is changed?

10 **What are the boundaries of the system?**
The boundaries of the system need to be clear and to make sense. Given the undesirability of multiple purposes, it is the general rule that systems be smaller rather than larger.

11 **What are the linkages with other systems?**
Systems often interact with each other. It is a design issue to make sure that the way they interact helps both fulfil their purpose.

12 **What structural boundaries does it cross?**
If systems need to cross the boundaries between different organizations or departments, there can be confusion and inefficiency. So, such crossovers need to be as few as possible or really carefully designed.

13 **Is the system one of transfer or transformation?**
Systems are there to transform – for example, ordination training to change a candidate into someone who can do the job – or to transfer – annual reports to communicate accurate numbers of church attendance. If the training makes no difference or the numbers get inflated, the system is doing the wrong thing.

14 **Is system authority and accountability consistent with role?**
Does the system make it difficult for people to do their work by not giving them enough authority yet still holding them accountable? Or does it run the risk of chaos by allowing people too much authority without being aware of the ramifications of their decisions?

15 **Are there proper controls built into the system?**
A control checks that a system is operating as it should, that people are doing the right thing at the right time.

16 **Is there an effective audit process?**
Audit is different from control in that it checks from time to time that the controls are in place and working. It also reviews whether the system is achieving its purpose and is the best way to achieve that purpose.

17 **Has the social process analysis been done?**
This looks at how the new system will be seen and valued. What reactions will it encourage? Will the way people feel about it help or hinder its operation?

18 **Is there a fully outlined flow chart?**
Is there enough detail in a flow chart to be clear exactly what should be happening at each step?

19 **Is there full system documentation?**
Often the way systems work is stored in people's heads. There needs to be some documentation that can be shared which shows what is supposed to happen, who is accountable for what, who can make decisions, what the controls and audits are, and so on.

20 **What is the implementation plan?**
Often really good systems fail because their implementation is poorly planned. Implementation needs careful detailing around communication, training, resourcing and supporting symbols.

21 **What is the final cost of design and implementation?**
It is important to check the final cost as the promised benefits may be outweighed by how much it is going to cost in financial and social terms.

Bibliography

J. Adair and J. Nelson (eds), 2004, *Creative Church Leadership*, London: Canterbury Press.

B. Adams, 2008, *Christ in the Marketplace*, Watford: THP Publishing.

Anglican Consultative Council, 1984, *Bonds of Affection*, Proceedings of ACC–6, Badagry, Nigeria.

G. Arbuckle, 1993, *Refounding the Church*, Maryknoll, NY: Orbis Books.

A. Bandura, 1977, 'Self-Efficacy: Toward a Uniting Theory of Behavioral Change', *Psychological Review* 84, pp. 191–215.

Baptist Churches of NSW and ACT, 2007, *Church Consultancy Manual*, available at www.baptistnsw.asn.au/evangelism_church_developme/church_consultancy_manual.pdf.

Baptist Union of Great Britain, 2005, *Mission Consultancy* (internal resource).

T. R. Batten, 1967, *The Non-Directive Approach in Group and Community Work*, London: Oxford University Press.

P. Bayes, 2010, Paper 3: 'The Weddings Project', *Resourcing Mission Bulletin*, July 2010, www.cofe.anglican.org.

R. Beckhard, 1969, *Organization Development: Strategies and Models*, Reading, MA: Addison-Wesley.

R. M. Belbin, 1993, *Team Roles at Work*, Oxford: Butterworth-Heinemann.

E. Berne, *Games People Play: The Basic Handbook of Transactional Analysis*, New York: Ballantine Books.

W. Bion, 1961, *Experiences in Groups*, London: Routledge.

R. R. Blake and J. S. Mouton, 1983, *Consultation,* 2nd edn, Reading, MA: Addison-Wesley.

P. Block, 2000, *Flawless Consulting: A Guide to Getting Your Expertise Used*, 2nd edn, San Francisco, CA: Pfeiffer.

D. Bosch, 1991, *Transforming Mission: Paradigm Shifts in Theology of Mission*, Maryknoll, NY: Orbis Books.

P. Boxer, and B. Palmer, 1994, 'Meeting the Challenge of the Case', in R. Casemore, G. Dyos, A. Eden, K. Kellner, J. McAuley, S. Moss (eds), 1994, *What Makes Consultancy Work: Understanding the Dynamics*, London: South Bank University Press, pp. 358–71.

D. S. Browning (ed.), 1983, *Practical Theology*, San Francisco, CA: Harper and Row.

S. Bruce, 2003, 'The Demise of Christianity in Britain', in G. Davie, P. Heelas, L. Woodhead (eds), 2003, *Predicting Religion: Christian, Secular and Alternative Futures*, Aldershot: Ashgate.

G. R. Bushe, 1998, 'Appreciative Inquiry in Teams', *Organization Development Journal* 16:3, pp. 41–50.

H. Cameron, 2004, 'What Contribution Can Organisational Studies Make to Congregational Studies?', in M. Guest, K. Tusting, L. Woodhead (eds), 2004, *Congregational Studies in the UK: Christianity in a Post-Christian Context*, London: Ashgate.

H. Cameron, 2010, *Resourcing Mission: Practical Theology for Changing Churches*, London: SCM Press.

H. Cameron, D. Bhatti, C. Duce, J. Sweeney, C. Watkins, 2010, *Talking about God in Practice*, London: SCM Press.

H. Cameron, P. Richter, D. Davies, F. Ward (eds), 2005, *Studying Local Churches*, London: SCM Press.

D. Campbell and C. Huffington (eds), 2008, *Organizations Connected: A Handbook of Systemic Consultation*, London: Karnac.

S. Canback, 1998, 'The Logic of Management Consulting', *Journal of Management Consulting* 10:2, November 1998, pp. 3–11.

W. Carr, 1985, *The Priestlike Task*, London: SPCK.

W. Carr and S. Kemmis, 1986, *Becoming Critical*, Lewes: Falmer Press.

J. W. Carroll, C. S. Dudley, W. McKinney (eds), 1986, *The Handbook for Congregational Studies*, Nashville, TN: Abingdon Press.

R. Casemore, G. Dyos, A. Eden, K. Kellner, J. McAuley, S. Moss (eds), 1994, *What Makes Consultancy Work: Understanding the Dynamics*, London: South Bank University Press.

P. B. Checkland, 1981, *Systems Thinking, Systems Practice*, Chichester: Wiley.

P. B. Checkland and J. Scholes, 1990, *Soft Systems Methodology in Action*, Chichester: Wiley.

Convocations of Canterbury and York, 2003, *Guidelines for the Professional Conduct of the Clergy*, London: Church House Publishing.

D. L. Cooperrider, D. Whitney, J. M. Stavros, 2008, *Appreciative Inquiry Handbook*, 2nd edn, Brunswick, OH: Crown Custom Publishing.

G. Cray, 2004, *Mission-Shaped Church*, London: Church House Publishing.

W. Critchley and H. Stuelten, 2008, 'Starting When We Turn Up: Consulting from a Complex Responsive Process Perspective', draft in preparation for publication Ashridge Consulting.

S. Croft, 2008, *Ministry in Three Dimensions. Ordination and Leadership in the Local Church*, 2nd edn, London: Darton, Longman and Todd.

G. Davie, 2006, 'Is Europe an Exceptional Case?', *The Hedgehog Review* 8:1–2.

G. Davie, P. Heelas, L. Woodhead (eds), 2003, *Predicting Religion: Christian, Secular and Alternative Futures*, Aldershot: Ashgate.

S. Denning, 2005, *The Leader's Guide to Storytelling: Mastering the Art and Discipline of Business Narrative*, San Francisco, CA: Jossey Bass.

B. Dick, 1999, *What Is Action Research?* Available online at www.scu.edu.au/schools/gcm/ar/whatisar.html.

D. Donnelly, 1992, 'Pilgrims and Tourists: Conflicting Metaphors for the Christian Journey to God', *Spirituality Today* 44:1, pp. 20–36.

V. Donovan (2001), *Christianity Rediscovered*, London: SCM Press.

A. Dulles, 1974, *Models of the Church*, New York: Doubleday.

M. Duncan, 2007, *Kingdom Come*, London: Monarch.

M. Durran, 2006, *Regenerating Local Churches*, London: Canterbury Press.

C. Elliott, 1999, *Locating the Energy for Change: An Introduction to Appreciative Inquiry*, Winnipeg: International Institute for Sustainable Development.

B. Farran, 1994, *A New Vision for Our Church: Becoming Ministering Communities*, Perth, Australia: Archdiocese of Perth.

L. Festinger, 1957, *A Theory of Cognitive Dissonance*, Stanford, CA: Stanford University Press.

L. Festinger and J. M. Carlsmith, 1959, 'Cognitive Consequences of Forced Compliance', *Journal of Abnormal and Social Psychology* 58, pp. 203–11.

L. Francis and M. Robbins, 2004, *Personality and the Practice of Ministry*, Cambridge: Grove Books.

C. Gempf, 2003, *Jesus Asked: What He Wanted to Know*, Grand Rapids, MI: Zondervan.

H. H. Gerth and C. Wright Mills (trans. and eds), 1991, *From Max Weber: Essays in Sociology*, London: Routledge.

E. Graham, H. Walton, F. Ward, 2005, *Theological Reflection: Methods*, London: SCM Press.

L. Greiner and R. Metzger, 1983, *Consulting to Management: Insights to Building and Managing a Successful Practice*, Englewood Cliffs, NJ: Prentice Hall.

M. Grundy, 2003, *What They Don't Teach You at Theological College*, London: Canterbury Press.

M. Grundy, 2007, *What's New in Church Leadership*, London: Canterbury Press.

M. Guest, K. Tusting, L. Woodhead (eds), 2004, *Congregational Studies in the UK: Christianity in a Post-Christian Context*, London: Ashgate.

M. Haralambos and M. Holborn, 1990, *Sociology: Themes and Perspectives*, 2nd edn, London: Collins.

M. Harris, 1998, *Organizing God's Work: Challenges for Churches and Synagogues*, London: Macmillan.

P. Hawkins and R. Shohet, 2000, *Supervision in the Helping Professions*, Maidenhead: Open University Press.

J. F. Hopewell, 1987, *Congregation: Stories and Structures*, Philadelphia, PA: Augsburg Fortress Press.

B. Hopkins and F. Hedley, 2008, *Coaching for Missional Leadership*, Sheffield: ACPI.

J. Hull, 2006, *Mission-Shaped Church: A Theological Response*, London: SCM Press.

J. Hutton, 2003, 'Working with the Concept of Organisation-in-the-Mind', paper presented to The Grubb Institute, London.

E. Jaques, 1976, *A General Theory of Bureaucracy*, London: Heinemann.

E. Jaques, 1990, 'In Praise of Hierarchy', *Harvard Business Review*, January–February 1990, pp. 127–33.

E. Jaques, 1994, *Five Special Organizational Studies: Church Clergy, Military Commanders, University Professors, Hospital Doctors, Partnerships*, Working Paper 3002, Gloucester, MA: Cason Hall and Co.

E. Jaques, 2010, 'In Praise of Hierarchy', in J. M. Shafritz and J. S. Ott (eds), 2010, *Classics of Organization Theory*, 9th edn, Belmont, CA: Wadworth.

S. Karpman, 1968, 'Fairy Tales and Script Drama Analysis', *Transactional Analysis Bulletin* 7: 26. Available at www.karpmandramatriangle.com.

H. Kirschenbaum and V. Henderson (eds), 1989, *The Carl Rogers Reader*, Boston, MA: Houghton Mifflin.

D. Knoke and D. Prensky, 1984, 'What Relevance Do Organization Theories Have for Voluntary Associations?', *Social Science Quarterly* 65, pp. 3–20.

D. A. Kolb, 1984, *Experiential Learning: Experience as the Source of Learning and Development*, Englewood Cliffs, NJ: Prentice Hall.

A. Korzybski, 1995[1933], *Science and Sanity: An Introduction to Non Aristotelian Systems and General Semantics*, 5th edn, Institute of General Semantics.

J. Kotter, 1996, *Leading Change*, Boston, MA: Harvard Business School Press.

K. Koyama, 1980, *Three Mile an Hour God*, Maryknoll, NY: Orbis Books.

E. Kübler-Ross, 1969, *On Death and Dying*, New York: Macmillan.

M. Kubr (ed.), 2002, *Management Consulting: A Guide to the Profession*, 4th edn, Geneva: ILO.

W. G. Lawrence, 1994, 'The Politics of Salvation and Revelation in the Practice of Consultancy', in R. Casemore, G. Dyos, A. Eden, K. Kellner, J. McAuley, S. Moss (eds),1994, *What Makes Consultancy Work*, London: South Bank University Press.

J. Leach and M. Paterson, 2010, *Pastoral Supervision*, London: SCM Press.

K. Lewin, 1951, *Field Theory in Social Science*, New York: Harper and Row.

R. Lewin and B. Regine, 2000, *Weaving Complexity and Business: Engaging the Soul at Work*, New York: Texere.

L. Lindon, 1995, 'Linking an Intervention Model to the Myers- Briggs Type Indicator, Consultancy and Managerial Roles', *Journal of Managerial Psychology* 10:4, pp. 21–9.

G. Lippitt and R. Lippitt, 1986, *The Consulting Process in Action*, 2nd edn, San Diego, CA: University Associates.

G. Lovell, 1991, *Diagrammatic Modelling: An Aid to Theological Reflection in Church and Community Development Work*, 2nd edn, Avec Occasional Paper No. 4.

G. Lovell, 1994, *Analysis and Design*, London: Burns and Oates.

G. Lovell (ed.), 1996, *Telling Experiences*, London: Chester House.

G. Lovell, 2000, *Consultancy, Ministry and Mission: A Handbook for Practitioners and Work Consultants in Christian Organizations*, London: Burns and Oates.

G. Lovell, 2005, *Consultancy Modes and Models*, Calver: Cliff College Publishing.

J. Luft and H. Ingham, 1955, 'The Johari Window, a Graphic Model of Interpersonal Awareness', *Proceedings of the Western Training Laboratory in Group Development*, Los Angeles: UCLA.

C. Lundberg, 1997, 'Towards a General Model of Consultancy', *Journal of Organizational Change Management* 10:3, pp. 193–201.

I. Macdonald, C. Burke, K. Stewart, 2006, *Systems Leadership; Creating Positive Organizations*, London: Gower.

S. Macdonald, 2006, 'From Babes and Sucklings: Management Consultants and Novice Clients', *European Management Journal* 24:6, pp. 411–21.

C. J. Margerison, 2001, *Managerial Consulting Skills: A Practical Guide*, 2nd edn, Aldershot: Gower.

O. Meier, 2010, *Management Intercultural*, 4th edn, Paris: Dunod.

P. Minear, 1960, *Images of the Church in the New Testament*, Philadelphia, PA: Westminster Press.

H. Mintzberg, B. Ahlstrad, J. Lampel, 1998, *Strategy Safari: The Complete Guide through the Wilds of Strategic Management*, London: Prentice Hall.

BIBLIOGRAPHY

I. Mobsby, 2007, *Emerging and Fresh Expressions of Church*, London: Moot Community Publishing.

G. Morgan, 2006, *Images of Organization*, Thousand Oaks, CA: Sage.

J. Nelson (ed.), 2008, *How to Become a Creative Church Leader*, London: Canterbury Press.

E. Nevis, 1987, *Organizational Consulting: A Gestalt Approach*, New York: Gardner Press.

H. R. Niebuhr, 1951, *Christ and Culture*, New York: Harper and Row.

A. Obholzer and V. Zagier Roberts (eds), 1994, *The Unconscious at Work: Individual and Organizational Stress in the Human Services*, London: Routledge.

S. Pattison, 1997, *The Faith of the Managers*, London: Cassell.

M. Percy, 2010, *Shaping the Church: The Promise of Implicit Theology*, London: Ashgate.

T. Peters and R. H. Waterman, 1982, *In Search of Excellence*, New York: HarperCollins.

B. Reed, 1978, *Dynamics of Religion*, London: Darton, Longman and Todd.

G. Rendle and A. Mann, 2003, *Holy Conversations: Strategic Planning as a Spiritual Practice for Congregations*, Herndon, VA: Alban Institute.

C. R. Rogers, 1957, 'The Necessary and Sufficient Conditions of Therapeutic Personality Change', *Journal of Consulting Psychology* 21, pp. 95–103.

C. R. Rogers, 1959, 'A Theory of Therapy, Personality, and Interpersonal Relationships as Developed in the Client-centered Framework', reprinted in H. Kirschenbaum and V. Henderson (eds), 1989, *The Carl Rogers Reader*, Boston, MA: Houghton Mifflin.

C. R. Rogers, 1961, *On Becoming a Person*, Boston, MA: Houghton Mifflin.

P. Rudge, 1964, *Ministry and Management: The Study of Ecclesiastical Administration*, London: Tavistock.

M. Saarinen, 1998, *The Life Cycle of a Congregation*, Herndon, VA: Alban Institute.

S. Savage and E. Boyd-Macmillan, 2007, *The Human Face of the Church: A Social Psychology and Pastoral Theology Resource for Pioneer and Traditional Ministry*, London: Canterbury Press.

E. Schein, 1990, 'A General Philosophy of Helping: Process Consultation', *Sloan Management Review* 31:3, Spring 1990, pp. 57–64.

E. Schein, 1997, *The Concept of Client from a Process Consultation Perspective: A Guide for Change Agents*, Working Paper No. 394.

E. Schein, 2000, *Process Consultation*, vols I and II, Cambridge, MA: Addison Wesley.

D. Schön, 1991, *The Reflective Practitioner*, London: Ashgate.

J. Seddon, 2008, *Systems Thinking in the Public Sector*, Axminster: Triarchy Press.

J. M. Shafritz and J. S. Ott (eds), 2010, *Classics of Organization Theory*, 9th edn, Belmont, CA: Wadworth.

E. Shapiro, 1995, *Fad Surfing in the Boardroom: Reclaiming the Courage to Manage in the Age of Instant Answers*, London: HarperCollins.

P. Shaw, 2002, *Changing Conversations in Organisations: A Complexity Approach to Change*, London: Routledge.

A. Shier-Jones, 2009, *Pioneer Ministry and Fresh Expressions of Church*, London: SPCK.

M. Smith, 2006[1999], 'Keeping a Learning Journal', *the encyclopaedia of informal education*, www.infed.org/research/keeping_a_journal.htm.

M. Snow, 2009, *Leading Change in the Church*, Cambridge: Grove Books.

M. Snow, and H. Thomas, 2008, *Coaching in the Church*, Cambridge: Grove Books.

J. Thompson, 2008, *SCM Studyguide: Theological Reflection*, London: SCM Press.

M. Torry, 2005, *Managing God's Business: Religious and Faith-Based Organizations and their Management*, London: Ashgate.

D. Tracy, 1983, 'The Foundations of Practical Theology', in D. S. Browning (ed.), 1983, *Practical Theology*, San Francisco, CA: Harper and Row, pp. 61–82.

M. F. Van Assen, G. J. J. B.van den Berg, P. Pietersma, 2009, *Key Management Models: The 60+ Models Every Manager Needs to Know*, 2nd edn, Harlow: Pearson Education Publishers/FT Prentice Hall.

P. Walker, 2005, *Mission Accompaniment*, Cambridge: Grove Books.

F. Ward, 2005, *Lifelong Learning: Theological Education and Supervision*, London: SCM Press.

G. Ward, 2010, *Understanding Postmodernism*, London: Teach Yourself.

R. Warren, 2004, *The Healthy Churches' Handbook*, London: Church House Publishing.

C. Watkins, D. Bhatti, H. Cameron, C. Duce, J. Sweeney, 2009, 'Living Church: Practical Theology as a Locus for Ecumenical Learning', a short paper for the conference 'Receptive Ecumenism and Ecclesial Learning: Learning to be Church Together', held at Ushaw College, Durham.

M. Wheatley, 2001, *Leadership and the New Science: Discovering Order in a Chaotic World*, 2nd edn, San Francisco, CA: Berrett-Koehler.

C. Widdicombe, 2000, *Meetings that Work: A Practical Guide to Teamworking in Groups*, Cambridge: Lutterworth Press.

D. Winnicott, 1965, *The Maturational Process and the Facilitating Environment*, London: Karnac.

J. Woodward and S. Pattison, 2000, *The Blackwell Reader in Pastoral and Practical Theology*, Oxford: Blackwell.

J. W. Worden, 2009, *Grief Counselling and Grief Therapy: A Handbook for the Mental Health Practitioner*, 4th edn, New York: Springer.

World Council of Churches, 1999, *The Nature and Purpose of the Church: A Stage on the Way to a Common Statement*, Geneva: World Council of Churches.

Index of Subjects